997

MAP CONTENTS

HOW TO USE THIS BOOK

Whether you're a visitor, a new resident, or a Milwaukee native, you'll find the *City • Smart Guidebook: Milwaukee* indispensable. Author Ann Angel brings you an insider's view of the best Milwaukee has to offer.

This book presents the city in five geographic zones. The zone divisions are listed at the bottom of this page and shown on the map on the following page. Look for a zone designation in each listing and use it to help you locate the listing on one of the zone-specific maps included in each chapter.

Example:

BRADLEY CENTER
1001 N. 4th St., Milwaukee
414/227-0400   **DA**

Zone Abbreviation = DA
The Bradley Center is located on the Downtown Area
map unless otherwise noted.

Milwaukee Zones

DA—Downtown Area, bordered on the east by Lake Michigan, on the west by 35th Street, on the north by Capitol Drive, and on the south by Lincoln Avenue.

ES—East Side, including Whitefish Bay, Fox Point, and the eastern edge of Glendale; the East Side is north of the Downtown Area.

NS—North Side, including Glendale, River Hills, Brown Deer, and Menomonee Falls; extends into Ozaukee County to include Mequon, Thiensville, Germantown, Cedarburg, and Grafton.

WS—West Side, including Wauwatosa, Elm Grove, and Brookfield.

SS—South Side, including General Mitchell International Airport, West Milwaukee, West Allis, Greenfield, Greendale, Hales Corners, and New Berlin.

MILWAUKEE ZONES

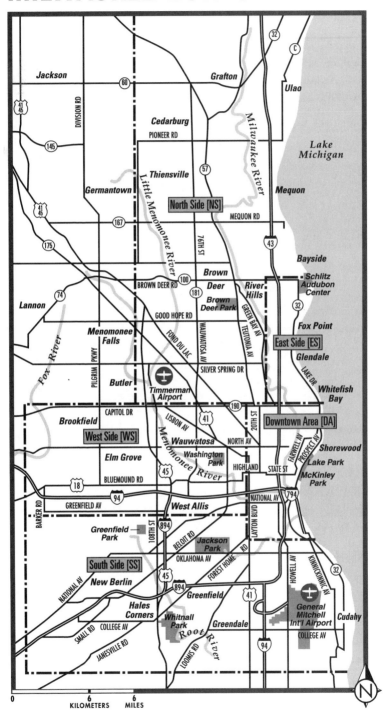

1

WELCOME TO MILWAUKEE

Lake Michigan's pristine waters and the surrounding rolling hills and farm meadows frame Milwaukee's brass-crowned cathedrals, church spires, art deco office buildings, and contemporary skyscrapers, giving visitors the picture of a city rich in history, tradition, and abundant natural beauty. Perhaps because of all these attractive qualities, the people of Milwaukee love to celebrate. Each year, summer festivals are held on the lakefront at Henry W. Maier Festival Park. Visitors from all over the United States flock here to join the celebrations during Milwaukee's temperate summer.

But winter's cold doesn't stop Milwaukeeans from celebrating—they participate in Winterfest, or just head indoors to see the Holiday Folk Fair or to enjoy the symphony or a performance by one of the many regional theater companies. Some watch Admirals hockey or Bucks basketball. Whatever the time of year, Milwaukeeans look for any opportunity to enjoy their diverse ethnic, cultural, and sports traditions. These traditions, along with strong employment ratings, good schools, and an outstanding system of county parks, make Milwaukee a great place to raise a family. And while the city has gained a reputation for knowing how to host the country's biggest outdoor parties, it also retains its renown as a city of manufacturing. Whether you're coming here to attend a festival, to sightsee, to visit family, or to work, you'll find out why Milwaukee is called a Great City on a Great Lake.

A Brief History of Milwaukee

The Early Days

Long before European immigrants came to Milwaukee, the Potawatomi, Fox, and Mascouten Indians hunted in the swampy areas and prairies. They fished in Lake Michigan and built their tribal villages along the Milwaukee, Menomonee, and Root Rivers. They made "wigwams," low houses of straw and mud, which protected them from Milwaukee's bitter winters. Despite those winters, Milwaukee's four seasons made it a good place to live. In fact, Milwaukee is an Algonquin Indian word that means "good land." Fur traders made note of arriving at "Mahnawaukee seepe," which they believed meant "the gathering place by the river." The official Chamber of Commerce interpretation is "the place where rivers meet."

People other than the natives thought the land was good. In 1674, French Jesuit priest Father Marquette, who was exploring the Midwest, stopped in Milwaukee. He liked the many rivers that made the land rich for growing, and he realized that the waters' easy navigation would also make this place good for trade. He loved its beauty, and he told people in Canada about the extraordinary area surrounded by rivers and a lake. Soon French Canadian fur traders came from the north, and from 1712 to 1740, these newcomers fought the Fox Indians for control of the Wisconsin River. The first French Canadian Settler was a man named Jacques Vieau, who brought his family and set up a trading post. Vieau's daughter Josette fell in love with Solomon Juneau, a fur trader who worked at the post. They were married, and the young couple built a home east of the Milwaukee River in 1818. This became Juneau Town, ensuring Solomon Juneau's place in history as the founding father of the

Henry W. Maier Festival Park

Early Rivalries

Despite economic growth, the rivalry between Walker's Point and Kilbourntown, called the East Ward and West Ward of the Town of Milwaukee, grew increasingly volatile. Each ward had five trustees who elected their own president. The autonomous subdivisions fought to maintain control over bridge maintenance, causing tempers to flare and a violent confrontation after a town board meeting in which the West Ward trustees declared the bridge a menace to river navigation. On the night of May 7, 1845, a West Ward mob started to tear down the Chestnut Street bridge. Incensed East Siders brandished guns and rolled a cannon to the riverbank, threatening to blow up Byron Kilbourn's house. They cooled down considerably when a West Ward spokesperson met them with the news that Kilbourn's daughter had died the night before and the house was in mourning. The violence served to warn the community leaders, though, and they worked to end the rivalry. A charter was drawn up that created legislation for a city government with five wards, two on the East Side, two on the West Side, and Walker's Point. The Milwaukee Charter became effective January 31, 1846.

city, despite the fact that his father-in-law was actually the first European settler. As more settlers arrived to trade in this part of the Northwest Territory, it was set up as three communities: Juneau Town, Kilbourntown, and Walker's Point.

Kilbourntown and Walker's Point were established by settlers interested in land speculation and opportunity because of diminishing resources on the crowded East Coast. Byron Kilbourn arrived from Connecticut via Ohio sometime before the 1830s and settled west of the Milwaukee River. George Walker came from Virginia as a fur trader about the same time and settled south of the Menomonee River. These men were accompanied by groups of Yankees, many of whom were college-educated people, who controlled the city and businesses for many years.

Intense rivalry existed between the towns' founders, though. Walker and Kilbourn set out to promote business in their own areas, each one fighting to locate county government within his own community. The results of this rivalry are still evident today. Streets were laid out so they would not align properly at the river, making construction of a bridge almost impossible. Nevertheless, a bridge was erected at Chestnut Street, now Juneau Avenue. Meanwhile, Solomon Juneau avoided confrontations with Kilbourn and Walker and quietly gathered donations to build the county courthouse in his own town. Finally, in 1846, the three areas combined to form the City of Milwaukee.

Word spread quickly from the East Coast to Europe that Milwaukee's rivers made this an ideal area in which to manufacture and sell metals. It was also a good place to grow and ship grains, such as wheat and barley, and the land was cheap. In the 1830s, German, Norwegian, Swiss, and even Dutch families flocked to Milwaukee to make their homes. East Coast immigrants remained in Juneau Town, which soon became known as Yankee Hill. In the 1840s, the Irish flocked to the area now called the Historic Third Ward, and by 1850, 14 percent of the city's 20,000 people were of Irish descent.

The Birth of the Brews, and Other Milwaukee Industries

The new arrivals began some of the first retail establishments, breweries, and grain operations in Wisconsin. The first industry was brewing, established by three Welshmen who, in 1840, opened the Milwaukee Brewery on the city's East Side to sell their ale and porter. A year later, Simon Reutelschofer, a German, started a lager-beer brewery in Walker's Point. For reasons unknown, Reutelschofer left the city in financial ruin. Still, Milwaukee was fated to become "Beertown." In 1844, Jacob Best and his sons opened Empire Brewery. One of Best's granddaughters married a ship captain named Frederick Pabst, who joined the company and renamed it Pabst Brewery. The Schlitz Brewery was founded in 1851.

Industrial Perfumes

In the early days, booming growth wasn't all roses for Milwaukeeans. New and less than lovely industrial odors wafting through the city caused some olfactory distress. When the wind came from the south, where the leather tanneries were, Milwaukeeans complained about the smells of the tanning chemicals and leather hides. Winds from the west brought the aroma of brewer's yeast, which, although equally pungent, was considered less offensive by the populace. Menomonee Valley became the site of added complaint when John Plankinton chose this area to locate and build his slaughterhouse. The young entrepreneur went into the business with Frederick Layton, who later partnered meat packing plants with Phillip Armour and Patrick Cudahy.

According to local legend, foundry workers William, Walter, and Arthur Davidson and their friend William S. Harley created a bicycle with an engine to "take the work out of bicycling." The company produced 150 motorcycles a year. They produced 18,000 as part of the World War I effort in 1917.

Abundant labor and easily accessible international transportation routes continued to attract industry. One of the most innovative industrial centers, A.P. Allis Company, opened for business in 1846. Although the company originally manufactured flour-mill supplies, Allis foresaw the impact that machining would have on the world, and he adapted the plant to manufacture heavy sawmill and mining machinery. The company still exists today as Allis-Chalmers. The leather-tanning business, begun by Yankees, also took off at around this time. By 1859, nine tanneries in the Menomonee Valley were turning out more than $200,000 worth of products annually. Iron and steel production, the first large-scale industry, was developed in 1867 by Michigan industrialist Eber Brock Ward, who began the Milwaukee Iron Company and Bessemer Steel. In 1878, partners Filer and Stowell organized the Cream City Iron Works, specializing in the manufacture of sawmill and milling machines. Milwaukee Harvester Company began production of mowers, harvesters, and binders in 1882. And in 1907, Harley-Davidson Motor Company was incorporated.

Twentieth-Century Milwaukee

Industrial growth ensured Milwaukee's place in American history as a key presence in the Industrial Belt. Throughout the nation, industrial progress often brought corruption to city government—and Milwaukee was no exception. Between 1898 and 1906, muckrakers—people who sought out and publicly exposed wrongdoers—dug deep. Although they could not prove allegations that the city's mayor David Rose was guilty of anything, a grand jury investigation into City Hall and the police department led to a series of indictments against high-ranking Democratic and Republican officials for collusion. Most of the indictments were for granting favors and "fixing" tickets with police officials.

Citizens soon had more than shady politics to worry about, though. Prohibition knocked the breweries for a loop when the national Volstead Act took effect in 1919. Some of Milwaukee's breweries switched to malt production, but most closed and jobs were lost. Unemployed Milwaukeeans and sympathizers held funerals on street corners for "John Barleycorn." Home breweries started up, malt and hops were sold in retail stories, and

TRIVIA

wine-making became a favored hobby. Area saloons sold "near-beer," a weak parody of the alcoholic brew.

Unemployed brewers were joined by unemployed foundry workers, machinists, and bankers when the Great Depression took hold in 1929. Mayor Michael Hoan opened soup kitchens to aid the homeless and vagrants, but unemployment brought Milwaukee's blue-collar neighborhoods to their knees. In 1930, only 1,000 families needed some type of welfare assistance. By 1933, the number had grown to 140,000 families. Even the return of beer operations in April of 1933 didn't help the city's morale; only eight breweries reopened.

Because Milwaukee was, and still is, a center of capital-goods manufacturing, the Depression hit the city a bit later than it did the rest of the country, but its effects lasted longer. In 1935, the Federal Government took over relief efforts. Soon, Public Works Administration projects were underway. By 1937, Park Lawn, the city's first public housing, was completed. A water-filtration plant was constructed on Lincoln Memorial Drive in 1939, under the same program. Milwaukee's city parks increased between 1934 and 1937, when they merged with parks from five local jurisdictions into a county park system run by a county park commission.

Milwaukee skyline

Milwaukee Convention & Visitors Bureau

Industrial growth continued as the country entered each war. During the 1940s, many of the city's plants converted to war production. For example, Allis-Chalmers produced transformers and motors for the armed forces. Postwar growth yielded to the suburbs and failed to help the central city. Following the wars, and especially after World War II, suburban growth was incredible: eight new suburbs incorporated between 1950 and 1957. Milwaukee's public-school system felt the brunt of urban flight. Public-school enrollment declined from a high of 81,700 in 1940 to 68,091 in 1947.

Port of Milwaukee

Milwaukee's location on the shores of Lake Michigan and the Milwaukee River attracted manufacturers and entrepreneurs, who looked to settle in areas that were accessible to storage and shipping. Built in 1857, the port originally serviced the Great Lakes and the Milwaukee River. Numerous multi-story warehouses, freight sheds, and storage yards line the riverbanks, testifying to half a century of grain-, lumber-, and heavy machinery-shipping between Milwaukee and other Great Lakes ports. Lumber mills, leather tanneries, agricultural merchants, and metal manufacturing industries used the port to ship their products south to Chicago and St. Louis, and east to New York.

The 1959 opening of the enlarged St. Lawrence Seaway route made the Port of Milwaukee an international port. An enlarged draft at Montreal created a direct route for ships harbored in Milwaukee to pass from the Great Lakes all the way to northwestern European, Mediterranean, and Caribbean ports. The Harbor Commission developed several general cargo breakbulk piers and terminals and a "heavy lift" wharf equipped with cranes to transfer bulk cargo and heavy machinery, making this port the most efficient of all the Great Lakes ports. In recent years the port has served as many as 350 cities worldwide, and port commerce totals over 2.9 million tons a year. Seasonal freezes hinder year-round shipping and limit the port's annual operations. For further information, call the Port of Milwaukee, 414/286-3511.

Still, people looking for work flocked to Milwaukee, and new opportunities for these as well as long-time residents seemed to increase. Although parts of the Milwaukee River were closed to navigation in the early 1950s, the St. Lawrence Seaway's opening, in 1959, brought new life to the Port of Milwaukee, allowing ships loaded with Milwaukee-machined metal products and local agricultural products to navigate the Great Lakes and reach the Atlantic Ocean, and making Milwaukee an international seaport.

Other growth and community improvements occurred, as well. In 1957, the Milwaukee Art Museum opened, expanding the cultural scene. That same year, Mayor Henry W. Maier created an urban renewal program to breathe life back into the central city. This program encouraged Marine Bank to build its 22-story headquarters in the downtown area. Maier was also responsible for beginning Summerfest, inspiring Milwaukee's many ethnic festivals; today, when warm weather arrives, the city's squares, beaches, and streets fill with mini-celebrations and exhibits. Current mayor John Norquist has begun plans for a Milwaukee Riverwalk to expand the celebrations. The Milwaukee Repertory Theater group has been joined by Theater X, the Skylight Theater, the Milwaukee Chamber Theater, and a number of volunteer theater groups, including theater for children. In addition, the Milwaukee Symphony and Milwaukee Ballet offer world-class talent to Milwaukeeans and their visitors.

On the sports scene, the Milwaukee Braves baseball team was sold to Atlanta in 1959, and an aggressive search brought the Milwaukee Brewers to the stadium in 1970. Milwaukee enhanced its reputation as a sports town when the National Basketball Association's Milwaukee Bucks began playing here in 1968. The Milwaukee Admirals National Hockey League team joined the sports scene in 1973. The Milwaukee tradition of sports still includes the Admirals; the Bucks; the Brewers; the Wave indoor soccer team; the Mustangs indoor football team; and Marquette University's Golden Eagles basketball team, which won the 1977 NCAA championship.

The People of Milwaukee

Milwaukee residents are a rich cultural mix. Although Irish, German, and Polish immigrants have dispersed throughout the metropolitan community, their heritage is kept alive in folk theaters and dancing troupes as well as in ethnic festivals. Irish music can still be heard on the South Side, and almost everyone proclaims an Irish ancestor or two on St. Patrick's Day. The city's Irish dancers participate in every parade and have performed nationally.

German immigrants owned homes on the North Side, the South Side, and, later, the West Side, and their influence is visible in many of the city's

Ship loading cargo in the Port of Milwaukee, page 7

Port of Milwaukee

Milwaukee Time Line

Father Pierre Marquette stops in Milwaukee on his travels along the Mississippi River. **1674**

Solomon Juneau and Josette Vieau marry. The young couple builds a home and trading center east of the Milwaukee River. **1818**

Byron Kilbourn arrives from Connecticut via Ohio and settles west of the Milwaukee River. George Walker comes from Virginia and settles south of the Menomonee River as a fur trader about the same time. **1830**

Three Welshmen begin brewing ale and porter at the Milwaukee Brewery. **1840**

Jacob Best and his sons open Empire Brewery, later to become the Pabst Brewery. **1844**

The Kilbourns build their home; today it's located in Juneau Park and open to the public during the summer as a historical sight. **1844**

The Milwaukee Curling Club forms. Curling, a winter game that entails sliding a 40-pound rock toward a target painted on ice, is first played on the frozen Milwaukee River. **1845**

A West Ward mob tries to demolish the Chestnut Street bridge, the only connection between the east and west sides of the river. **1845**

Juneau Town, Kilbourntown, and Walker's Point sign the Milwaukee Charter, combining the three communities into the City of Milwaukee. **1846**

The Schlitz Brewery begins brewing lager beers. **1851**

John Plankinton and Frederick Layton open slaughterhouse operations in the Menomonee Valley. **1852**

The Cream City Baseball Club—with its reputation for losing—comes to Milwaukee. **1860**

A full-time Milwaukee fire department is hired. **1871**

The Milwaukee Grain Exchange is built on Michigan Street, guaranteeing continued economic growth for Milwaukee agriculture. **1879**

Facilities to house the insane, the indigent, prison inmates, and homeless children are in operation. **1880**

The Bennett Law, calling for compulsory school attendance for children 16 and under, is passed. **1889**

Dr. Allen Herron, an African American physician, establishes his practice. **1896**

Socialist Party of America is founded in Milwaukee by Victor Berger and Frederic Heath. **1901**

Time Line

1902–52	The original Milwaukee Brewers, members of the American Association of Baseball, play baseball for the city's fans.
1907	Harley-Davidson Motor Company, a manufacturer of motorcycles, incorporates.
1919	Prohibition puts thousands of brewery workers out of business when Milwaukee's brewers are forced to halt production.
1931	A Milwaukee County hospital is built east of 92nd on West Wisconsin Avenue.
1932	One-half of the city's home owners, devastated by the Depression, fail to pay property taxes.
1933	Prohibition no longer includes beer consumption. Only eight Milwaukee breweries reopen; many change hands: for example, Miller buys Gettelman, and Pabst buys Blatz.
1934–37	The city's parks merge with parks from five other jurisdictions to form the Milwaukee County Parks System.
1934	More than 100 crafts and building-trade workers' groups, allied with the American Federation of Labor, strike against a variety of Milwaukee businesses.
1935	The Federal Government takes over the city's Depression relief responsibilities, bringing Public Works programs to Milwaukee.
1949	The City Auditorium is built.
1953	The Boston Braves move to Milwaukee to play in the newly constructed Milwaukee County Stadium, with a seating capacity of more than 36,000.
1957	Henry Aaron, Eddie Mathews, and Warren Spahn help the Braves beat the New York Yankees to win the World Series.
1959	The Milwaukee Symphony is formed.
1967	The first Summerfest is held.
1967	A five-hour race riot breaks out, leaving three dead and 100 injured. More than 1,500 people are arrested, most for curfew violation.
1976	A court order requires the city to desegregate public schools.
1979	Voluntary busing of students to magnet and specialty schools begins.
1995	The Mustangs indoor football team moves to Milwaukee.
1996	The city slips to ninth place in beer production nationally.

most historic restaurants and hotels, such as the five-star Pfister Hotel on East Wisconsin Avenue and Historic Turner Hall on West Third Street. German influence is especially evident in Old World Third Street, where sausage hangs in the Usinger family's storefront, and the Mader family still runs the historic Mader's German Restaurant nearby. Beer gardens, bandshells, and rousing music are a part of every summer festival and many family celebrations, too.

Mexican Fiesta

In 1896, Dr. Allen Herron, an African American physician, established a practice that thrived for nearly 50 years. Milwaukeean Louis Hughes memorialized civil-rights freedom fights with his autobiography, *Thirty Years a Slave*. Isaac T. Bryan fought discrimination in Milwaukee by filing suit in the Wisconsin Supreme Court in 1896 because he was denied service in a local establishment. During the mid-1900s, more African Americans came to Milwaukee from the South to find work in factories. African American heritage is preserved at the Black Holocaust Museum on Martin Luther King Drive.

A large Native American population also exists in Milwaukee's central city. In fact, over 20 percent of the state's Native Americans have taken advantage of jobs and housing in Milwaukee. Many Native Americans still live in the area immediately south of I-94 in the Menomonee River Valley, home to the Potawatomi Bingo Casino.

In the last 50 years, people have migrated to Milwaukee from Mexico, Puerto Rico, and Cuba to find jobs and a safe community for raising their families. After the Vietnam War, a new group of immigrants—war survivors —came to the area from Laos and Vietnam. In each case, these families brought their own traditions and languages. They purchased homes, set up shops to sell delicacies from their homelands, and built buildings that resembled the ones they left behind. Today, if you walk on the streets of Milwaukee near the South Side, you might hear Spanish, Laotian, Vietnamese, Polish, and sometimes even a bit of German.

Business and Economy

Industry remains a viable means of earning a living in today's Milwaukee. In fact, the global economy is alive and well here. Harley-Davidson Motor Company, home of American-made motorcycles, maintains production sites on Milwaukee's West Side, exporting Harley "choppers" and clothing to Europe and Japan as well as across the United States. Square D Company manufactures electric power equipment for the world's consumption. While Bucyrus Erie builds earthmoving equipment used to lay the groundwork for roads here and abroad, A.O. Smith produces structural components for everything from baby carriages to cars and ships.

However, the global economy is not necessarily in the best interests of the working class. The news frequently announces that local factories are closing, and some production sites have been moved to countries outside the United States. This is especially true since the recent U.S./Mexican trade agreements. Most recently, Briggs and Stratton, a manufacturer of engine parts, moved manufacturing facilities south of the border. Fred Stratton, the corporation's owner, said the move was based largely on increasing employee costs. While Milwaukee's unemployment rate should remain one of the lowest in the country, it appears that current employment opportunities are most plentiful in the service and food industries.

The family-friendly environment continues to encourage newcomers' moves into the community, but most will gravitate toward suburban areas. Despite rehabilitation of some central city areas such as the Historic Third Ward and the Riverwest neighborhoods, overcrowding in the public schools coupled with other problems that confront cities throughout the nation convince many that the city is not the most desirable area for raising children.

Meanwhile, Mayor John Norquist is working hard to create positive change in the central city by spearheading efforts to attract businesses and industry and to clean up the central city area. One plan is to create a river walk that encompasses the breadth of the city along the Milwaukee River. Although his interest in some city issues, such as education, has not always been welcome, he works to create and maintain a strong family environ-ment in the community. With the cooperation of the city's law-enforcement agencies, school administrators, and industrial leaders, his attempts to improve the community's image should pay off.

Additional Reading

Beertown Blazes: A Century of Milwaukee Fire Fighting, by R.L. Nailen and James S. Haight

The Fifties and Beyond in Milwaukee, by Harold Gauer

Milwaukee: At the Gathering of the Waters, by Harry H. Anderson and Frederick I. Olson

This is Milwaukee, by Robert W. Wells

Trading Post to Metropolis: Milwaukee County's First 150 Years, edited by Ralph Aderman

Cost of Living

Milwaukee's cost of living is approximately 4 percent above the United States national average. This compares with costs of living which are 27 to 124 percent above average in major Northeastern cities and 17 to 50 percent above average in major West Coast cities. Grocery and health-care costs are near the average, while miscellaneous goods and services and utility costs are lower than average. Overall, housing and transportation costs are above average.

Typical costs of everyday items and services include:
- 5-mile taxi ride: $10
- Hotel double rooms: $60 at a budget hotel; $160 and even $225 at the more exclusive hotels
- Dinner: $15 per person
- Movie admission: $6.50 for full-price adult tickets
- Daily newspaper: 50 cents; Sunday paper: $1.75
- 16-oz. tube of brand-name toothpaste: $3.49
- 6-pack of Miller beer: $3.99
- 1 pound of bratwurst: $2.99

Housing

Average housing costs vary, based on the area. In metro Milwaukee, the average house sold for $115,000 in 1996. Recently the market has seen a number of houses in River Hills, Lake Country, and Elm Grove top the million-dollar mark. In fact, suburbanites are purchasing small, older homes in Elm Grove and tearing them down to build four- and five-bedroom mansions valued at over $700,000, earning the area the nickname "the Beverly Hills of Milwaukee."

Taxes

Sales tax is 5.6 percent, and state corporate tax is 7.9 percent. The average metro Milwaukee homeowner can expect to pay between $20.19 and $41.95

per $1,000 of assessed valuation. Property tax is higher in central Milwaukee than in the suburbs because of the cost of maintaining the Milwaukee Public School system. Manufacturing machinery and equipment are exempt from property taxation. There is no property tax on nonbusiness personal property. Wisconsin inheritance tax has also been phased out.

Milwaukee Weather

Milwaukee has four distinct and surprising seasons. Spring can be chilly and rainy, but it's usually temperate by the end of April, when the high reaches an average 53 degrees and the low gets to be about 35 degrees. Lined jackets, gloves, and umbrellas are all useful at this time of year. March, April, and May average about 3 inches of precipitation per month.

Only die-hard swimmers enter Lake Michigan's chilly 65-degree waters before June 1. In fact, early summer lakefront festivals require sweaters and sometimes even winter jackets. By mid-July, the lake is warmer and the city is downright hot: highs reach an average of 78 degrees, and lows drop to about 59 degrees. Summer rains can be torrential but are sandwiched between days of sunshine and heat. Humidity tends to be high, so mild temperatures feel much warmer than in drier climates. The rain and humidity are probably responsible for the emerald-green lawns and leaves that seem to remain vibrant until late August. Average precipitation for June, July, and August is 3.5 inches per month.

Monthly Average Temperatures

	High (°F)	Low (°F)
January	26	11
February	30	16
March	40	26
April	53	36
May	64	45
June	75	55
July	80	62
August	78	61
September	71	53
October	59	42
November	45	31
December	31	17

(Information courtesy of the Midwestern Climate Center, Wisconsin State Climatology Office)

Fall is one of the prettiest seasons in Milwaukee, luring many tourists to this area to enjoy the fall colors. Milwaukeeans head toward lake country, where they can get their fill of bright orange, copper, and red leaves. The fall high averages 59 degrees; the low is 41, with average temperatures hovering at about 50 degrees. Average precipitation for September, October, and November is fewer than 3 inches.

Downhill and cross-country skiing and ice skating usually start right after Thanksgiving. Winter highs average 29 degrees; the low is usually around 15 degrees, with average temperatures of 22 degrees. Al-

Marquette Golden Eagles Mascot

though winter visitors need to bring plenty of warm clothing, they might be fortunate enough to experience a winter thaw that brings false spring breezes to the city. The best advice for visitors is to be prepared for just about anything. Even in summer, it's best to pack a sweater or sweatshirt.

City Dressing

Milwaukee's typical style is conservative but casual. You're more likely to see jeans skirts and khaki pants than leather and lace. Summer festivals are extremely casual. T-shirts and shorts or jeans seem to be the uniform. However, Milwaukeeans do like to dress up for special occasions. Although you'll see people wearing jeans at cultural events, you're also likely to see a variety of dressier choices, from sport coats and ties for men to skirts and even a few evening dresses on women.

Visitors should be cautioned that average temperatures can be deceiving—Lake Michigan breezes can create weather extremes. Bitterly cold winter days occur with temperatures of 0 or 10 below zero and wind-chills of 40-below. Hot and humid summer weather in the 90s can suddenly drop 30 degrees when winds shift off the lake. The lake has been kindly referred to as the city's air conditioner, but summer cold fronts are not so kind, and weather forecasters mean it when they call sudden temperature changes "pneumonia fronts."

2

GETTING AROUND THE CITY

Milwaukee is located 90 miles north of Chicago on the western shore of Lake Michigan. The city covers 96 square miles; Milwaukee County is 242 square miles. The metropolitan Milwaukee area consists of the city itself and four counties: Milwaukee County, Waukesha County to the west, and Ozaukee and Washington Counties to the north.

Finding Your Way Around

Milwaukee's street and land grids were determined by late-eighteenth- and early-nineteenth-century settlement patterns. Rectangular streets and roads became common grids throughout the Midwest because of a government decision to avoid settlements that relied on nuclear villages from which farmers commuted outward to their fields. Keeping this in mind, the U.S. Continental Congress adopted a rectangular land-survey and subdivision pattern in 1785 and 1787. These decisions created the rectangular land parcels and streets evident in Milwaukee County today. Street designs have benefited from this pattern because the absence of acute angles increases traffic safety.

Milwaukee's streets are divided into east/west and north/south categories at the intersection of the Milwaukee River and I-794. East/west-running streets are preceded by East (E.) or West (W.), depending on whether they are east or west of that cross; the bulk of the streets are to the west. North/south-running streets are preceded by North (N.) or South (S.); most north-south streets west of the river are numbered, making the city easy to navigate. Streets east of the river are named. The building addresses indicate how far north or south of I-94/I-794 (or the East-West

Freeway) they are: 3300 N. 67th St., for example, is approximately 33 blocks north of I-94 and 67 blocks west of the Milwaukee River.

Note: Don't confuse these east/west, north/south street categories with the zones used in this book. The Downtown Area (DA) alone has streets in all four directional categories, and the East Side (ES) has a few west-named streets.

Horse drawn carriage in front of the
Pabst Theater

Milwaukee Convention & Visitors Bureau

Public Transportation

The Milwaukee County transit system keeps people moving with more than 69 routes placing 90 percent of county residents within one-quarter mile of bus service. Special bus service is often scheduled for festivals, sporting events, and other special happenings.

Bus Service

Bus 30 travels north to south from the University of Wisconsin-Milwaukee through downtown, then heads west to 35th Street. Bus 10 travels from Bayshore on the city's East Side to Brookfield Square on the West Side. Bus 15 travels south from downtown Milwaukee to Bayshore. Bus 67 is routed from Northridge on the city's north to 92nd and Cold Spring Road, on the far South Side. On New Year's Eve and Day, buses run later than usual and offer free transportation, thanks to a program co-sponsored by Miller Brewery. Miller Free Rides runs from 8 p.m. New Year's Eve until 4 a.m. New Year's Day. A "freeway flyer" provides efficient transportation

TRIVIA

Milwaukee's first electric trolley line opened on April 3, 1890. The trolley made two round trips daily from 12th and Wells Streets to 34th Street. By February 1, 1896, 310 cars operated on more than 1,000 miles of track, Milwaukee's main means of mass transit. The trolleys were slowly abandoned because they interfered with freeway and highway expansion. The most impressive trolley route ran across the Menomonee Valley on a double track viaduct that rose 90 feet above the valley floor and was 2,085 feet long. This track was abandoned in 1956, and the viaduct was removed by 1962.

for suburban commuters into the central city, with park-and-ride lots located at strategic freeway junctures. Bus service is available on holidays and Sundays. For route and fare information, call the Milwaukee County Transit System, 414/344-6711. A bus ride is $1.35 for adults; 65 cents for children under 12. Carry exact change.

Rapid Transit
Rapid Transit remains a controversial topic in Milwaukee. Some taxpayers believe that rapid transit will become reality despite heavy opposition because it's one of Mayor Norquist's pet projects. Until the issue is resolved, bus and automobile transportation remain the easiest ways to see the city and much of the metropolitan area.

Taxis
A number of cab companies operate in the region, but they're not as accessible from the street as they are in such major cities as Chicago and New York. Unless you're disembarking from a plane or train, it's best to call ahead and establish a pickup point for taxi service. Although taxi service is generally limited to airport and train runs, a number of companies offer 24-hour service in the metropolitan Milwaukee area.

The largest cab companies with service available in the Metro area include Yellow Cab Co-op, 414/271-1800; Checker Taxi of Milwaukee, 414/438-1638 or 800/547-8294; and City Veterans Taxi Cab Cooperative, 414/291-8080.

Driving in Milwaukee

Even drivers unfamiliar with Milwaukee routes can easily navigate downtown and suburban areas. Although traffic can occasionally slow to a crawl, especially flowing from downtown to the suburbs, the freeway and highway systems adequately support most daily traffic. Morning jams tend

---

Limousine Services

A1 Transportation, Inc.

Waukesha:	414/272-1955
Wisconsin Limousine Services, Inc.	
Manitowoc and Two Rivers:	414/931-1982
Metropolitan Milwaukee:	414/769-9100
Oconomowoc and Lake Geneva:	414/769-9100
Sheboygan and Kohler:	414/931-1982

TIP

I-43 south of Milwaukee County Stadium is closed until late 1998 because the new Miller Park Stadium construction will change the location of this section of the highway. During construction, use the 35th Street exit and follow the "Detour" signs.

to be most severe on the East-West Freeway (I-94) between 7:15 and 8 a.m.; evening traffic bottlenecks on the same freeway from 4:50 to 5:45 p.m. Other routes that slow from congestion are northerly-southerly Highway 100, or 108th Street, and Blue Mound Road and Wisconsin Avenue, two east-west routes. Traffic tends to stream steadily on most other main streets.

Highways

The East-West Freeway (I-94) runs across the city until it hits the Marquette Exchange, at about 10th Street and St. Paul Avenue (just west of the Milwaukee River), where it merges briefly with the North-South Freeway (I-43) and veers south to Mitchell International Airport, through Racine County, and then on to Chicago. I-43 travels approximately parallel to Lake Michigan and the Milwaukee River, from Cedarburg and Grafton through downtown Milwaukee to the Marquette Exchange, where it merges with I-94 and continues south until just before the airport, when it veers west and heads out through the southwestern part of metro Milwaukee.

Badger Coaches bus, page 25

Badger Coaches

Driving Tips

Wisconsin Avenue, Milwaukee's main east-west street through the central downtown area, is frequently marked with "No left turn" signs. Watch for them. It's legal to make a right turn on a red light unless the intersection is marked otherwise. Right turns on red lights are restricted in heavily populated areas, especially near schools. The speed limit decreases from 25 mph to 15 mph in school zones. U-turns are permitted unless there is a sign indicating otherwise.

When driving downtown, you do need to watch for one-way streets, especially near schools. Drivers should also be aware that many schools are surrounded by one-way streets to ease the traffic flow during school opening and closing times. If you happen upon a one-way street, rest assured that a street going the opposite direction is only a block away.

Be forewarned that driving in Brookfield on Blue Mound Road (Highway 18), with its series of strip malls, movie theaters, retail establishments, and offices, can be hazardous. It's consistently ranked the most dangerous street in the metro Milwaukee area; drivers are cautioned to avoid making left turns. This is especially true near the intersection of Barker and Blue Mound Roads, nicknamed Goerkes Corners, where rear-end collisions are commonplace.

Pedestrians have the right-of-way as long as they are walking in a designated crosswalk. (Jaywalkers are ticketed.)

Parking Tips

Downtown Milwaukee has lost parking to new buildings, so spaces are becoming increasingly precious. A few multilevel parking structures exist on side streets near the Bradley Center, the Federal Building, the Wisconsin Center, and Marquette University. Meter parking is available except on Wisconsin Avenue. Limited parking is available in all suburban areas.

TiP Radio station WTMJ, 620 AM, gives the most complete traffic updates during rush hours, providing emergency traffic bulletins, lane closing reports, and construction information throughout the day.

Biking in Milwaukee

Milwaukee has one of the most scenic bike routes in Wisconsin. Called the 76 Route, it was constructed by the Milwaukee County Park system in observance of the country's bicentennial. The 76-mile route follows a series of abandoned rail tracks and rail right-of-ways, winding along the Milwaukee River and through Lake Park along Lake Michigan's shore.

While lots of scenic trails make biking an enjoyable way to see Milwaukee, using bikes as the primary method of getting around town isn't always practical. Seasonal cold and snow can make city streets and bike paths completely inaccessible. Even in good weather, downtown streets are often congested and narrow. Suburban politicians in some areas originally fought bike paths, fearing the asphalt or concrete would make the communities appear too urban. Although these suburbs have become more bicycle-friendly, many Brookfield, Elm Grove, and Mequon street paths are actually lanes painted with white lines along the side of main roads. This has created bike paths fraught with dangers, such as sewer grates or asphalt pavement that's cracked and buckling over soft road shoulders. In addition, lanes narrow to become almost nonexistent at railroad crossings and intersections. Bicycle riders should wear helmets and assume drivers do not see them. Ride defensively.

General Mitchell International Airport

General Mitchell International Airport, the region's primary commercial airport, is located 8 miles south of Milwaukee's business center. General Mitchell is served by eight major air carriers and nine regional carriers, reaching 100 nonstop and direct destinations daily. The airport serves over 55 million passengers each year and offers direct freight service through United Parcel Service, the U.S. Post Office, and Federal Express. Several military aviation groups maintain air bases at the field, but Mitchell has never sustained the kind of air traffic typical of an airport in a city the size

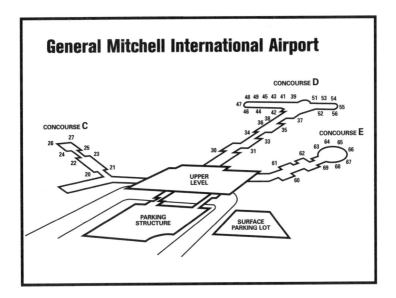

General Mitchell International Airport

Why General Billy Mitchell Had an Airport Named for Him

General Mitchell International Airport was named for World War I hero General William "Billy" Mitchell. Mitchell planned the largest aerial assault of the war when he combined the efforts of 1,481 Allied planes and the U.S. Navy to help the Allied fleets during the Battle of Mihiel. During this battle, airplanes, traveling at speeds of 150 mph, fought dogfights in the sky while the navy picked off German submarines. Air gunners were also responsible for sinking a number of German warships.

Despite his heroism, Mitchell had a career peppered with controversy. While working as assistant chief of the Air Service after the war, Mitchell frequently became violent and argumentative, especially when his superiors didn't agree with his ideas. He was court-martialed in 1925 for defying his superiors and chose to resign from the army rather than accept a five-year suspension.

Mitchell was the grandson of Milwaukeean Alexander Mitchell, a prominent figure in Milwaukee County's early transportation developments.

of Milwaukee because Chicago's O'Hare International Airport, one of the busiest in the country, is located only 90 minutes away. Mitchell is ranked about thirty-fifth in the nation, but expansion projects and plans may change that.

A new Airport Systems cargo complex was opened in October 1989 to provide security and ground-support services for cargo carriers. The complex also provides services for loading and unloading freight and houses a vehicle maintenance shop for ground-support equipment.

Mitchell International responded to increasing air-traffic demands and growing airline service needs by expanding its gate area in 1990. A 16-gate addition to Concourse D opened in December of that year. The additional 16 gates boost Mitchell's total number to 42. In addition, a $6-million, 425-foot moving walkway was constructed to transport passengers swiftly from the Concourse D entrance to the new gate area.

For airport information, call General Mitchell International Airport: 414/747-5300. Ground transportation services are available from Mitchell to communities throughout Wisconsin and Northern Illinois. Ground transportation information (recorded message): 414/747-5308.

Getting to Mitchell International

The airport is just 8 miles from downtown Milwaukee; take I-94 to Exit 318, which leads straight into the airport's parking structure. Parking is free for the first 30 minutes. One multistructure lot allows indoor parking and accesses the airport through a walkway. A nearby second lot offers long-term outdoor parking. Covered parking costs $5 per day. These lots tend to fill early in the morning, so additional remote parking has been added; shuttles travel between the airport and remote parking every 15 minutes.

DCD/David LaHaye

Ferry loading passengers on the Milwaukee River

Getting Around Mitchell International

The lower level of the two-story terminal has two sections with a ticketing/check-in road that flows between them. The west section contains baggage claims, car rentals, and visitor information booths, while the east section has ticketing and check-in counters. From both sections, elevators and escalators carry visitors upstairs to the airport's gates and a skywalk to the parking structure. The terminal's upper level, where the concourses and gates are located, also offers many amenities to travelers. A cocktail lounge and food court are part of a concession mall. The Mitchell Gallery of Flight, retail shops, a 24-hour postal station, conference rooms, and flight information are all accessible and clearly marked.

Major Airlines Serving Mitchell International

For major airline service, contact Midwest Express Airlines at 414/570-7000 or American/American Eagle at 800/223-5436; Spanish language information, 800/228-8356. Other major airlines that service the Milwaukee metropolitan area include Continental, 800/421-2456; Delta, 800/325-1999; United, 800/722-5243; and USAir/USAir Express, 800/428-4322.

The Mitchell Gallery of Flight

The Mitchell Gallery of Flight is located in the upper level of the airport terminal. Here, the story of Billy Mitchell's flamboyant life is told through pictures, personal memorabilia, and reproductions of his many awards. The history of flight, beginning with a model of a flying dinosaur, the pteranodon, tells the story of humankind's interest in flight. A flyable 1911 Curtiss Pusher

ATA Airlines, a low-fare, vacation-oriented airline, offers direct service between Milwaukee and a small number of vacation destinations, including Florida: 800/225-2995.

and the peace mural made by the people of St. Petersburg, Russia, are integral to the museum collection. The museum's unique collection of scale models includes a giant model of the Graf Zeppelin II airship, a Boeing 757, Milwaukee's early Layton Avenue terminal, and a SE-210 Sud Caravelle airliner cockpit. Milwaukee's contribution to flight is also captured through the work of Alfred W. Lawson, a pioneer in his efforts from 1919 to 1921 to establish a national commercial airline in Milwaukee. Many old photographs, historic documents, and a large-scale model tell the Lawson story.

Aerospace technology displays include Project JULIE, Milwaukee's St. Mary's Hospital's space-shuttle experiment, and the Airbus A320, one of the latest airliners to enter service. In all likelihood, a coming exhibit will feature the 1996 experiments of Marquette University's Dr. Robert Fitz on long-term weightlessness and its effects on loss of muscle mass and strength.

Travelers are also encouraged to take a walking tour of concession mall exhibits, which include an Alexander Calder sculpture and the International Peace-through-Art Project.

Railways

Milwaukee is served by three railroads that provide freight service to other important cities throughout the Midwest and North America. Amtrak passenger service is available to all of the United States and Canada. Currently, daily commuter service is available between Chicago and Milwaukee; travelers can connect to cities almost everywhere in the country from Chicago, with daily connections to Detroit and to Springfield, Illi-

Other Airports

Lawrence J. Timmerman Field, on the city's North Side at 92nd Street and Grantosa Boulevard, is a second county-owned airport offering charter passenger service and daily regional flights. For information, call 414/461-3222. Metro Milwaukee is served by six other, smaller aviation airports.

The International Peace-through-Art Project, "Clay: A Healing Way"

On July 30, 1989, the people of Leningrad gathered on the banks of the Neva River to stomp clay used to form a mural as part of the American-Soviet mural project, "Clay: A Healing Way." On July 11, 1989, 5,000 Milwaukeeans gathered on the Summerfest grounds to mold a similar friendship mural, which is displayed in the Riverport in Leningrad. The project was conceived by Hartland, Wisconsin, ceramic artist and teacher Joel Pfeiffer, who realized that in order to create living clay, people needed to support each other physically while mixing the powdered clay and water. He believed this was a powerful symbol of the interconnectedness and interdependence of humankind. "Clay: A Healing Way" is on permanent display at Mitchell International Airport.

nois. Amtrak is considering opening routes to northern Wisconsin over the next few years. For passenger service, call Amtrak: 800/872-7245.

Interstate and Regional Bus Service

The Greyhound Bus terminal is downtown at 606 N. 7th St., on the corner of 7th Street and Michigan Avenue, with buses to most major Wisconsin cities. Travelers can also catch a Greyhound at the Goerkes Corners park-and-ride in Brookfield.

The Badger Coaches terminal is directly across the street from the Greyhound terminal, at 635 N. 7th St. This regional bus makes daily express trips between Madison and Milwaukee and charters group tours anywhere in the United States and Canada. Badger also picks up and delivers passengers at 84th and Michigan and at Goerkes Corners.

Wisconsin Coach Lines bill themselves as "employee shuttle specialists," offering daily commuter service between Waukesha County and downtown Milwaukee, with service to Mitchell International Airport.

Greyhound Bus fare and schedule information, 800/231-2222; Spanish-language information, 800/531-5332. Badger Coaches, 414/276-7490. Wisconsin Coach Lines, 414/544-6503.

Ellingsen & Brady

3

WHERE TO STAY

Whether you're an executive planning an extended business stay and seeking efficiency and affordability or a couple craving a romantic getaway, you'll find that Milwaukee's innkeepers extend their hospitality in a variety of ways. From bed and breakfasts with cozy fireplaces and whirlpool baths to efficiency apartments located on golf courses to elegant and even opulent hotels, there are accommodations within the metropolitan Milwaukee area to suit almost every taste and budget.

Downtown Milwaukee's early growth and industry are evident in the architecture and size of some of the city's grandest hotels. This area hosts many conferences and conventions, so a number of world-class hotels have been built here. Festivals also draw tourists to the downtown area from all over the country. Be forewarned that even with these hotels and the planned addition of Hotel Metro in the next few years, downtown space is extremely limited. Metropolitan Milwaukee also has limited hotel space, so make your reservations well in advance of special events and festivals. Disabled access is indicated by &.

Price rating symbols:
$ **Under $50**
$$ **$50 to $75**
$$$ **$76 to $125**
$$$$ **$126 and up**

Note: Prices reflect a general range and may fluctuate depending on season and availability.

DOWNTOWN AREA

HAMPTON AV

Milwaukee River

Estabrook Park

57

WILSON DR

OAKLAND AV

MARYLAND AV

Atwater Park

57

ATKINSON AV

9TH ST

25TH ST

CAPITOL DR

190

HOPKINS ST

TEUTONIA AV

43

KEEFE AV

BURLEIGH ST

HOLTON ST

HUMBOLDT BLVD

Kern Park

Univ. of Wis. Milw.

DOWNER AV

LAKE DR

LOCUST ST

CENTER ST

KENWOOD ST

27TH ST

16TH ST

25TH ST

20TH ST

FOND DU LAC AV

MEINECKE

5TH ST

4TH ST

MARTIN LUTHER KING JR DR

Kilborn Park

Riverside Park

BRADFORD AV

NORTH AV

12TH ST

RESERVOIR

PLEASANT

BRADY ST

FARWELL AV

PROSPECT AV

LINCOLN MEMORIAL DR

McKinley Park

57

VLIET AV

WALNUT ST

6TH ST

ASTOR

OGDEN ST

JUNEAU AV **6**

Veterans Park

7

HIGHLAND BLVD

13

9 **1**

KILBOURN AV

STATE ST

5

VAN BUREN ST

WELLS ST

11

PLANKINTON

WISCONSIN AV

4

3

MICHIGAN AV

Marquette Univ.

2 **8**

2ND ST

10

HARBOR DR

94

12

MILWAUKEE ST

WATER ST

CANAL ST

CHICAGO ST

— *Summerfest Location*

Mitchell Park

VIRGINIA ST

OREGON ST

Lake Michigan

PIERCE ST

NATIONAL AV

16TH ST

11TH ST

1ST ST

794

LAPHAM ST

Jones Island

MITCHELL ST

Lodging in Downtown Milwaukee

1 Astor Hotel
2 Holiday Inn Milwaukee – City Centre
3 Hotel Metro
4 Hotel Wisconsin
5 Hyatt Regency Milwaukee

6 The Knickerbocker on the Lake
7 Manegold Mansion Bed and Breakfast
8 Milwaukee Hilton
9 Park East Hotel
10 The Pfister Hotel

11 Plaza Hotel and Apartments
12 Ramada Inn – Downtown
13 Wyndham Milwaukee Center Hotel

0   1.5   1.5
KILOMETERS   MILES

N

DOWNTOWN AREA

Hotels and Motels

ASTOR HOTEL
924 E. Juneau Ave.
Milwaukee 53202
414/271-4220
$$$ DA
The Astor embodies turn-of-the-century elegance. Built in 1918, the landmark hotel is listed on the National Register of Historic Places. Stained glass in a floral motif lights the domed entrance and is repeated in a skylight over the reception area. The hotel has 66 traditionally furnished rooms and 30 suites with full kitchens. Catering to business executives, it offers extended-stay programs and apartments. Amenities include complimentary cable, shuttle, affiliate health-club passes, and a daily newspaper.

HOLIDAY INN MILWAUKEE–
CITY CENTRE
611 W. Wisconsin Ave.
Milwaukee 53203
414/273-2950 or 800/HOLIDAY
$$ DA
A spring 1996 effort to remodel all the rooms at this hotel has made it one of the more enjoyable, affordable, all-service places to stay. Its 245 rooms and suites offer in-room coffeemakers. Easy on/off freeway access, ten minutes from Mitchell International, and close to the Grand Avenue Mall. Meeting and banquet rooms available for groups of up to 250 people. &

HOTEL METRO
411 E. Mason St.
Milwaukee 53202
(no phone yet)
$$$$ DA
This art deco–style luxury hotel is scheduled to open in late 1997. Until its fall 1996 purchase by a limited liability corporation set up by developers, this building housed Mariner Realty Co. The building was designed in 1937 by local architects Eschweiler & Eschweiler. Developers plan to recapture the elegance of the period

---

The Hotel Metro Opening Brings an Art Deco Treasure to the Area

According to developers, the Hotel Metro's interior, from operations to furnishings, will reflect the art deco style evident in the curvature of the building's northwest corner and the ornamental brass detailing found throughout the interior. Plans call for everything from uniforms to staff demeanor to reflect the art deco theme, even down to some of the language of that time (employees are being trained by watching movies from the period). Across from the Pfister Hotel and within walking distance of just about everything, the Metro is sure to be a welcome addition to downtown-area hospitality.

---

when they turn the office building into an all-suites hotel. &

HOTEL WISCONSIN
720 N. Old World Third St.
Milwaukee 53203
414/271-4900
$$ **DA**

This vintage and campy hotel used to be a salesman's delight: large rooms allowed salesmen to lay out sample tables and invite clients to peruse their wares. Nowadays, these large rooms appeal to families on short visits and touring theater groups. Members of the touring *Phantom of the Opera* cast stayed here. Not a franchise, its reputation is word-of-mouth. Built in 1913, ongoing restoration has maintained the quirky charm, while new wallpaper and drapes have freshened the rooms. Ten floors contain 125 rooms intended for short stays. Children stay free and parking is free. An additional 75 extended-stay rooms are set aside for long-term visitors. The hotel is home to Café Mélange, which frequently hosts the National Public

The Stagecoach Inn, page 37

The Stagecoach Inn

Radio show *Hotel Wisconsin* from the lobby. A multimillion-dollar renovation effort planned for 1997 should bring this hotel back to its original glory. Hotel Wisconsin is 1 block from the new Wisconsin Center. &

HYATT REGENCY MILWAUKEE
333 W. Kilbourn Ave.
Milwaukee 53203
414/276-1234 or 800/233-1234
$$$ **DA**

An enclosed skywalk connects this 484-room hotel with the Wisconsin Center and Grand Avenue Shopping Center. Its 18-story open atrium makes the registration area one of the most awe-inspiring lobbies in the city. With lounges and conference rooms surrounding the atrium, it is also the site of many local gala fundraisers, weddings, and dinner auctions. Children stay free. The choice of well-heeled business travelers and conventioneers, the hotel also includes three restaurants and three cocktail lounges. Its revolving cocktail lounge is a great choice for late-night brandies and a view of the evening-lit city. &

THE KNICKERBOCKER ON THE LAKE
1028 E. Juneau Ave.
Milwaukee 53202
414/276-8500
$ **DA**

One of Milwaukee's historic lodgings, this was the second hotel built on downtown's East Side at the turn of the century. Not considered as grand as the neighboring Astor Hotel, this is still a graceful location. Rooms and apartments are available at daily, weekly, and monthly rates. &

MILWAUKEE HILTON
509 W. Wisconsin Ave.

Milwaukee 53203
414/271-7250 or 800/HILTONS
$$$ DA
Originally built by Milwaukeean
Walter Schroeder, this hotel's grand
ballrooms and exquisite rooms were
stellar additions to Milwaukee hos-
pitality when it opened in the 1920s.
It retained its reputation for ele-
gance through successive owners
and despite an aging interior. A mul-
timillion-dollar renovation has re-
stored it to its original grandeur. The
marble flooring, gold filigree,
wrought-iron stair railings, and
crystal chandeliers remind visitors
of the city's manufacturing wealth.
With more than 30,000 square feet
of conference and banquet ser-
vices, the Hilton hosts many area
weddings and social events. The
lavish Crystal Ballroom can accom-
modate gatherings of up to 1,000.
The hotel's 500 deluxe rooms offer
up-to-date and secure amenities.
An indoor pool and fitness center
help guests relax. &

PARK EAST HOTEL
916 E. State St.
Milwaukee 53202
414/276-8800 or 800/328-7275
$$$ DA
Computer hookups and health-club
passes attract a steady stream of
business clients to this hotel. Summer tourists enjoy the lake views
from many of the 160 newly remodeled rooms; many with whirlpool tubs
keep guests coming back. Videocas-
sette players, free parking, and shuttle service are added features. &

THE PFISTER HOTEL
424 E. Wisconsin Ave.
Milwaukee 53202
414/273-8222 or 800/558-8222
$$$$ DA
This four-star hotel has been Milwaukee's grandest since its opening
in 1893. Despite its opulent elegance, it is also one of the friend-
liest establishments in the city.
Every detail is attended to by a
courteous staff. This is the hotel that

A History of Elegance at the Pfister

*Back in the late 1880s, Guido Pfister set out to build the "Grand
Hotel of the West." The elegant landmark hotel, the Pfister, has been
visited by every U.S. president since McKinley. First-time visitors are
usually awestruck by the massive gilded lobby; the hotel's motto,
Salve, a Latin term of greeting and farewell, is set in the gilded plas-
ter as a promise to all who pass through the doors that this will be a
pleasurable stay. The corridors and public sitting galleries contain
the largest nineteenth-century Victorian art collection on display in
any hotel in the world. Each room and suite attends to guest needs,
with a variety of amenities ranging from Jacuzzi baths and personal
sitting rooms to Godiva chocolates on guest pillows.*

Top Ten Historically Famous Guests Who Have Made the Pfister Their Home away from Home

1. President McKinley
2. President Theodore Roosevelt
3. Vince Lombardi and the Green Bay Packers
4. President John F. Kennedy
5. Prince Henry Hohenzollern of Prussia
6. Sir David Lloyd George, past Prime Minister of Great Britain
7. Sarah Bernhardt
8. Lillian Russell
9. John L. Sullivan
10. "Buffalo Bill" Cody

sports teams and celebrity guests prefer for their Milwaukee visits. Valet parking. ♿

PLAZA HOTEL AND APARTMENTS
1007 N. Cass St.
Milwaukee 53202
414/276-2101
$$ DA

Located near Lake Michigan, many of the furnished rooms contain full kitchens. Reduced rent for long-term stays. Parking is available. Daily, weekly, or monthly rates. ♿

RAMADA INN–DOWNTOWN
633 W. Michigan St.
Milwaukee 53203
414/272-8410 or 800/228-2828
$$ DA

Three blocks from the arena, Bradley Center, and Wisconsin Center, this Ramada is also convenient to I-94 and County Stadium. Located 1 mile from the Potawatomi Bingo Casino and Summerfest grounds, the hotel fills quickly during summer festivals and charges higher rates during special events. This downtown high-rise with large lobby, fitness center, and indoor pool is typical of hotels and motels built in the 1960s and '70s. The 155 rooms and suites were recently remodeled. ♿

WYNDHAM MILWAUKEE CENTER HOTEL
139 E. Kilbourn Ave.
Milwaukee 53202
414/276-8686 or 800/WYNDHAM
$$$ DA

In Milwaukee's exciting theater district and near the Bradley Sports Center, the Wyndham's 221 gracious guest rooms in a modern 10-story high-rise make it an attractive location for sports buffs, as well. The Midwestern cuisine at the Kilbourn Restaurant offers an attractive stopover for less adventurous guests. Free use of the in-house health/fitness facilities, two lounges, laundry, valet service, and full-service cable TV indicate that this hotel is geared to the business traveler during the week. Weekend theatergoers find the hotel's theater packages enticing and the location, divine. &

Bed and Breakfasts

MANEGOLD MANSION BED AND BREAKFAST
3009 W. Highland Blvd.
Milwaukee 53208
414/344-5655
$$$ DA

Previously the Highland House Bed and Breakfast, this historic 1897 home was built by William and Milhelda Manegold. One of ten mansions built on Highland Boulevard in the late 1800s and early 1900s, the building has 17 rooms, four baths, two fireplaces, and, typical of houses built at the turn of the century, a third-floor ballroom. While the fireplace warms winter visitors, an enclosed porch and two outdoor porches make this a pleasant all-season stay.

The Hyatt Regency, page 29

The Hyatt Regency Milwaukee

EAST SIDE

Hotels and Motels

EXEL INN OF MILWAUKEE
5485 N. Port Washington Rd.
Glendale 53217
414/961-7272 or 800/356-8013
$ ES

Convenience makes this comfortable economy motel a good choice for visitors interested in shopping at the Bay Shore Mall or visiting the northeast suburbs. All Exel Inns provide inside halls for security and free continental breakfast every day. Located immediately off I-43 at Silver Spring Drive East (Exit 78), this inn provides some rooms with whirlpools and allows pets under 25 pounds. Children under 18 may stay in a separate room with a single rate for both. Lake Michigan is 1 mile away; Summerfest grounds are 5 miles. &

MANCHESTER EAST
7065 N. Port Washington Rd.
Glendale 53217
414/351-6960
$$ ES

This 133-room all-suite hotel caters to business clients during the week. An indoor pool and exercise room are just a few of the amenities the hotel provides. Close to downtown businesses and festivals, the hotel also accommodates visitors planning to take in Milwaukee's performing arts, sights, and events. &

WOODFIELD SUITES
5423 N. Port Washington Rd.
Glendale 53217
414/962-6767
$$$ ES

This new suite hotel provides guests with coffeemakers, refrigerators, microwaves, and hair dryers in every

EAST SIDE

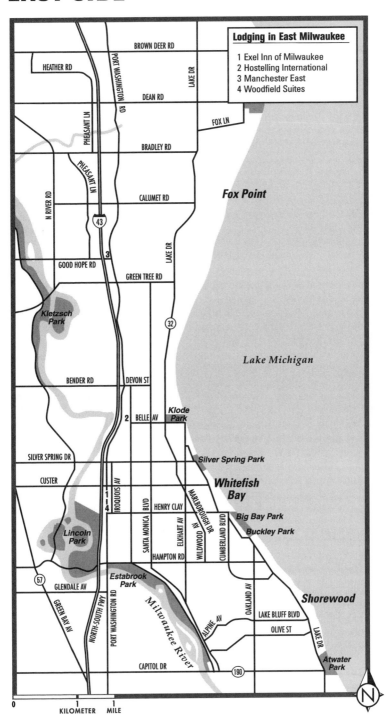

Lodging in East Milwaukee

1 Exel Inn of Milwaukee
2 Hostelling International
3 Manchester East
4 Woodfield Suites

BROWN DEER RD

HEATHER RD

PORT WASHINGTON RD

LAKE DR

DEAN RD

FOX LN

PHEASANT LN

BRADLEY RD

PHEASANT LN

N RIVER RD

CALUMET RD

Fox Point

43

3

GOOD HOPE RD

LAKE DR

GREEN TREE RD

Kletzsch Park

32

Lake Michigan

BENDER RD

DEVON ST

2 BELLE AV

Klode Park

SILVER SPRING DR

Silver Spring Park

CUSTER

IROQUOIS AV

Whitefish Bay

1
1
4

SANTA MONICA BLVD

HENRY CLAY

MARLBOROUGH DR

ELKHART AV

WILDWOOD AV

CUMBERLAND BLVD

Big Bay Park

Lincoln Park

Buckley Park

HAMPTON RD

57

GLENDALE AV

Estabrook Park

OAKLAND AV

Shorewood

GREEN BAY AV

NORTH-SOUTH HWY

PORT WASHINGTON RD

Milwaukee River

ALPINE AV

LAKE BLUFF BLVD

OLIVE ST

LAKE DR

CAPITOL DR

190

Atwater Park

0   1   1
KILOMETER MILE

N

room. Large work desks equip each suite, as do full-size ironing boards, irons, and data-port hookups for computers, making this the ideal site for corporate guests. Deluxe continental breakfasts each morning and cocktails each evening are included in the room price. The suites include an indoor pool, fitness facility, and whirlpool. Several nearby restaurants serve guests. Children under 17 stay free with their parents. &

Hostels

HOSTELLING INTERNATIONAL
5900 N. Port Washington Rd.
Glendale 53217
414/961-2525 ES

HI is the largest system of lodgings in the world right now, providing inexpensive and unusual lodging experiences for travelers of all ages, with lower rates for those over 50. Membership is $25 for the first year and $20 after that, with family and youth memberships available. HI offers places to stay worldwide, including a dairy barn in Milwaukee; a sailing ship in Stockholm, Sweden; lighthouses throughout the United States; and even a jail in Ottawa, Canada. Talk about educational travel! The hostel service is working on obtaining downtown Milwaukee, Eagle (Old World Wisconsin), Lapham Peak, and Madison locations.

NORTH SIDE

Hotels and Motels

BREEZE INN TO THE CHALET MOTEL
10401 N. Port Washington Rd.
Mequon 53092
414/241-4510 or 800/343-4510

$$$ NS

This north-suburban motel promises comfort and affordability in its 142 newly renovated rooms. Billed as clean, safe, and conveniently located to Historic Cedarburg, it ensures that guests enjoy their stay without worries. Some rooms include whirlpool tubs. The inn is 20 minutes from County Stadium, the Domes, Milwaukee County Zoo, and the Milwaukee Public Museum. Fifteen minutes north of Downtown Milwaukee on I-43, the motel is less convenient to downtown than some hotels, but it offers visitors with Northshore interests a great locale.

BUDGETEL INN
5442 N. Lovers Lane Rd.
Milwaukee 53225
414/535-1300 or 800/428-3438
$ NS

This inn and its 142 newly renovated guest rooms is close to a number of Menomonee Falls industrial parks. Complimentary continental breakfast is delivered to rooms daily. Some rooms, called "leisure suites," contain refrigerators and microwaves. Each room has a coffeemaker. The inn is immediately off of Highway 45 on Silver Spring Drive. &

MANCHESTER SUITES–NORTHWEST
11777 W. Silver Spring Dr.
Milwaukee 53225
414/462-3500 or 800/723-8280
$$ NS

This living-room setting with refrigerator, wet bar, and microwave caters to business clients and motor travelers. Its attractive lobby and hallways make this an appealing choice. Complimentary made-to-order breakfast is served daily. Free HBO, CNN, ESPN, and local calls. A Denny's and

NORTH SIDE

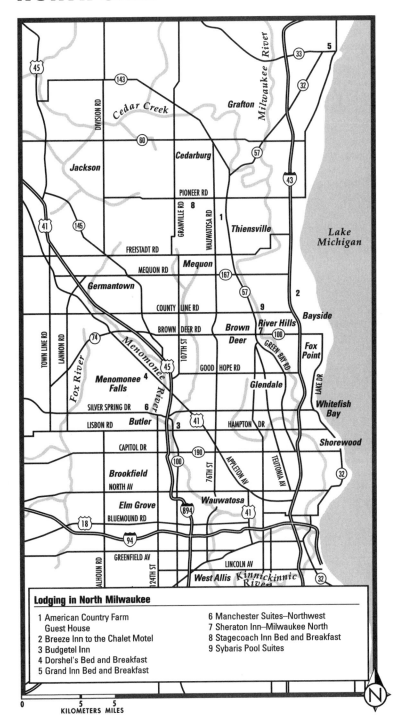

Lodging in North Milwaukee

1 American Country Farm
   Guest House
2 Breeze Inn to the Chalet Motel
3 Budgetel Inn
4 Dorshel's Bed and Breakfast
5 Grand Inn Bed and Breakfast

6 Manchester Suites–Northwest
7 Sheraton Inn–Milwaukee North
8 Stagecoach Inn Bed and Breakfast
9 Sybaris Pool Suites

0   5   5
KILOMETERS MILES

other convenience restaurants are located nearby. Children under 14 stay free. The Highways 45 and 100 location makes this a convenient stopover for travelers. &

SHERATON INN–MILWAUKEE NORTH
8900 N. Kildeer Ct.
Brown Deer 53209
414/355-8585 or 800/325-3535
$$$ NS
Some rooms contain king-size beds and pull-out sofas. With 149 rooms, restaurant, lounge, indoor pool, and whirlpool and sauna on premises, the Sheraton attracts corporate guests during the week, and wedding or extended-family guests on weekends. Pay-per-view cable is available in all rooms. Seasonal rates follow occupancy patterns with lower fall and winter rates. Lower rates also apply to holiday specials and New Year's packages. Since it's near the Schroeder Aquatic and Athletic Center, soccer and swim coaches tend to put their teams up here on weekends and during tournaments. Locals also house their visiting family here. Free van service to the airport is provided. &

SYBARIS POOL SUITES
10240 Cedarburg Rd.
Mequon 53092
414/242-8000
$$$$ NS
A romantic country setting with modern conveniences and incredible amenities makes this the perfect spot for romantic getaways. Rooms and suites incorporate whirlpools and full-size pools into the decor and are priced accordingly. The romantic Victorian room has a country-style decor with a queen-size bed, Ben Franklin fireplace, double whirlpool, mi-crowave, refrigerator, and patio with a grill. Three deluxe swimming pool suites are available. The original swimming-pool suite contains a 22-foot swimming pool—in the room! The Chalet holds a 26-foot swimming pool with a cascading waterfall, a slide from balcony to pool, a double whirlpool in the bedroom, and a steam room in the pool area. Couples who have stayed at the Sybaris say that their worldly problems seem to disappear the moment they enter their rooms, where quiet luxury seems to prevail. Management offers tours each afternoon from 1 until 5. &

Bed and Breakfasts

AMERICAN COUNTRY FARM GUEST HOUSE
12112 N. Wauwatosa Rd.
Mequon 53097
414/242-0194
$$$ NS
A stone cottage set in a wooded cove, this a private and cozy place to stay. A patio, twin or king-sized bed, wood-burning fireplace, kitchen, private bath, air conditioning, and color TV provide convenience, as well. Located 4 miles from Cedarburg, guests can take advantage of the location and see the covered bridge, tour Pioneer Village, and hike and bike North Side trails. &

DORSHEL'S BED AND BREAKFAST GUESTHOUSE
W140 N7616 Lilly Rd.
Menomonee Falls 53051
414/255-7866
$$ NS
Three traditionally decorated rooms accented with antiques provide a homey ambiance. Full breakfast is served each morning, and fresh flowers are placed around the house

daily. Guests are provided with Wisconsin cheeses, home-baked pastries, and candies in their room. Dorshel's is minutes from the freeway and close to tourist areas around Milwaukee, including Holy Hill, the Cedarburg Winery, Milwaukee County Zoo, and Brewers Stadium.

GRAND INN BED AND BREAKFAST
832 Grand Ave., Hwy. 33
Port Washington 53074
414/284-6719
$$$ **NS**

A turn-of-the-century Queen Anne house, this inn contains five bedrooms and a carriage house. The beautifully restored inn is located in one of the state's most quaint Lake Michigan ports. A master suite features a sitting room with a fireplace, a porch, and a king-sized bed. Some other rooms have fireplaces, whirlpools, and sitting rooms or private porches. The inn is near Harrison Beach State Park, Riveredge Nature Center, and Lake Michigan. Children are not invited.

STAGECOACH INN BED AND BREAKFAST
W61 N520 Washington Ave.
Cedarburg 53012
414/375-0208 or 888/375-0208
$$$ **NS**

Just 20 minutes north of Milwaukee, this spacious inn has 12 rooms, three on the first floor. A country inn, the historic building has been restored with antiques and amenities. Six rooms have whirlpool tubs. Guests are within walking distance of Cedarburg's shops, the winery, restaurants, and galleries. The Riveredge Nature Center, Pioneer Village, and Cedar Creek Settlement are also nearby.

WEST SIDE

Hotels and Motels

CAMELOT INN
10900 W. Blue Mound Rd.
Wauwatosa 53226
414/258-2910
$$ **WS**

Located near Milwaukee County Zoo, this 66-room inn features full cable TV, complimentary coffee in the lobby, and a restaurant. The location is good but the aging inn could benefit from a face-lift. Discounted zoo tickets are available at the desk.

COURTYARD BY MARRIOTT
16865 W. Blue Mound Rd.
Brookfield 53005
414/821-1800 or 800/321-2211
$$$ **WS**

Designed so the lobby and rooms are built around a courtyard inside the hotel, this Marriott offers a quaint gazebo complete with lawn chairs and chaise longues, making the courtyard a quiet respite for visitors. The courtyard is not accessible from the outside. The classically decorated mauve and paisley lobby opens to a dining area that serves daily breakfast buffets. Large rooms contain refrigerators and cable TV. Colonial Williamsburg furnishings and decorating make this a charming but classic place to stay. This particular hotel, on Blue Mound Road, is surprisingly quiet considering that it sits on one of the most congested streets in metropolitan Milwaukee. It's convenient to Brookfield Square and strip malls that offer varied and unique shopping. &

DAYS INN
11811 W. Blue Mound Rd.

WEST SIDE

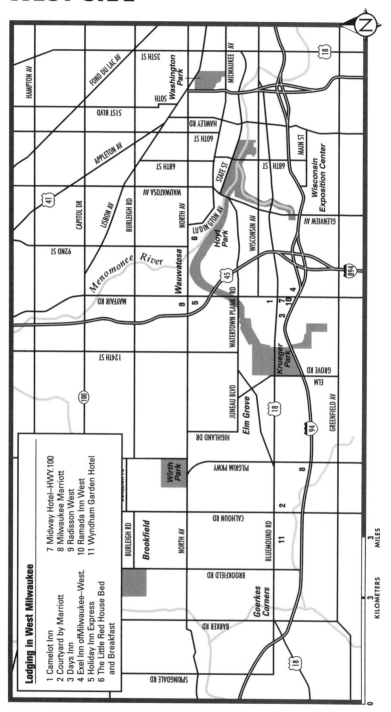

Lodging in West Milwaukee

1 Camelot Inn
2 Courtyard by Marriott
3 Days Inn
4 Exel Inn of Milwaukee—West.
5 Holiday Inn Express
6 The Little Red House Bed and Breakfast
7 Midway Hotel—HWY.100
8 Milwaukee Marriott
9 Radisson West
10 Ramada Inn West
11 Wyndham Garden Hotel

Wauwatosa 53226
414/771-4500 or 800/329-7466
$ (Sept–May)
$$ (June–Aug) **WS**

Minutes from Milwaukee County Stadium, State Fair Park, Pettit Ice Center, and Milwaukee County Zoo, a wooded backdrop gives this 156-room inn a suburban feel. Rooms are newly carpeted. Although this is a Days Inn, it is still locally owned. The glassed-in lobby, looking onto a courtyard and indoor swimming pool, makes this an attractive resting spot. Amenities include a sauna, coffee shop, cocktail lounge, and the attached Christy's restaurant. Considered a leisure hotel, the inn caters to families and weddings. Located close to Highway 100 and I-94, this is an especially nice stopover for tourists and Milwaukee Brewers' fans. Of special note to Packers fans: Brett Favre put Christy's on the local map when he signed shirts and memorabilia there in October 1996. Smoking and nonsmoking rooms are available. ⅄

EXEL INN OF MILWAUKEE–WEST
115 N. Mayfair Rd.
Wauwatosa 53226
414/257-0140 or 800/356-8013
$ **WS**

A no-frills lodging with an inside hall for added security, this motor hotel is located directly off of I-94 (Exit 304B-Mayfair Rd.) on Highway 100, and 1 block south of Blue Mound Road, convenient to Milwaukee County Zoo, State Fair Park, and Pettit Ice Center. Its location in a treed valley makes this hotel more attractive than many others along Highway 100. Continental breakfasts and hot coffee are among the inn's amenities. A few whirlpool suites are available for $100 a night; some nonsmoking rooms are

available. Nearby restaurants include a Ground Round, Oscar's, and Eduardo's Pizza. ⅄

HOLIDAY INN EXPRESS
11111 W. North Ave.
Wauwatosa 53226
414/778-0333 or 800/HOLIDAY
$$ **WS**

Located near Mayfair Mall, Harley-Davidson, Briggs and Stratton, the Wisconsin Medical College, and Froedtert Hospital and the attached research park, this 122-room hotel tends to attract business clients. A complimentary breakfast bar provides coffee and pastries for guests on the move; same day laundry service and a copier meet additional business needs. An adjacent Denny's provides meal service 24 hours a day. ⅄

MIDWAY HOTEL–HIGHWAY 100
251 N. Mayfair Rd.
Wauwatosa 53226
414/774-3600 or 800/528-1234
$$–$$$ **WS**

This hotel, one of the first motor lodges along the Highway 100 strip, retains its comfortable charm. The hospitable staff makes this a pleasant haven on the bustling hotel corner. Appealing to both corporate and weekend family guests, the hotel lobby overlooks an atrium filled with live trees, an indoor pool, and Ping-Pong and pool tables. Holiday packages are available. Banquet rooms can accommodate up to 300 for theater-style events. Small meeting rooms seat groups of 5 to 25. The hotel's updated decor is teal and cream, with oak trim lining the atrium. Oscar's Restaurant is located on the premises. ⅄

MILWAUKEE MARRIOTT
375 S. Moorland Rd.

Brookfield 53005
414/786-1100 or 800/228-9290
$$ **WS**
Adjacent to the Brookfield Square parking lot and I-94, this full-service hotel was one of the first west-suburban hotels. Brookfield Hills Golf Course, an easy and attractive 18-hole course adjacent to the hotel, provides readily available reasons to turn a stay here into a golf get-away. The elegantly decorated hotel still attracts families on weekends and corporate clients during the week. Whitney's restaurant and Rumors Lounge on the premises. &

RADISSON WEST HOTEL
2303 N. Mayfair Rd.
Wauwatosa 53226
414/257-3400 or 800/333-3333
$$$ **WS**
An upscale corporate environment, this 150-room hotel is convenient to I-94. A major renovation enlarged the lobby area and added a deli and state-of-the-art fitness center. An in-

door pool and sauna, banquet facilities for 300, and complimentary air-port transportation make this a haven for corporate clients. Because the hotel is adjacent to Mayfair Mall, shopping is an easy option while staying here. Structural changes increased the number of king-size rooms from 50 to 90. Sixty rooms contain two double beds. &

RAMADA INN WEST
CONVENTION AND CONFERENCE
CENTER
201 N. Mayfair Rd.
Wauwatosa 53226
414/771-4400 or 800/531-3965
$$ **WS**
This is another motor hotel on the corner of Highway 100 and Blue Mound Road near I-94. Heated indoor pool, sauna, whirlpool, and exercise room provide corporate guests with relaxation and stress relief. A game room, complete with Ping-Pong and video games, entertains families. A restaurant and

Wyndham Garden Hotel, page 41

Wyndham Garden Hotel

lounge located on the premises and weekend packages make this an attractive hotel option. Close to Milwaukee County Stadium, Pettit Ice Center, Milwaukee County Zoo, and State Fair Park, its 235 rooms have recently been remodeled. &

WYNDHAM GARDEN HOTEL
18155 Blue Mound Rd.
Brookfield 53045
414/792-1212 or 800/WYNDHAM
$$$ **WS**

Guest rooms and public rooms in this upscale hotel were recently made over to create a rich and sophisticated decor. Oriental rugs grace the oak-trimmed lobby. Although this hotel caters to weekday corporate travelers, it maintains a steady stream of weekend leisure traffic, as well. Weekend packages are available at reduced rates. An indoor three-lane lap pool with a Jacuzzi whirlpool and an exercise room with a full line of workout equipment (including treadmill, weights, and stationary bikes) make this an elite fitness center that guests appreciate. In-room amenities include full-size ironing boards and irons, coffeemakers, hair dryers, pay-per-view TV, data ports for laptops, and voice mail. The Garden Café serves breakfast, lunch, and dinner. The hotel also accommodates small and large groups in its lounge, a 2,200-square-foot conference room, and an executive boardroom that seats up to 12 people. While the hotel is home to many weekday corporate clients, it also hosts weekend reunions and weddings. &

Bed and Breakfasts

THE LITTLE RED HOUSE BED
AND BREAKFAST

The Grand Milwaukee Hotel

The Grand Milwaukee Hotel, page 43

9212 Jackson Park Blvd.
Wauwatosa 53226
414/479-0646
$$ **WS**

Wauwatosa's first bed and breakfast, the Little Red House opened in 1996. This tiny establishment really is a red house on a quiet residential street. Guest quarters are two comfortable rooms, with a shared bath. Amenities include central air and sensational homemade breakfasts. Guests are promised easy freeway access. Wauwatosa is within minutes of all Greater Milwaukee attractions, area restaurants, Mayfair Mall, and Wauwatosa's specialty shops.

SOUTH SIDE

Hotels and Motels

BEST WESTERN WOODS VIEW
INN
5501 W. National Ave.
Milwaukee 53214
414/671-6400 or 800/528-1234

SOUTH SIDE

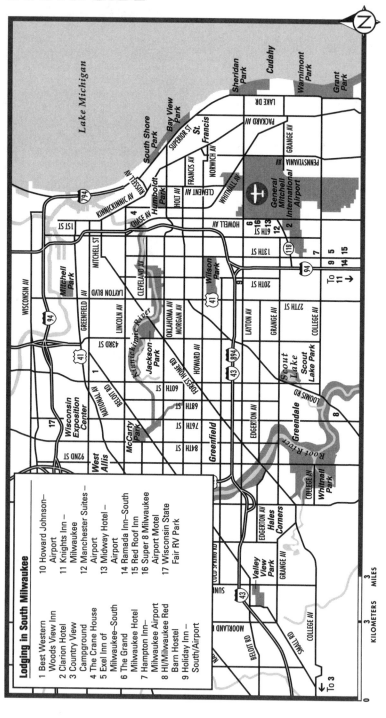

Lodging in South Milwaukee

1 Best Western Woods View Inn
2 Clarion Hotel
3 Country View Campground
4 The Crane House
5 Exel Inn of Milwaukee–South
6 The Grand Milwaukee Hotel
7 Hampton Inn–Milwaukee Airport
8 HI/Milwaukee Red Barn Hostel
9 Holiday Inn–South/Airport
10 Howard Johnson–Airport
11 Knights Inn–Milwaukee
12 Manchester Suites–Airport
13 Midway Hotel–Airport
14 Ramada Inn–South
15 Red Roof Inn
16 Super 8 Milwaukee Airport Motel
17 Wisconsin State Fair RV Park

The Pfister Hotel, page 30

$$ **SS**

Located near the South Side, this newly remodeled inn is within 8 blocks of County Stadium, 3 blocks of Veterans Administration, 1 mile of Pettit Ice Center, and 3 miles of Milwaukee County Zoo. Convenient amenities in this 62-unit complex include an indoor pool and an on-premises restaurant. Kitchenettes are available.

CLARION HOTEL
5311 S. Howell Ave.
Milwaukee 53207
414/481-2400 or 800/221-2222
$$ **SS**

Across from the airport, this 180-room hotel with 1-, 2-, and 3-room suites provides inviting accommodations for travelers. Extras include free cocktails and daily, round-the-clock airport limousine service. The hotel has an indoor pool, sauna, and satellite TV. Complimentary continental breakfast is served daily. In keeping with its efforts to accommodate air travelers, the hotel offers long-term secured parking on-site.

Children stay free. The hotel also provides a banquet and conference center for up to 800 people for sit-down affairs, 1,000 people for buffets. The convention center is maintained through ongoing remodeling, with the latest major renovation an addition of a new wing. ♿

EXEL INN OF MILWAUKEE–SOUTH
1201 W. College Ave.
Oak Creek 53154
414/764-1776
$ **SS**

This no-frills inn is a convenient airport hotel. Long-term parking and free 24-hour shuttle service to and from Mitchell International make this 110-room guest house especially attractive to Wisconsinites on their way to other cities. Additional amenities include daily continental breakfast, and remote control TV with HBO. Kids under 17 stay free. The hotel offers smoking and non-smoking accommodations. ♿

THE GRAND MILWAUKEE HOTEL
4747 S. Howell Ave.

When staying in local hotels, be sure to ask about kids' rates. Many Milwaukee area hotels offer free accommodations and meals for children under 18 if they are accompanied by a parent.

Milwaukee 53207
414/481-8000 or 800/558-3862
$$$ **SS**
The Grand offers free airport limousine service, 510 rooms, and convention facilities for up to 500 people. A health club, tennis and racquetball, indoor/outdoor pools, saloon, gourmet dining, and a coffee shop are part of the facilities. &

HAMPTON INN–MILWAUKEE AIRPORT
1200 W. College Ave.
Milwaukee 53221
414/762-4240
$$ **SS**
In a beautifully landscaped business/airport location 1.5 miles from the airport and 11 miles south of downtown, this Hampton offers an indoor pool and whirlpool along with complimentary full continental breakfast and 24-hour shuttle service, cable TV with free HBO, and a 100-percent-satisfaction guarantee: if you aren't completely satisfied, the cost of your night's stay is cheerfully refunded. No food or beverage service on-site, but a Shoney's restaurant is within walking distance. &

HOLIDAY INN–SOUTH/AIRPORT
6331 S. 13th St.
Milwaukee 53221
414/764-1500 or 800/HOLIDAY
$$ **SS**
A Holidome Fun Center gives guests ample opportunity to relax and rest, with an indoor pool, whirlpool, and table and video games. The fun center in this 158-room hotel makes it a great family-centered place to stay. Children under 18 stay free with parents. Facilities are available for meetings and banquets for up to 300 people. &

HOWARD JOHNSON–AIRPORT
1716 W. Layton Ave.
Greendale 53221
414/282-7000 or 800/446-4656
$ (Sept–May)
$$ (June–Aug)   **SS**
Another airport convenience hotel, this 96-room lodging accommodates smokers and nonsmokers. Howard Johnsons once graced many of Milwaukee's freeway on- and off-ramps, but most have slowly given way to all-suite hotels. This one offers free HBO and CNN, an outdoor pool, guest laundry, and a courtesy car to and from the airport. &

KNIGHTS INN–MILWAUKEE
9420 S. 20th St.
Oak Creek 53154
414/761-3807 or 800/843-5644
$ **SS**
Located at I-94 and Ryan Rd. (Exit 322), this hotel is close to the state's largest rummage sale, along Seven-Mile Road, and offers 115 rooms; free cable TV, local calls, and stays for children under 18; truck and trailer parking; and senior discounts. AAA approved. &

MANCHESTER SUITES–AIRPORT
200 W. Grange Ave.
Milwaukee 53207
414/744-3600 or 800/723-8280
$$ SS

Suitable for air and business travelers, this 100-suite hotel is across from the airport. A courtesy airport shuttle transports air travelers day and night. A newer hotel, its comfortable suites offer a living-room setting complete with a refrigerator, wet bar, and microwave. Guest service includes complimentary made-to-order breakfast every day, and free HBO, ESPN, CNN, and local calls. &

Courtyard by Marriott, page 37

MIDWAY HOTEL–AIRPORT
5105 S. Howell Ave.
Milwaukee 53207
414/769-2100 or 800/528-1234
$$$ SS

This hotel has 139 rooms and on-site dining room and lounge. Midways developed a reputation during the early to mid-1970s of offering family-centered recreation areas, each equipped with an indoor pool, sauna, and whirlpool. The recreation areas are centered in the hotels' atriums, providing an almost-tropical holiday atmosphere. &

RAMADA INN–SOUTH
6401 S. 13th St.
Milwaukee 53221
414/764-5300 or 800/228-2828
$$$ SS

This Milwaukee hotel and convention center caters to business seminars and symposiums. The hotel has 191 rooms and three suites. A restaurant, coffee shop, and cocktail lounge are part of the center. The 2,000-square-foot ballroom—with 14-foot ceilings and an unobstructed view—adapts to large

business gatherings. A separate executive symposium accommodates smaller groups. Eighteen-foot breakout rooms are at ground level, allowing the facility to host a number of speakers or workshops simultaneously. The convention center is freeway-accessible, and a free airport shuttle runs 24 hours a day. An indoor pool, sauna, whirlpool, and indoor and outdoor recreation are as offer guests opportunities for relaxation. &

RED ROOF INN
6360 S. 13th St.
Oak Creek 53154
414/764-3500 or 800/THE ROOF
$ SS

A no-frills hotel with 108 rooms, this Red Roof, part of the national chain, offers free ESPN, Showtime, daily morning paper, and coffee. Children under 18 stay free with parents. &

SUPER 8 MILWAUKEE AIRPORT MOTEL
5253 S. Howell Ave.
Milwaukee 53207

414/481-8488 or 800/800-8000
$$ SS

This is another no-frills airport hotel, located directly across the street from Mitchell International. Only 5 miles from downtown, this motel was designed with suites. Pets are welcome with permission of the staff, and nonsmoking rooms are available by request. Free cable TV, HBO, and continental breakfast daily. Whirlpool, guest laundry, fax, airport shuttle, and free parking make this basic but convenient motel popular with travelers. Children under 18 stay free with parents. &

Bed and Breakfasts

THE CRANE HOUSE
346 E. Wilson St.
Bay View 53207
414/483-1512
$$ SS

This bed and breakfast, owned and operated by local couple Paula Tirrito and Steven Skavroneck, is just south of downtown in Bay View, within walking distance of South Shore Park on Lake Michigan. The four guest rooms, decorated in vintage themes, offer guests an eclectic choice. The Beach Room contains seashells and wicker. The Radio Room houses Skavroneck's antique radio collection. Both of these rooms provide queen-size beds. The Hat Room, with one full-size and one twin bed, is decorated with men's and women's hats from the 1930s, '40s, and '50s. The Bea Room has an antique bedroom set, a gift from Tirrito's Aunt Bea. A three-course breakfast and coffee are delivered to guests' doors every morning. The Crane House does have a shared bathroom. The owner-operators keep a file of local restaurants for their guests' consideration.

Hostels

HI/MILWAUKEE RED BARN HOSTEL
6750 W. Loomis Rd.
Greendale 53221
414/529-3299
$ SS

Although a bit drafty in winter, this hostel gives travelers a real look at life on a Wisconsin dairy farm. Weary travelers can rest their heads with the cows—the barn serves as sleeping quarters. Fees are $10 plus tax for members; an additional $3 if you're not a member.

Camping

COUNTRY VIEW CAMPGROUND
S110 W226400 Craig Ave.
Mukwonago 53149
414/662-3654
$ SS

This privately owned campground rents wooded and open-view sites with hookups. A swimming pool, playground, and game room make this a feasible family spot. Groceries, snacks, laundry facilities, and a pavilion ensure additional convenience. The campground is open mid-April through mid-October. &

WISCONSIN STATE FAIR RV PARK
I-94 and West 84th Street
Milwaukee 53214
414/266-7035
$ SS

Open April 1–October 31, State Fair RV Park is the city's only urban RV camp. The park features 128 sites, showers, restrooms, dumping stations, and electrical hookups. Only minutes from most city attractions, the park fills quickly during the summer months—reservations are recommended. Pets are permitted. &

Ellingsen & Brady

4

WHERE TO EAT

Friday night means Fish Fry Night in Milwaukee. Traditionally, this is the night that locals gather with friends at the corner pub to fill up on beer-battered or breaded deep-fried fish dipped in tartar sauce. Usually the dish is served all-you-can-eat family-style, with accompaniments of cole slaw, French fries, and rye bread. Many local restaurants put aside their standard menus on Fridays in order to keep the deep fryers smoking with fish and fries. This tradition is so deeply ingrained that Milwaukeeans express shock when they discover that the fish fry fails to excite the national palate.

Any other night, the city is hopping with gastronomic choices. You can dine on traditional German fare at one of the city's fine old establishments; treat yourself to a champagne brunch while cruising on Lake Michigan; enjoy a cozy meal at a neighborhood trattoria; or sample a range of more exotic cuisines, from African to Vietnamese. Explore and you'll find that this Mid-western city, smack in the middle of the country's grain belt, offers refreshing surprises that reflect the ethnic and cultural diversity of its inhabitants. Mil-waukee, in fact, brings culinary experts to their feet with applause again and again.

This chapter begins with a list of restaurants organized by the type of food each offers. For details about each restaurant, see pages 53–72, where retau-rants are listed alphabetically by geographical zone. Dollar sign symbols indi-cate how much you can expect to spend per person for an entree at each restaurant. Disabled access is indicated by ＆.

Price rating symbols:
$ Under $10
$$ $11 to $20
$$$ $21 and up

John Ernst, page 53

John Ernst

Stackner Cabaret (DA), p. 55

East Indian

Taste of India (WS), p. 66

Fish Fry

Alioto's (WS), p. 61
Balistreri's Bluemound Inn (WS),
   p. 62
Café Mélange (DA), p. 52
Great National Saloon
   & Restaurant (SS), p. 67
Historic Turner Hall
   & Restaurant (DA), p. 53
The Red Mill (WS), p. 66
Smith Brothers Fish Shanty (NS),
   p. 61

Frozen Custard

Gilles Frozen Custard Drive-In
   (WS), p. 64
Kopps (SS), p. 69
Leon's Frozen Custard Drive-In (SS),
   p. 69

German

John Ernst (DA), p. 53
Karl Ratzsch's Restaurant (DA),
   p. 53
Kegel's Inn (SS), p. 67–69
Mader's German Restaurant (DA),
   p. 54

Italian

Alioto's (WS), p. 61
Ann's Italian Restaurant (SS), p. 66
Balistreri's Bluemound Inn (WS),
   p. 61–62
Balistreri's Italian-American
   Ristorante (WS), p. 62
Bartolotta (WS), p. 62
Buca Little Italy (DA), p. 51
Mama Mia's on Blue Mound (WS),
   p. 65

Mimma's Café (DA), p. 54
Salvatore the III (SS), p. 69

Lunch Counters

George Webb's (NS), p. 59
Gollash Pharmacies (SS), p. 67
Heinemann's (WS), p. 65

Mexican/South American

Conejito's Place (DA), p. 52
Hector's, A Mexican Restaurant
   (WS), p. 64–65
La Fuente Restaurant (SS), p. 69
Palomas Restaurant
   & Banquet Hall (DA), p. 54–55

Seafood

The Anchorage, Milwaukee River
   Hilton Inn (ES), p. 56
Scotty's Crab House (ES), p. 55
Smith Brothers Fish Shanty (NS),
   p. 61

Serbian

Old Town Serbian
   Gourmet House (DA), p. 54
Three Brothers Bar & Restaurant
   (SS), p. 69–70

Tea

Watts Tea Shop (DA), p. 56

Vegetarian

Abu's Jerusalem Restaurant (DA),
   p. 51
Beans & Barley Market
   & Café (DA), p. 51
Chip & Py's (NS), p. 59
East Side Ovens (DA), p. 52
Palomas Restaurant
   & Banquet Hall (SS), p. 55
Taste of India (WS), p. 66
West Bank Café (DA), p. 56

Dining in Downtown Milwaukee

1 Abu's Jerusalem Restaurant
2 African Hut
3 Beans & Barley Market & Café
4 Boulevard Inn
5 Buca Little Italy
6 Café Marché
7 Celebration Yacht of Milwaukee
8 Conejito's Place
9 East Side Ovens
10 Edelweiss Cruise Dining
11 The English Room
12 Grenedier's
13 Historic Turner Hall & Restaurant
14 John Ernst
15 Karl Ratzsch's Restaurant
16 Mader's German Restaurant
17 Mimma's Café
18 Miss Katie's Diner
19 Mr. Perkin's Family Restaurant
20 Old Town Serbian Gourmet House
21 Palomas Restaurant & Banquet Hall
22 Sanford Restaurant
23 Scotty's Crab House
24 Stackner Cabaret
25 Thai Palace
26 Third Street Pier Restaurant
27 Watts Tea Shop
28 West Bank Café

0   1.5   1.5
  KILOMETERS   MILES

DOWNTOWN AREA

ABU'S JERUSALEM RESTAURANT
1978 N. Farwell Ave., Milwaukee
414/277-0485
$ **DA**
Winner of *Milwaukee Magazine*'s Readers' Choice Award, Abu's specializes in Middle Eastern cuisine. Vegetarian eggplant and spinach specialties as well as lamb and beef dishes are available. Combination plates allow a taste of each. Decor reflects the casual atmosphere, so dress down. Call for hours. &

AFRICAN HUT
1107 N. Old World Third St.
Milwaukee
414/765-1110
$ **DA**
African meat pies, a spicey dish of *jollof* rice, and African wines make this trendy downtown restaurant an authentic taste of Africa. Contemporary African art hangs on the walls of this culturally experiential establishment. Currently the place to be seen. Open Mon–Sat for lunch and dinner; closed Sun. &

BEANS & BARLEY MARKET & CAFÉ
1901 E. North Ave., Milwaukee
414/278-7878
$ **DA**
This vegetarian deli has developed a reputation for preparing incredibly delicious soups and sandwiches. Homemade soups and breads daily. Favorites include burritos and tofu burgers. Some meat dishes are available. Although much of the noon business is takeout, plenty of seating is available. Open daily for breakfast and lunch. No reservations required. &

BOULEVARD INN
925 E. Wells St., Milwaukee
414/765-1166
$$$ **DA**
Another *Milwaukee Magazine* Critics' and Readers' Choice award-winner, the Boulevard's owners have served Milwaukeeans for decades. One of Milwaukee's finest dining establishments, with the wine list rating among the city's best. The Caesar salad, chilled and hot soups, and regional fare are worth tasting. Open for lunch and dinner. Sunday brunch. Reservations recommended. &

BUCA LITTLE ITALY
1233 N. Van Buren St., Milwaukee
414/224-8672
$$ **DA**
A shrine to Frank Sinatra, Italian singalongs, and a party atmosphere make this Southern Italian restaurant a performance/dining experience. Spaghetti and meatballs, outstanding baked ravioli, and garlic mashed potatoes are served family-style, with portions so large even big groups take food home. The spumoni, dotted with pieces of fresh fruit, is the best in the city. Open for dinner seven days a week. &

CAFÉ MARCHÉ
143 N. Broadway, Milwaukee
414/273-4411
$$ **DA**
This 1996 entry into the dining business has become the downtown Historic Third Ward's golden child. Veal Marché and ahi tuna are must-haves. The emphasis here is on blended spices and fresh ingredients. Open for breakfast, lunch, and dinner. Outdoor seating in summer; Sunday brunch. Attractively set in a historic corner building; reservations required. &

CELEBRATION YACHT OF MILWAUKEE
502 N. Harbor Dr., Milwaukee
414/272-2628
$$ **DA**

Open April through October, the Celebration allows guests to view Milwaukee's skyline from an open upper deck or while dining. Private charters and daily excursions available. &

CONEJITO'S PLACE
539 W. Virginia St., Milwaukee
414/278-9106
$ **DA**

Paper plates, a jukebox, and a wall of people ready to pounce on your spot await you at the best place in Milwaukee to get cheap, authentic Mexican food. Although the ambiance is "early tavern," the price is right and the chopped-meat tacos and combination plates can't be beat. *Huevos rancheros* make this the best Sunday dining spot north of the border. Open for lunch and dinner; breakfast on Sunday only. No reservations. No credit cards accepted. &

EAST SIDE OVENS
322 E. Michigan St., Milwaukee
414/224-7770
$ **DA**

Recipes for breads and pastries have been passed down from the family bakery located here for over 50 years. The deli, which opened in 1995, features vegan foods (no dairy products, lard, red meat, fish, or poultry). Daily specials include soups, stews, and barbecues, all minus the meat.

EDELWEISS CRUISE DINING
1110 N. Old World Third St.
Milwaukee
414/272-DOCK
$$$ **DA**

A bit more elegant than the Celebration dinner cruise, the Edelweiss offers a prix fixe menu for cruising the downtown harbors. Four cruise choices include lunch, dinner, and cocktail cruises daily in June, July, and August, and a champagne brunch on Sunday. May, September, and October cruises run Thursday through Sunday. Cost of the cruise, meal, and gratuity are included in prices. Call for reservations. The Edelweiss is available for charter.

THE ENGLISH ROOM
The Pfister Hotel
424 E. Wisconsin Ave.
Milwaukee
414/273-8222
$$$ **DA**

The English Room has been the Pfister Hotel's fine-dining room since 1892. Though certainly an elegant dining experience, in which guests find themselves surrounded by rich tapestry, lush oak trim, and nineteenth-century artwork, the restaurant has

TRIVIA

The English Room at the Pfister Hotel has developed a popular tradition of holiday and pre-theater dining. Thankgiving meals provide traditional "pilgrim's feasts," while Christmas menus offer a "Dickens of a Christmas," complete with tickets to the Milwaukee Rep's production of *A Christmas Carol*. Additional holiday and special event theme meals can be arranged.

cut back individual service and table-side presentations for food preparation, and many English Room regulars miss the wine steward whose wit and charm helped them make selections from an extensive list. Open for lunch Mon–Fri. Dinner every night. Reservations recommended. Tea is also served in the Pfister lobby. ♿

GRENADIER'S
747 N. Broadway, Milwaukee
414/276-0747
$$$ **DA**

This restaurant deserves its dual Critics' and Readers' Choice Awards from *Milwaukee Magazine*. The opulent French-Victorian atmosphere, complete with uniformed doorman and tuxedoed waiters, can be downright stuffy, and the staff has a reputation for being patronizing to some, but chef Knut Apitz is one of the most gifted in the business. Grilled loin of lamb, roast breast of duck, and blue-corn crepes with goat cheese are three current menu favorites. Open for lunch Mon–Fri. Dinner and piano entertainment nightly. Reservations required. ♿

HISTORIC TURNER RESTAURANT
1034 N. 4th St., Milwaukee
414/276-4844
$$ **DA**

Long known as one of the best downtown locations for a Friday night fish fry, Turner Restaurant expanded its menu when it was renovated to keep up with its new neighbor, the Bradley Sports Center. Now the menu offers a full compliment of appetizers, meals, and desserts. Try the deep-fried chicken fingers on the appetizer menu. The pasta and salads are a hit, too. Of note is the gyro salad, an abundant helping of tomatoes, onions, cucumbers, and Greek olives smothered with cucumber dressing. After-sporting-event crowds will love the wide selection of beers, including Milwaukee's micro-brewed Sprechers. Open daily for lunch and dinner. ♿

JOHN ERNST
600 E. Ogden Ave., Milwaukee
414/273-1878
$$ **DA**

Considered one of the best fine-dining restaurants in the city, John Ernst has a German flavor without relying only on its German heritage to draw customers. Patrons relish the casual Old World ambiance found in the leaded-glass windows, dark oak trim, and wall murals. Prime steaks and continental cuisine offer exceptional choices. The hospitable staff and nightly piano and accordion music make this a traditional special-occasion choice for many Milwaukeeans. Friday night fish frys. Closed Mon. Lunch and dinner served Tue–Sat. Sunday brunch. Reservations are recommended.

KARL RATZSCH'S RESTAURANT
320 E. Mason St., Milwaukee
414/276-2720
$$$ **DA**

This German legend has been operating successfully since 1904. The delectable German and continental entrees have made it a *Holiday* magazine and annual Distinguished Restaurant of North America (Dirona) award-winner since the award's inception in 1990. Leaded glass, hand-painted murals, and an impressive beer-mug collection give the place an authentic German ambiance. Gracious staff make this worth a repeat visit. Valet parking available. Open Mon–Sat for dinner. ♿

> A great secondary source for Milwaukee diners is Cari Taylor-Carlson's book *Milwaukee Eats*, available at the Harry W. Schwartz shops or the Little Read Book in Wauwatosa.

MADER'S GERMAN RESTAURANT
1037 N. Old World Third St.
Milwaukee
414/271-3377
$$$ DA

Enter this restaurant, complete with suits of armor, beer steins, and massive platters of veal schnitzel and sauerbraten, and you'll think you've entered a Teutonic castle. A great stop for tourists. The food tends to be abundant and calorie-laden. A few heart-healthy items have been added to the menu in recent years. Excellent veal dishes. Open for lunch and dinner daily. Friday night fish frys. Sunday brunch. Reservations recommended. &

MIMMA'S CAFÉ
1307 E. Brady St., Milwaukee
414/271-7337
$$ DA

This Italian café, which specializes in pasta dishes, is a low-keyed delight. The risotto and polenta are delicious, and the ravioli stuffed with prosciutto and mushrooms is truly memorable. Reservations required. Open for lunch Tue–Thur; dinner nightly. &

MISS KATIE'S DINER
1900 W. Clybourn St., Milwaukee
414/344-0044
$ DA

President Clinton ate here. Miss Katie's menu includes meat loaf, barbecued ribs, malts, and shakes. Hearty omelets grace the breakfast menu. Blue Plate Specials and waitresses in '50s uniforms contrast with the versatile menu's lemon chicken, Italian specialties, and full-service bar. Fish fry Friday. Open daily for all meals. &

MR. PERKIN'S FAMILY RESTAURANT
2001 W. Atkinson Ave.
Milwaukee
414/447-6660
$ DA

Sweet-potato pie made Mr. Perkin's reputation, and country ham and biscuits, chitterlings, chicken and dressing, greens, and peach cobbler that satisfy the largest appetite keep this business hopping. Worth a visit but be warned: this is not the safest neighborhood. Open Mon–Thur from 5 a.m.–5 p.m.; Fri and Sat 5 a.m.–7 p.m.; and Sun 7 a.m.–noon. &

OLD TOWN SERBIAN GOURMET HOUSE
522 W. Lincoln Ave., Milwaukee
414/672-0206
$ DA

Moussaka, chicken *paprikash,* and *burek* are just a few of the Serbian delights served along with distinctive wines and beers in this ethnically decorated restaurant. Open for lunch Tue–Fri; dinner Tue–Sun. Entertainment. Reservations accepted.

PALOMAS RESTAURANT & BANQUET HALL
611 W. National Ave., Milwaukee
414/649-2565
$$ DA

Latin American and vegetarian cuisine representing Chile, Puerto Rico, and the Caribbean is served in a romantic, elegant atmosphere. Tapas on Tuesday. Lunch buffets are offered weekdays. Open for dinner Tue–Sat. Reservations recommended. Accepts MasterCard and Visa.

SANFORD RESTAURANT
1547 N. Jackson St., Milwaukee
414/276-9608
$$$ **DA**

Award-winning chef Sanford D'Amato and his wife, Angie, provide Milwaukee with elegance, classic flair, and fine European food at this 50-seat storefront restaurant. Certainly one of the most consistently fine restaurants in the city, it is a winner of both Readers' and Critic's Choice Awards from *Milwaukee Magazine*. The seasonal menu and personalized wine list change daily. Open for dinner Mon–Sat; closed Sun. &

SCOTTY'S CRAB HOUSE
1533 E. Belleview Pl., Milwaukee
414/964-5400
$$$ **DA**

Serving Creole delights in a building that feels more like Key West than Milwaukee, this casual establishment provides the best Creole dining experience in the city. Large platters of shrimp and jambalaya are just spicy enough, without being heavy-handed, to make this a dynamic choice. Open Tue–Sat for dinner. Visa and MasterCard accepted. Reservations required.

STACKNER CABARET
108 E. Wells St., Milwaukee
414/244-9490 or 414/272-1994
$$ **DA**

Milwaukee's only authentic cabaret dinner theater provides casual dining

English Room at the Pfister Hotel, page 52

and a full-service bar. Located within the Milwaukee Theater complex, the cabaret serves lunch and dinner. Private parties are welcomed. Call for tickets and times. &

THAI PALACE
838 N. Old World Third St.
Milwaukee
414/224-7076
$$ **DA**

If you've been craving a good Chaopraya River prawn, this is the place to put on your restaurants-to-try list. Other specialties include lobster with "holy basil," a divine basil-flavored oil. An interesting variety of Thai choices, offered within walking distance of most downtown attractions and hotels. Open for lunch Mon–Fri; open for dinner daily. Reservations recommended. &

THIRD STREET PIER RESTAURANT
1110 Old World Third St.
Milwaukee
414/272-0330
$$$ **DA**

Select a steak or seafood entree

and prepare to enjoy a candlelight dinner while watching river traffic float along the Milwaukee River. The food is good; the ambiance is exceptional. More than 200 wines. Excellent choice of sandwiches and soups for lunch. Friday night fish frys. Open for lunch Mon–Fri; for dinner, daily. Outdoor dining during summer. Entertainment. Reservations accepted. &

WATTS TEA SHOP
761 N. Jefferson St., Milwaukee
414/291-5120
$$ **DA**

Located above George Watts' china shop, this cheerfully decorated tearoom provides graceful luncheon and tea service. The classic menu items include chicken salad, chicken pot pie, chicken divan, and salmon croquettes. The courteous staff pays close attention to every detail, making this a delightful way to wile away the afternoon. &

WEST BANK CAFÉ
732 E. Burleigh St., Milwaukee
414/562-5555
$ **DA**

This trendy Riverwest café specializes in Vietnamese cuisine with a European flair. Many choices are vegetarian, but fresh seafood and meats are also on the extensive menu. A few uncommon beer and wine choices round out your meal. Open daily for dinner. Reservations accepted; as word gets out, they may be necessary. &

EAST SIDE

THE ANCHORAGE
Milwaukee River Hilton Inn
4700 N. Port Washington Rd.
Glendale
414/962-4710
$$$ **ES**

Long considered Milwaukee's premiere seafood restaurant, with fresh seafood flown in from both coasts three times a week, the Anchorage suffered a slight dip in quality when taken over by the Hilton hotel chain. Still, specials often include dolphin fish, mahimahi, bluefish, and swordfish. Pasta and casserole dishes fill out the menu. The Anchorage overlooks the Milwaukee River and the pleasant wood and stained-glass decor still makes this a nice stop for seafood fans. Open early to catch the breakfast crowd on weekends, it also serves weekday lunches. &

BENJI'S DELICATESSEN & RESTAURANT
4156 N. Oakland Ave., Shorewood
414/332-7777
$ **ES**

Considered one of the best kosher delis in Milwaukee, Benji's offers pastrami, corned beef, homemade soups, and herring to die for.

BENTLEY'S RESTAURANT & LOUNGE
Manchester East Hotels & Suites
7065 N. Port Washington Rd.
Glendale
414/351-6960
$ **ES**

Steaks, sandwiches, and salads with Saturday night prime rib specials define the steakhouse atmosphere here, while the prices belie the upscale surroundings and attractive decor. Open for lunch and dinner Mon–Sat. &

CHINA PALACE RESTAURANT
4511 N. Oakland Ave., Shorewood
414/332-2024

EAST SIDE

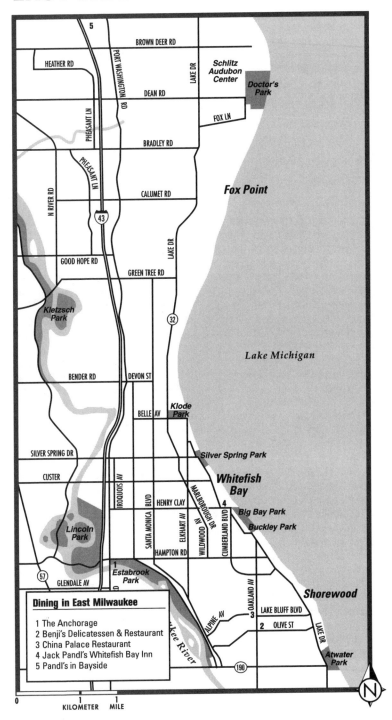

BROWN DEER RD

HEATHER RD

PORT WASHINGTON RD

LAKE DR

Schlitz Audubon Center

Doctor's Park

DEAN RD

PHEASANT LN

FOX LN

BRADLEY RD

PHEASANT LN

CALUMET RD

Fox Point

N RIVER RD

43

LAKE DR

Kletzsch Park

GOOD HOPE RD

GREEN TREE RD

32

Lake Michigan

BENDER RD

DEVON ST

BELLE AV

Klode Park

SILVER SPRING DR

Silver Spring Park

CUSTER

IROQUOIS AV

SANTA MONICA BLVD

HENRY CLAY

MARLBOROUGH DR

Whitefish Bay

4

Big Bay Park

Lincoln Park

ELKHART AV

WILDWOOD AV

CUMBERLAND BLVD

Buckley Park

HAMPTON RD

57

GLENDALE AV

1

Estabrook Park

OAKLAND AV

Shorewood

ALPINE AV

LAKE BLUFF BLVD

LAKE DR

Dining in East Milwaukee

1 The Anchorage
2 Benji's Delicatessen & Restaurant
3 China Palace Restaurant
4 Jack Pandl's Whitefish Bay Inn
5 Pandl's in Bayside

3

2 OLIVE ST

Milwaukee River

190

Atwater Park

N

0   1   1
    KILOMETER   MILE

Java Jive

The West Coast coffee craze has reached Milwaukee. Your best downtown bet for the caffeine brew is **La Boulangerie**, *a French bakery and deli on Broadway near Buffalo Street. Wauwatosa residents find their favorite java at* **Jitterz** *on State Street. Elm Grove and Brookfield residents head for the corner of North Avenue and Calhoun Road, where* **That Coffee Place** *brews the richest beans. But new shops—some chains, some tiny entrepreneurial establishments—are opening throughout the area.*

$　　　　　　　　　　　　　　　**ES**

Specializing in Szechuan and Hunan dishes, the China Palace menu also offers Cantonese and Mandarin dishes. One of the city's better Chinese restaurants, its most popular item seems to be moo shu pork, a taco-like meal of shredded pork, cabbage, bean sprouts, egg, and green onions. Meal comes hot-as-you-like-it.

JACK PANDL'S WHITEFISH BAY INN
1319 E. Henry Clay St.
Whitefish Bay
414/964-3800
$$　　　　　　　　　　　　　　　**ES**

German pancakes are the cornerstone of Pandl's Friday night fish frys. The Wiener schnitzel and broiled whitefish are also patrons' top choices. Winner of *Milwaukee Magazine*'s Critic's Choice Award, this restaurant is furnished with oak tables and Tiffany lamps and windows, providing elegant comfort and charm. Open Mon–Sat for lunch and dinner; closed Sun. Reservations recommended.

PANDL'S IN BAYSIDE
8825 N. Lake Dr., Bayside
414/352-7300
$$　　　　　　　　　　　　　　　**ES**

An excellent Sunday brunch choice, this 25-year-old family-owned restaurant offers customers a refined dining experience. The dining room, decorated in forest green with antiques and candles, provides patrons with a pastoral view of wooded hills. Homemade rolls and muffins prepare diners for a wide variety of well-prepared meals. Open for lunch and dinner Mon–Sat; Sunday brunch. Reservations recommended. &

NORTH SIDE

BODER'S ON THE RIVER
11919 N. River Rd., Mequon
414/242-0335
$$$　　　　　　　　　　　　　　　**NS**

This country-home-turned-restaurant has provided the setting for any number of Milwaukee garden weddings. Weeping willows dot the rolling grounds that slope to the river. The regional country menu provides interesting entrees served with attractive touches, such as homemade muffins, corn fritters, and seasonal fruit. A Milwaukee favorite for celebrating special occasions and romantic evenings. Sunday brunch; Friday night buffet. Open for lunch and dinner Tue–Sun; closed Mon. Reservations recommended. &

CHIP & PY'S
1340 Town Square Rd., Mequon
414/241-9589
$$ **NS**
Eclectic gourmet cuisine that pleases enough palates that it survived a move from the near South Side to its present location. Daring diners will enjoy trying vegetarian and pasta entrees seasoned with liquors or Cajun spices. Pleasing contemporary decor. Open for lunch Tue–Sat; for dinner, Tue–Sun. Closed Mon. Piano music on weekends. &

CLUB FOREST
4200 W. County Line Rd. 96N
Mequon
414/238-0876
$$$ **NS**
According to legend, the farm couple who once owned this farmhouse—itself once a speakeasy and brothel—still haunts the place. The most recent incarnation as a restaurant has put both the building and ghosts to exceptionally good use. USDA Prime Grade steaks, wood-grilled fresh fish, daily specials, and homemade desserts make having eaten here a sweet memory that spurs plans to return. Open daily for dinner. Outdoor dining during summer. Entertainment. Reservations recommended. &

GEORGE WEBB'S
9002 W. Silver Spring Dr.
Milwaukee
414/462-1780
$ **NS**

These local chain restaurants can be found in storefronts and strip malls and on city corners throughout metropolitan Milwaukee. Breakfast at Webb's, whether it's at 10 a.m. or 2 a.m., has become a Milwaukee tradition. The chili and hamburgers aren't bad, either. Each fluorescent-lit restaurant contains booth and counter seating. Look for the double clocks on the wall—a Webb's trademark—and you'll know you've found Milwaukee's best greasy spoon. Open 24 hours a day, every day. No credit cards accepted. &

RANGE LINE INN
2635 W. Mequon Rd., Mequon
414/242-0530
$$$ **NS**
A charming New England farmhouse setting enhances this casual dining experience. Steaks and seafood grace the menu. Try the potato puff, a twice-baked puff potato served in its own casserole dish. The melted-cheese center is a divine surprise. Open evenings.

THE RED MILL EAST
4034 W. Good Hope Rd.
Milwaukee
414/228-6800
$$ **NS**
With a reputation for providing the best live jazz in the city, the rustic Red Mill East is sometimes overlooked for its outstanding beer-batter fish and onion rings. Filets are outstanding, too. The mill does a bustling fish-fry business on Friday. Open for lunch Mon–Fri; for dinner Mon–Sat; closed Sun. Reservations are recommended but be prepared to wait a bit on Friday, even with reservations.

RIVERSITE RESTAURANT
11120 N. Cedarburg Rd., Mequon
414/242-6050

NORTH SIDE

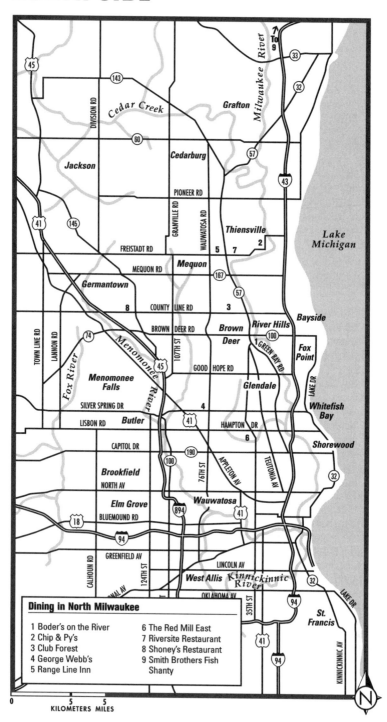

Dining in North Milwaukee

1 Boder's on the River
2 Chip & Py's
3 Club Forest
4 George Webb's
5 Range Line Inn
6 The Red Mill East
7 Riversite Restaurant
8 Shoney's Restaurant
9 Smith Brothers Fish Shanty

0   5   5
KILOMETERS MILES

Jack Pandl's Whitefish Bay Inn, page 58

$$$ **NS**

This inn provides quality food in an attractive setting, with lots of seafood and wild-game specials. Choose wine from an extensive list. Semiformal attire is appropriate at this upscale establishment. Friday night fish frys. Outdoor dining available in summer. Open Mon–Sat for dinner. Reservations recommended. &

SHONEY'S RESTAURANT
10400 W. Silver Spring Dr.
Milwaukee
414/466-1155
$ **NS**

Highway café dining here. The Shoney's restaurants are clean, affordable, and hospitable, a good bet for single travelers, families, and truckers. Open daily. &

SMITH BROTHERS FISH SHANTY
100 N. Franklin Pl.
Port Washington
414/284-5592
$ **NS**

Watch sailboats catch a breeze while you enjoy fresh seafood and homemade desserts. Situated in the quaint city of Port Washington, the Shanty overlooks Lake Michigan. The casual atmosphere makes dining here relaxing. Friday night fish frys. Open for lunch and dinner daily. Outdoor dining in summer. Reservations taken except Fri. &

WEST SIDE

ALIOTO'S
3041 N. Mayfair Rd., Wauwatosa
414/476-6900
$$ **WS**

A great place for veal dishes and Sicilian steak, this Italian supper club also provides fish-fry lovers with deep-fried cod and perch. This second-generation family-owned restaurant serves large portions and traditional Southern Italian pastas. &

BALISTRERI'S BLUEMOUND INN
6501 W. Blue Mound Rd.
Milwaukee
414/258-9881
$$ **WS**

Called the Bluemound Inn until this steakhouse changed hands in 1995, it remains a favorite fish-fry locale. The Balistreri's Italian influence is reflected in the menu, but steaks, prime rib, and deep-fried shrimp keep this casual restaurant running in supper-club style.

BALISTRERI'S ITALIAN-AMERICAN RISTORANTE
812 N. 68th St., Wauwatosa
414/475-1414
$ WS

Recognized by most Milwaukeeans as a favorite corner pizza parlor, Balistreri's offers a thin-crust pizza in a busy, red-and-green environment. Plans to enlarge were postponed when Balistreri purchased the nearby Bluemound Inn, but the hustle and bustle only add to this establishment's neighborhood charm. Open for dinner daily.

BARTOLOTTA
7616 W. State St., Wauwatosa
414/771-7910
$$$ WS

Recipient of both the Critics' Choice and Readers' Choice Awards from *Milwaukee Magazine*, Bartolotta gained popularity with a menu of rustic Italian cuisine. The best choices include *brodetto di pesce,* fish with Italian seasonings, and *gamberoni all' acqua pazza,* or "shrimp in crazy water," a delectable poached shrimp dish served with garlic- and chili flake-marinara. The location used to be called "Wauwatosa's five points," until one of the five streets leading to the point was closed off and turned into a pedestrian walk. Open for dinner. Closed Sun. Entertainment on weekends. Reservations recommended well in advance.

BRUNO'S VINTAGE INN
17700 W. Capitol Dr., Brookfield

414/790-1980
$$$ WS

European dining at its finest can be found here, but this restaurant has yet to find its clientele. Perhaps it's a location problem—Bruno's is tucked away in Stonewood Village, a small shopping area that just can't seem to make a mark in the community. The menu is gourmet eclectic, including exotic choices (such as ostrich) and more common selections (like pork chops). Bruno's also contains a cigar room for smoking aficionados. Open daily.

CAFÉ CONTINENTAL
19035 W. Blue Mound Rd.
Brookfield
414/786-9095
$$ WS

Set in a strip mall, this café's location belies menu selections that are excellently prepared. From chicken in lingonberry sauce to spinach Florentine, meals are a casual and enjoyable experience. Open for lunch and dinner daily.

EDDIE MARTINI'S
8612 Watertown Plank Rd.
Wauwatosa
414/771-6680
$$$ WS

This 1950s-style formal supper club made its appearance to rave reviews in 1994. Refined dining and classic service mark this establishment's personality. Steak *au poivre* is outstanding. Fresh seafood dinners are also available. Beware the Eddie Martini—it packs a punch. Open for lunch Mon–Fri; for dinner, Thur–Sun. Reservations necessary.

ELM GROVE INN
13275 Watertown Plank Rd.
Elm Grove
414/782-7090

WEST SIDE

Dining in West Milwaukee

1. Alioto's
2. Balistreri's Bluemound Inn
3. Balistreri's Italian-American Ristorante
4. Bartolotta
5. Bruno's Vintage Inn
6. Café Continental
7. Eddie Martini's
8. Elm Grove Inn
9. The Fireside Restaurant & Playhouse
10. Gillies Frozen Custard Drive-In
11. Golden Star
12. Hector's, A Mexican Restaurant
13. Heinemann's
14. Jack's West Side Deli
15. Jake's in Brookfield
16. Loaf & Jug
17. Mama Mia's on Blue Mound
18. Old Country Buffet
19. The Red Mill
20. Saz's on State Street
21. Seigo's Japanese Steak House
22. Taste of India

MILES

KILOMETERS

$$$ **WS**

This historic stagecoach inn and Pony Express stop, perched on Elm Grove's main street, has provided fine country dining for years. Huge wooden booths and a large fireplace accent the New England decor. Meals are pricey and acoustics can be a problem, so request a booth or the back room if background noise bothers you. Still, this is a nice place to celebrate special occasions. Open Mon–Fri for lunch, Mon–Sat for dinner. Closed Sun. Reservations recommended. ⅋

THE FIRESIDE RESTAURANT & PLAYHOUSE
Business Highway 26 S., Fort Atkinson
414/563-9505 or 800/477-9505
$$$ **WS**

This dinner theater, located about 20 minutes west of Milwaukee, has been around forever. It remains Wisconsin's number-one year-round motorcoach attraction, providing diners with family hospitality, Broadway theater, and revues. Nine shows weekly, Wed–Sun.

GILLES FROZEN CUSTARD DRIVE-IN
7515 W. Blue Mound Rd.
Milwaukee
414/453-4875
$ **WS**

This remains one of Milwaukee's oldest and best custard stands and high-school hangouts. Gilles custard can be purchased in local supermarkets, but the stand provides atmosphere and hot sandwiches to complement ice-cream sundaes, sodas, and milk shakes. No credit cards. Open daily.

GOLDEN STAR
12460 W. Capitol Dr., Brookfield

Grenadier's, page 53

414/783-7500
$ **WS**

Al McGuire, of Marquette Warriors college basketball fame, eats here. He's joined by West Side Chinese-food lovers. Dine in or carry out. A buffet is often served, but fresh choices are available. Open for lunch and dinner daily. ⅋

HECTOR'S, A MEXICAN RESTAURANT
7118 W. State St., Wauwatosa
414/258-5600
$ **WS**

This Wauwatosa Mexican delight was met with enthusiasm by suburbanites tired of making the urban treck to Conejito's. The *taquitas* from the appetizer menu—deep-fried egg rolls filled with cream cheese, chicken, olives, and peppers, and dipped in a sweet and hot sauce— are worth a visit by themselves. Enchiladas are another good choice. Authentic Mexican served here. The casual establishment also provides a wide selection of Mexican beers and margaritas. Open Mon–Sat for lunch, daily for dinner. The dining room is small, and patrons are seated on a first-come, first-served basis.

HEINEMANN'S
317 N. 76th St., Milwaukee
414/258-6800
$ WS

This is Milwaukee's lunch-and-shopping stopping place. Most born-and-bred Milwaukeeans recall accompanying their mothers and grandmothers to the Heinemann's downtown or in Wauwatosa next to The Grand, a women's clothing store. Lunch and shopping still might include a visit to one of the seven Heinemann's locations, but you'll find business clients grabbing an omelette, roast turkey sandwich, or hamburger during power lunches. Each restaurant is attractively decorated with homey, traditional wallpapers and large booths. &

JACK'S WEST SIDE DELI
7312 W. Appleton Ave.
Milwaukee
414/527-1500
$ WS

This kosher-style deli lays claim to the best corned beef in Milwaukee. Open 10 a.m. to 4 p.m. Mon–Sat.

JAKE'S IN BROOKFIELD
21445 W. Capitol Dr., Brookfield
414/781-7995
$$ WS

Like the Jake's in Wauwatosa (6030 W. North Ave., 414/771-0550), this restaurant developed its reputation with shredded onion rings and filets. It's a mainstay in the area because of melt-in-your-mouth filets and delectable fresh seafood choices. A casually upscale dining experience, the restaurants are decorated with ever-changing artwork produced by lo-

cals. Warm touches include a fireplace and candles. Although reservations are taken only for large parties, cheese and crackers provided in the bar make the wait bearable. Open nightly for dinner. &

LOAF & JUG
17700 W. Capitol Dr., Brookfield
414/781-1789
$ WS

This Brookfield deli, located in Stonewood Village, may be the most thriving business in the Early American shopping mall. Patrons pick up a menu and pencil at the door, then check off their choices of meats, cheeses, bread, condiments, soups, salads, and homemade cookies. With a wide variety to make any sandwich your heart's desire, this is one of the best West Side delis. Open Mon–Sat for lunch. &

MAMA MIA'S ON BLUE MOUND
18880 W. Blue Mound Rd.
Brookfield
414/789-0277
$ WS

This original mom-and-pop pizza parlor first opened on Burleigh and recently expanded west to this location and south to 8531 W. Greenfield Ave. (414/475-0400). The thin-crust pizza has a spicy tomato-sauce base. Pitchers of beer and pop complement the meals. Although the garlic bread is a delicious specialty, it drips with oil. Spaghetti and lasagna are also good selections here. Open for lunch Mon–Fri. Open for dinner every night. Reservations accepted for parties of six or more. &

OLD COUNTRY BUFFET
16750B W. Blue Mound Rd.
Brookfield
414/786-2113

$ WS

All-you-can-eat buffets promise to satisfy diners with big appetites. The food is abundant, the prices reasonable, and the atmosphere friendly. A good family choice. &

THE RED MILL
1005 S. Elm Grove Rd., Brookfield
414/782-8780
$$ WS

The original Red Mill developed its reputation as a supper club with the best beer-batter onion rings, steak, and beer-batter fish in Milwaukee. The traditionally decorated club continues to earn its renown, and Friday night fish frys still deserve top billing. Open for lunch Mon–Fri; and for dinner, Mon–Sat. Closed Sun. Reservations accepted. &

SAZ'S ON STATE STREET
5539 W. State St., Milwaukee
414/453-2410
$ WS

The ribs and hot sandwiches are outstanding; the decor is Cheers bar. Buses run to County Stadium, the Bradley Center, and Maier Festival Park during summer festivals, making this a convenient stop before and after sports and other events. The late-night menu makes you want to stay for a brew and a bite. Open for lunch Mon–Sat; for dinner, daily. Sunday brunch. Friday night fish frys. &

SEIGO'S JAPANESE STEAK HOUSE
18380 W. Capitol Dr., Brookfield
414/781-2727
$$ WS

Tableside preparation of steaks, seafood, and chicken provides entertainment while diners await their meals. Traditional Japanese atmos-

phere. Open for dinner daily. Reservations accepted. &

TASTE OF INDIA
10900 W. Blue Mound Rd.
Wauwatosa
414/259-9200
$ WS

Authentic East Indian cuisine features vegetarian dishes, with some meat dishes available. Food here is a mix of well-blended spices and a delight for those who relish East Indian fare. The ambiance is plain, but service is friendly. Open for lunch Tue–Sun, and dinner daily. Reservations accepted. MasterCard and Visa accepted.

SOUTH SIDE

ANN'S ITALIAN RESTAURANT
5969 S. 108th Pl., Hales Corners
414/425-5040
$ SS

Thin-crust pizza, barbecued ribs, Italian specialties, and fine value make this an enjoyable casual dining experience. Originally a private house, the building has been remodeled and expanded to serve the growing clientele. Other specialties include manicotti, veal parmigiana, chicken cacciatore, and sandwiches. Open for dinner. Carryouts available. Reservations taken.

THE COLUMNS
3445 W. Edgerton Ave., Greenfield
414/281-4422
$$$ SS

Steak and prime-rib specials satisfy meat lovers while they enjoy elegant surroundings in the Crystal Dining Room. Seafood also on the menu. Banquet rooms available for 20 to 300 people. Open for dinner Tue–Sun, brunch on Sunday. Friday night fish frys. Entertainment. Reservations recommended. &

GOLLASH PHARMACIES
3027 S. 60th St., Milwaukee
414/541-2400
$ SS

This pharmacy chain with a lunch counter in each store brings back the past, when you could wait for a prescription while grabbing a quick and tasty bite. In addition to this South Side location, Gollash is in downtown, Elm Grove, Brookfield, and Delafield. Some locals can recall when these were Phillips Pharmacies and still return for French fries and cherry Cokes. Open Mon–Sat for breakfast, lunch, and dinner. Only fountain is open Sunday. No credit cards. &

GREAT NATIONAL SALOON
& RESTAURANT
6833 W. National Ave., West Allis
414/774-0042
$ SS

It's a good omen that Kenny Meurer,

the son of a retired Milwaukee baker, owns this establishment. Steaks, ribs, and seafood offer variety. Wednesday night is all-you-can-eat rib night for $6.95. The setting feels like a cozy stone cottage; the food is abundant and good. Nightly specials make the saloon as pleasant on your wallet as it is satisfying to your belly. Open Mon–Sat for lunch and dinner.

HAROLD'S RESTAURANT
The Grand Milwaukee Hotel
4747 S. Howell Ave., Milwaukee
414/481-8000
$$$ SS

Etched glass, rich reds, and deep greens make this Grand Hotel restaurant an elegant choice. Scampi Milano, rack of lamb, and steaks round out the menu. Large-scale hotel preparation often creates flaws here. Stick to simply prepared items and you won't be disappointed. Open daily for lunch and dinner. &

KEGEL'S INN
5901 W. National Ave., West Allis

The Fireside Restaurant and Playhouse, p. 64

Fireside Dinner Theatre

SOUTH SIDE

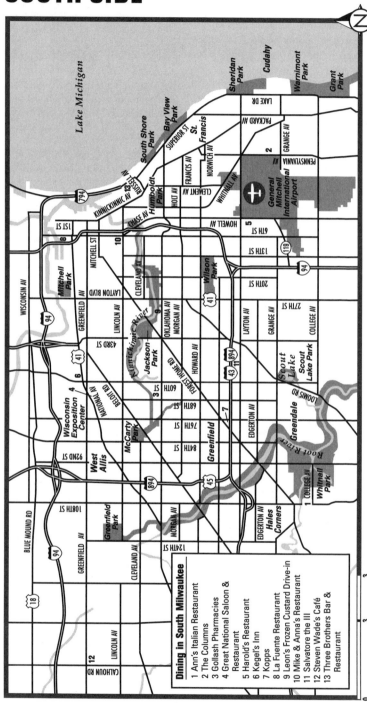

Lake Michigan

Sheridan Park

Cudahy

Warnimont Park

Grant Park

Bay View Park

South Shore Park

St. Francis

LAKE DR

PACKARD AV

SUPERIOR ST

FRANCIS AV

NORWICH AV

GRANGE AV

CLEMENT AV

MITCHELL AV

2

PENNSYLVANIA AV

HOLT AV

General Mitchell International Airport

KINNICKINNIC AV

RUSSELL AV

794

13

Humboldt Park

CHASE AV

HOWELL AV

1ST ST

MITCHELL ST

5

6TH ST

13TH ST

119

8

10

94

CLEVELAND AV

Mitchell Park

WISCONSIN AV

94

Wilson Park

41

20TH ST

27TH ST

LAYTON BLVD

LINCOLN AV

GREENFIELD AV

LAYTON AV

GRANGE AV

COLLEGE AV

OKLAHOMA AV

MORGAN AV

41

43RD ST

Kinnickinnic River

Jackson Park

HOWARD AV

43

894

11

Scout Lake

Scout Lake Park

6

BELOIT RD

NATIONAL AV

Wisconsin Exposition Center

4

3

FOREST HOME RD

60TH ST

68TH ST

7

EDGERTON AV

Greendale

LOOMIS RD

McCarty Park

76TH ST

84TH ST

Greenfield

Root River

West Allis

92ND ST

894

45

Whitnail Park

College AV

1

BLUE MOUND RD

108TH ST

Greenfield Park

MORGAN AV

EDGERTON AV

Hales Corners

94

GREENFIELD AV

CLEVELAND AV

124TH ST

18

LINCOLN AV

12

CALHOUN RD

Dining in South Milwaukee
1 Ann's Italian Restaurant
2 The Columns
3 Gollash Pharmacies
4 Great National Saloon & Restaurant
5 Harold's Restaurant
6 Kegel's Inn
7 Kopps
8 La Fuente Restaurant
9 Leon's Frozen Custard Drive-in
10 Mike & Anna's Restaurant
11 Salvatore the III
12 Steven Wade's Café
13 Three Brothers Bar & Restaurant

0   3   KILOMETERS

0   3   MILES

N

414/257-9999

$ SS

German and American cuisine set in Old World ambiance make this a strong contender among German restaurant choices. Fish frys on Fri. Opens 11 a.m. on Fri; otherwise, open for dinner. Closed Sun.

KOPPS
7631 W. Layton Ave., Milwaukee
414/282-4080

$ SS

Large hamburgers and daily custard specials make this a first choice for quick-stop dining. Try the chocolate soda or any flavor malt; turtle sundaes are also outstanding. Kopps has expanded to include three custard stands throughout the metropolitan Milwaukee area. Open daily for lunch, dinner, and dessert. &

LA FUENTE RESTAURANT
625 S. 5th St., Milwaukee
414/271-8595

$ SS

Shrimp soup, *ceviche,* and steak *ranchero* round out a menu that has gained a reputation with its seafood offerings. La Fuente has captured *Milwaukee Magazine*'s Reader's Choice Award three years in a row. Open Sun–Thur 10 a.m. to 10:30 p.m., Thur–Sat 10 a.m. to midnight. No reservations accepted. &

LEON'S FROZEN CUSTARD DRIVE-IN
3131 S. 27th St., Milwaukee
414/383-1784 SS

Offering different "flavors of the day," this drive-in has consistently been voted a favorite of *Milwaukee Magazine* readers. Whether in a dish, on a cone, or as a shake or malt, the custard is as good as it gets on a hot summer day. Open daily. &

MIKE & ANNA'S RESTAURANT
2000 S. 8th St., Milwaukee
414/643-0072

$$$ SS

A mix of elegance and humor (for a while there was a mannequin sitting at the register) greets patrons at this converted corner tap. The gourmet menu demonstrates creative use of spices, liquors, and sauces. The rack of lamb is always an outstanding choice here. Reservations required. Open Tue–Sat for dinner.

SALVATORE THE III
4950 S. 27th St., Milwaukee
414/281-0111

$$ SS

The Mediterranean ambiance prepares patrons for traditional Italian fare. Fish fry Fridays. Open for lunch Mon–Fri; for dinner daily. Outdoor dining during summer. Reservations recommended.

STEVEN WADE'S CAFÉ
17001 W. Greenfield Ave.
New Berlin
414/784-0774

$$$ SS

A daily changing gourmet menu offers continental dining in this small and charmingly elegant house-turned-café. Specialties include seafood, lamb, and duck. Desserts are a must. Recipient of *Milwaukee Magazine's* Critics' and Readers' Choice Awards. Open for dinner Mon–Sat; closed Sun. Reservations required.

THREE BROTHERS BAR & RESTAURANT
2414 S. St. Clair St., Milwaukee
414/481-7530

$$ SS

This family-run restaurant has been a favorite ethnic choice for decades. Formica tables gathered closely in a

turn-of-the-century tavern define the
casual atmosphere and belie outstanding *burek* and goulash. Roast
lamb, pork, and veal are superbly
prepared. Warning: if raw onions
don't love you, choose your entree
carefully. Open for dinner Tue–Sun.
Reservations recommended.

Pabst Mansion

5

SIGHTS AND ATTRACTIONS

To learn about the culture and community that truly is a "gathering place by the waters," start at the lakefront, where visitors spy sailboats and iron-ore freighters crossing paths, and where kites soar over picnicking families and cruising in-line skaters. Walk through parks and streets lined with historical churches scattered among skyscrapers, architecture that melds the decades with copper spires and concrete trim. Look up and you'll see colorful flags flying from steeples and skyscraper gardens, former-mayor Maier's attempt to highlight Milwaukee's more recent trademark, the City of Festivals. Visit the museum, the library, and "the Domes" at Mitchell Park Conservatory, and you'll join in the chorus of Milwaukee's admirers.

DOWNTOWN AREA

CATHEDRAL OF ST. JOHN THE EVANGELIST
802 N. Jackson St., Milwaukee
414/276-9814   **DA**
This cathedral, the seat of the Archdiocese of Milwaukee, was established in 1847 and rebuilt after a fire in 1935. Self-guided walking tours are available. A Noerhen pipe organ provides music for worship and for the choral and instrumental concerts often performed here.

CITY HALL
200 E. Wells St., Milwaukee
414/286-3200   **DA**
Between Market and Water Streets, this building mixes German Renaissance, Romanesque, and Flemish architectural styles. It's topped by a 393-foot clock tower. An eight-story atrium was screened in after distraught citizens jumped to their deaths during the Depression.

THE GRAIN EXCHANGE
Mackie Building

DOWNTOWN AREA

Sights and Attractions in Downtown Milwaukee

1 Cathedral of St. John the Evangelist
2 City Hall
3 Historic Turner Hall
4 Iroquois Boat Line
5 The Grain Exchange
6 Marquette University

7 The Midwest Express and Wisconsin Center
8 Milwaukee Journal Sentinel Tours
9 Milwaukee Maritime Center
10 Old St. Mary's Church
11 Pabst Mansion

12 Pabst Theater
13 Potawatomi Bingo Casino
14 St. Joan of Arc Chapel
15 Trinity Evangelical Lutheran Church
16 University of Wisconsin–Milwaukee

17 War Memorial Center
18 Wisconsin Conservatory of Music
19 Wisconsin Lake Schooner Education Association

0   1.5   1.5
KILOMETERS   MILES

225 E. Michigan St., Milwaukee
414/276-7840   **DA**
This three-story grain exchange has been renovated to its original gilded splendor. The 1879 Victorian Renaissance, 10,000-square-foot grain room is the site of some of Milwaukee's most elaborate weddings.

HISTORIC TURNER HALL
1034 N. 4th St., Milwaukee
414/272-1733   **DA**
This Cream City brick building, built between 1832 and 1833 to house the Milwaukee Turners' gymnastic club, remains the pride of German heritage in Milwaukee. Upstairs in the restaurant (see Chapter 4), hand-painted murals depict Germany's pastoral heritage. The Milwaukee Turners still practice on the lower level. The restaurant went through a major renovation in 1995, maintaining the building's fine wood interior while adding stained glass windows and brass railings. The exterior was returned to the original lannonstone and Cream City brick on the arched entry in 1996. Organized tours are available through the Milwaukee Turners' club, but if

you're only stopping in briefly, the restaurant's managers will invite you to take a look around.

IROQUOIS BOAT LINE
The Milwaukee River at Clybourn Street Bridge, Milwaukee
414/332-4194   **DA**
Enjoy a pleasant tour down the Milwaukee River and along the lake's shore, while the captain describes areas of historical significance. A double-decker boat with a canopied top and below-deck window viewing provides a 90-minute tour. A full bar and snacks are available. Open June 1–Labor Day. Special rates for schools, senior citizens, and private parties.

Top Ten Architectural Delights

1. Trinity Lutheran Church
2. The Pfister Hotel
3. St. Joan of Arc Chapel
4. The Grain Exchange
5. Historic Turner Hall
6. City Hall
7. Kilbourntown House
8. Pabst Mansion
9. Annunciation Greek Orthodox Church
10. St. Josephat Basilica

MARQUETTE UNIVERSITY
1442 W. Wisconsin Ave.
Milwaukee
414/288-7250 DA

This campus provides a Jesuit-based urban education for 10,500 degree candidates and an additional 8,000 continuing-education students. Located near the city's business and cultural centers, the campus houses St. Joan of Arc chapel, brought over in pieces from France and reconstructed on its present site; and Jesu Church, a Milwaukee cornerstone. Marquette University is one of Milwaukee's largest employers, and it's an integral part of the downtown environment.

THE MIDWEST EXPRESS AND WISCONSIN CENTER
500 W. Kilbourn Ave., Milwaukee
414/271-4000 DA

This convention and entertainment complex, located in the heart of downtown Milwaukee, has undergone major changes in the past few years and will continue to evolve to meet Milwaukee's convention and entertainment needs. Home of the annual Home Remodeling and Boat Shows, concerts, and other public events, the center is skywalk-accessible to hotels, shopping, dining, and parking. Call 414/271-2750 for recorded event information.

MILWAUKEE JOURNAL SENTINEL **TOURS**
333 W. State St., Milwaukee
414/224-2419 DA

Now Milwaukee's only daily newspaper, the *Milwaukee Journal Sentinel* schedules tours for large groups. These tours provide insight into the hows of newspaper production, from assigning stories to printing the paper. This is the home newspaper of syndicated columnist and best-selling author Jacquelyn Mitchard.

Top Ten Places to See Milwaukee's Skyline

by Elizabeth "Bo" Black, Executive Director of Milwaukee World Festival, Inc. (Summerfest/Winterfest)

1. The Sky Glider at Summerfest
2. The Ferris Wheel at Summerfest
3. Concourse at the Marcus Amphitheater
4. Brewer's Hill
5. Cudahy Tower Penthouse
6. The 40th floor of the Firstar Building
7. Polaris Restaurant at the top of the Hyatt Regency
8. Top of Lafayette Hill
9. A boat off the shore of Lake Michigan
10. Bay View Bike Trail

Giraffes at the Milwaukee County Zoo, page 80

MILWAUKEE MARITIME CENTER
500 N. Harbor Dr., Milwaukee
414/276-7700   **DA**
Watch a tall ship as it's being built. Learn about Great Lakes trade routes and infamous shipwrecks. The Maritime Museum helps tourists understand the significant role the Great Lakes have played in national shipping and trade.

OLD ST. MARY'S CHURCH
836 N. Broadway, Milwaukee
414/271-6180   **DA**
Built in 1865, the same year that Milwaukee became a city, this church is made of Cream City brick. King Ludwig of Bavaria donated the painting of the Annunciation that adorns the altar. St. Mary's is the oldest Catholic church in Milwaukee and is listed on the National Register of Historic Places.

PABST MANSION
2000 W. Wisconsin Ave.
Milwaukee
414/931-0808   **DA**
This French Renaissance–style man-

sion, constructed of etched glass, ironwork, and exquisite wood, was built for the Pabst founder in 1893. The interior public rooms have been carefully restored and are decorated seasonally. The house is an exceptional showpiece during the Christmas holidays. Tours daily 10–3:30, Sun, noon–3:30. Adults $8, children $3, senior citizens $6.

PABST THEATER
144 E. Wells St., Milwaukee
414/286-3665   **DA**
This showcase Victorian theater was built in 1895 on the same location as the Stadt Theater, which had been destroyed by fire. A National Landmark, remodeled in 1976, the theater features top musical and theatrical entertainment. A giant Austrian crystal chandelier, an original fixture, serves as a lighting centerpiece in the theater seating area. Many Milwaukee families make a traditional pilgrimage to this theater to view the annual Milwaukee Repertory production of *A Christmas Carol*. Free tour every Sat at 11:30; meet in the box office area near the Milwaukee Center. Private tours also available for a fee.

POTAWATOMI BINGO CASINO
1721 W. Canal St., Milwaukee
414/645-6888   **DA**
Milwaukee's only bingo and casino hall, Potawatomi awards over $3.6 million in prizes each day. A large variety of pull tabs are featured on the 200-reel Las Vegas–style slot machines. Food is served. Open daily.

ST. JOAN OF ARC CHAPEL
14th St. and Wisconsin Ave.
Milwaukee
414/288-6873   **DA**
A stone that Joan of Arc knelt upon

A 1939 Jaguar in the Brooks Stevens Collection, page 77

and kissed is said to be colder than any of the other stones that make up this chapel. You'll find it on the floor of a niche in the wall behind the altar. This fifteenth-century chapel was originally built in France and reconstructed on the Marquette University campus in 1965. Open daily 10–4, Sun 12–4. Closed all major holidays. Large groups should call ahead. Free tours.

TRINITY EVANGELICAL LUTHERAN CHURCH
North 9th Street and Highland Avenue, Milwaukee
414/271-2219   **DA**
American High Victorian Gothic and traditional German Gothic forms combine in their 1878 construction to create one of the most remarkable Lutheran churches in the country. Built of Milwaukee Cream City brick and trimmed with Illinois sandstone and ornamental sheet metal, this was considered one of the finest Lutheran churches when it opened. Trinity is the second-oldest Lutheran congregation in the city.

UNIVERSITY OF WISCONSIN-MILWAUKEE
414/229-1122   **DA**
Eleven UWM schools and colleges serve over 25,000 students each year. The university offers more than 100 undergraduate programs and sub-majors. The 93-acre Kenwood campus, located in a quiet residential neighborhood in the northeast part of downtown, offers a serene learning environment. Parking can be a problem, and many students opt to catch a bus at one of the city's park-and-ride lots rather than tangle with tight schedules and scarce parking. The university is just a few blocks from Lake Michigan.

WAR MEMORIAL CENTER
750 N. Lincoln Memorial Dr. Milwaukee
414/273-5533   **DA**
Built to honor Milwaukee's war veterans, the War Memorial Center serves under the credo "Honoring the Dead by Serving the Living." The center, overlooking Lake Michigan, is home to the Milwaukee Art Museum and

provides a focal point for various civic activities. Banquet halls and conference rooms can be rented here.

WISCONSIN CONSERVATORY OF MUSIC
1584 N. Prospect Ave., Milwaukee
414/276-5760   DA
Built as a family mansion in 1903, this architecturally significant house on the Milwaukee River has served as a music school since 1932. Tours are offered. Over 100 performances in the mansion's recital hall are open to the public annually. Recent performances have included jazz, blues, and all styles of instrumental recitals, many without admission fees.

WISCONSIN LAKE SCHOONER EDUCATION ASSOCIATION
500 N. Harbor Dr., Milwaukee
414/276-7700; fax 414/276-8838 DA
This not-for-profit education center is dedicated to constructing a traditional Great Lakes schooner at Milwaukee's Municipal Pier. The completed schooner will provide youth with hands-on experience through shore-based water programs and will serve as an ambassador for Wisconsin across distant seas. The association's goal was developed as part of Wisconsin's sesquicentennial project. The public is welcome to view the site.

EAST SIDE

KILBOURNTOWN HOUSE
4400 Estabrook Pkwy., Milwaukee
414/273-8288   ES
Located in Estabrook Park between Hampton Avenue and Capitol Drive, this 1844 home is listed on the National Register of Historic Places

and features nineteenth-century furnishings and decorative arts. The house is open to the public several times each year.

NORTH SIDE

BROOKS STEVENS AUTOMOBILE COLLECTION
10325 N. Port Washington Rd.
Mequon
414/241-4185   NS
Everyone loves the antique cars in a parade, and here you can view over 70 antique and classic cars daily. Weekdays 9–5, Sat and Sun 10–3. Senior citizen discounts and group rates available. Closed Sun, Dec 1–March 1. Cars are also available for rent for parties and weddings. Call for information.

WM. K. WALTHERS, INC.
North 60th Street and Florist
Avenue, Milwaukee
414/527-0770   NS
The world's largest wholesaler of model railroad equipment, Walthers maintains an open-door policy for

model railroad enthusiasts. The store and catalog center stock the widest selection of cars and accessories in the world. Manufacturing was once done on-site but has moved to Europe, where leading model railroad facilities exist. Tours of the warehouse and administrative offices are offered Mon–Sat at 10, 11, 12:30, 1:30, and 2:30 Labor Day–Memorial Day; call for hours the rest of the year. Free.

DCD/David LaHaye

Winterfest, page 90

WEST SIDE

ANNUNCIATION GREEK ORTHODOX CHURCH
9400 W. Congress St., Milwaukee
414/461-9400 **WS**
This Frank Lloyd Wright blue-domed church, Wright's last major building, is considered one of his grandest architectural achievements. Completed in 1961, the church was designed to reproduce a cross and circle. The nave, chancel, and sanctuary form the cross, while the cavernous interior, with its curved balconies and grillwork, forms the circle. One of the best ways to view the church is via tours scheduled the second weekend of July during the annual Greek Festival. Individuals may call ahead to join a scheduled group tour.

CALVARY CEMETERY
5503 W. Blue Mound Rd.
Milwaukee
414/258-0058 **WS**
Legend has it that a black marble angel with a missing hand stands sentry in the middle of this cemetery. She protects the final resting place of Milwaukee's first industrialists, political figures, and philanthropists. Vandals are warned: to enter the cemetery is to incur the wrath of the

hand. Established in 1853, Calvary holds Solomon Juneau, one of Milwaukee's first settlers, and a number of Pabst and Miller brewers.

GENESEE WOOLEN MILL
S40 W28178 Hwy. 59, Waukesha
414/521-2121 **WS**
Visitors can watch freshly shorn wool processed and made into finished products. The mill features 100 percent virgin lamb's wool, hand-tied comforters, and various other wool products and spinning supplies. Call for more information. Open Mon, Tue, Thur, Fri.

HARLEY-DAVIDSON FACTORY
11700 W. Capitol Dr., Wauwatosa
414/343-4056 **WS**
The first Harley-Davidson motorcycle was built in 1903 at 38th and Highland Boulevard in Milwaukee. Today, tourists can watch the assembly of engines and transmissions. Parts are shipped to the company's Philadelphia plant for final assembly. The engine plant tour takes about 60 minutes. Close-toed shoes are re-

WEST SIDE

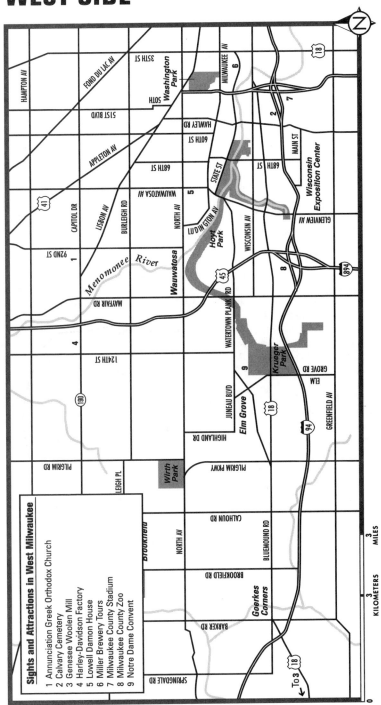

Sights and Attractions in West Milwaukee

1 Annunciation Greek Orthodox Church
2 Calvary Cemetery
3 Genesee Woolen Mill
4 Harley-Davidson Factory
5 Lowell Damon House
6 Miller Brewery Tours
7 Milwaukee County Stadium
8 Milwaukee County Zoo
9 Notre Dame Convent

TIP

Picnic areas, ponds, and a wooded path make the Milwaukee County Zoo a wonderful place to have a picnic. Bring a bag lunch and plan a quiet mid-day break. Be warned, though: wandering peacocks love to beg for leftovers.

quired; children must be at least 12 years old. No cameras. Tours: Jan–Sept Mon, Wed, and Fri at 9, 10:30, and 12:30. Oct–Nov, Mon and Fri, 9, 10:30, and 12:30. Closed the week before Christmas until the Mon after New Year's Day.

LOWELL DAMON HOUSE
2107 N. Wauwatosa Ave.
Wauwatosa
414/273-8288 **WS**
Wauwatosa's oldest home is a classic example of colonial architecture. Built in 1847, it is decorated with mid-nineteenth-century furniture and art. Caretakers employed by the Milwaukee County Historical Society live in an attached residence. Street parking is available. Wed 3–5, Sun 1–5.

MILLER BREWERY TOURS
4251 W. State St., Milwaukee
414/931-BEER **WS**
Ask a Milwaukeean to suggest the one place every visitor should tour, and you're sure to hear "the Miller Brewery"—yet most Milwaukeeans admit they've never been. They're missing something here. Miller tours include beer production, samples (if you're the right age), and a visit to the Miller gift shop, where souvenirs aplenty remind you that beer production gave Milwaukee its national name. Guided tours Tue–Sat, noon, 2, and 3:30. Gift shop open 9–4:30. Free.

MILWAUKEE COUNTY STADIUM
201 S. 46th St., Milwaukee

414/933-6100 **WS**
This stadium has been home to the Milwaukee Braves and the Milwaukee Brewers for over 40 years and holds slightly more than 35,000 fans. A walking tour provides a window view of Hank Aaron's retired number and an inside look at club mascot Bernie Brewer and its house and slide. Fans love to watch the large-headed brewmeister slide from his house into a foaming stein of beer whenever the Brewers hit a home run. A new stadium to replace this building will also house a historical exhibit; it is scheduled for completion in 2001.

MILWAUKEE COUNTY ZOO
10001 W. Blue Mound Rd.
Milwaukee
414/771-3040 **WS**
Visit five continents in one day and view predators and prey living in natural environments but separated by hidden moats. Sampson the gorilla was a favorite during the 1960s; a pictorial Sampson exhibit remains. Zoo officials have taken a proactive stand in raising and breeding endangered species. Animals inhabiting the zoo include koalas, bears, giraffes, and rhinos. Indoor bird, monkey, and reptile houses make the zoo a year-round experience. A zoo train and zoomobile tours are offered. Parking fee and admission charged.

NOTRE DAME CONVENT
Watertown Plank Road

The School Sisters of Notre Dame
by Sister Benilda Dix, SSND

The School Sisters of Notre Dame (SSND) is an international community of 6,000 religious women serving the church in 35 countries on five continents. Blessed Theresa of Hesys Gerhardinger founded the congregation in 1833 in Bavaria, Germany, to provide education and spiritual formation for girls. In 1847 the first School Sisters arrived in the United States. Three years later Mother Caroline Friess, just 26 years old, was put in charge of the North American missions and opened a motherhouse in Milwaukee. Today the Milwaukee Province has more than 600 vowed members and 45 men and women associates, as well as lay volunteers. The sisters work in North America, primarily Wisconsin, Michigan, and Indiana. We also serve Oceania, Central America, Africa, and Europe. We describe ourselves as women of prayer seeking to respond to God's call as it is expressed in the needs of our times, especially serving women, youth, and the poor. In the spirit of our founders, we focus on education, which means empowering people to reach the fullness of their potential, and developing a global vision based on Christian values. We serve in schools as teachers and administrators, from preschool to graduate levels. In parishes and diocesan offices we work in religious education, liturgy, and pastoral ministry. In many other settings we offer spiritual, social, legal, and health services.

Elm Grove
414/782-1450   **WS**

This eye-catching structure, actually modeled after a Bavarian castle, marks the junction of Watertown Plank Road and Juneau Boulevard in Elm Grove. The complex, towering over the neighborhood, has been there for more than 140 years. Currently it houses the provincial offices of the Milwaukee Province of the School Sisters of Notre Dame and provides assisted- and independent-living space for 170 sisters. Recent renovation has converted the retirement building from a nursing home setting into one of more communal living. The order's American founder, Mother Caroline Friess, and more than 2,000 sisters are buried in the

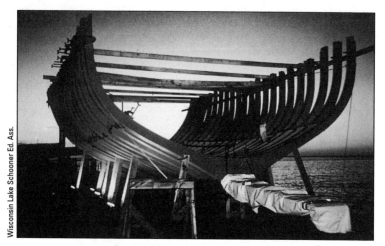

Wisconsin Lake Schooner Education Association, page 77

cemetery on the grounds, which cover 89 acres. Although the castle is not open for tours, a gift shop on the first floor near the bell tower is open daily 1–4 p.m.

SOUTH SIDE

JEREMIAH CURTIN HOUSE
South 84th Street and West Grange Avenue, Greendale
414/273-8288 **SS**
This charming limestone cottage was the boyhood home of diplomat and linguist Jeremiah Curtin. Built in 1846, the home is a fine example of Irish cottage architecture. Open in July and August. Call for days and hours. Free.

QUALITY CANDY/BUDDY SQUIRREL
1801 E. Bolivar Ave., Milwaukee
414/483-4500 **SS**
Chocolate lovers take note. See America's award-winning chocolates being made at this full-scale confectionery, open to groups. Chocolates, nuts, and popcorn—including free samples. Free tours with discounts for bus groups. Reservations required.

ST. JOSEPHAT BASILICA
2336 S. 6th St., Milwaukee
414/645-5623 **SS**
One of the finest examples of Renaissance Revival–style architecture in the country, the basilica reflects the determination of working-class Polish Americans to create a house of worship that reflected their cultural heritage. Limestone salvaged from the Chicago post office served as the facade for this copper-domed church. Art-glass windows imported from Austria and murals by Polish artist Zukotynski and Italian artist Gonippo Raggi ornament the gorgeous interior.

ST. SAVA SERBIAN ORTHODOX CHURCH
3201 S. 51st St., Milwaukee
414/545-4080 **SS**
This modern, Byzantine-style stone church, built in 1956, is widely known for its spectacular mosaics. St. Sava's roof is topped with five copper-clad

SOUTH SIDE

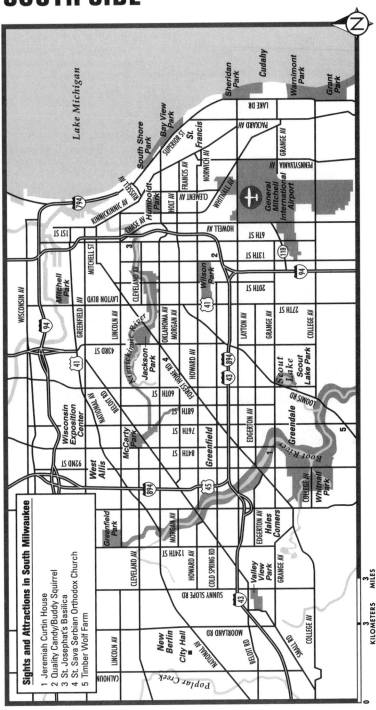

Sights and Attractions in South Milwaukee

1 Jeremiah Curtin House
2 Quality Candy/Buddy Squirrel
3 St. Josephat's Basilica
4 St. Sava Serbian Orthodox Church
5 Timber Wolf Farm

A wolf and handler on the grounds of the Timber Wolf Preservation Society

Timber Wolf Preservation Society, Inc.

domes on tall, windowed drums. Tall, thin, arched elements are repeated at each window and the portico, representing the Eastern architectural tradition. Since statuary is not part of the Orthodox Christian tradition, paintings (called "icons") and mosaics made in Ravenna, Italy, depict religious figures throughout the church.

TIMBER WOLF FARM AND PRESERVATION SOCIETY
6669 S. 76th St., Greendale
414/425-8264 **SS**
Dedicated to the preservation of wolves and located in an urban setting, this is the only center of its kind. The farm's staff offers education and training about this endangered species. Call for a tour schedule.

FESTIVALS

AFRICAN WORLD FESTIVAL
Henry W. Maier Festival Park
200 N. Harbor Dr., Milwaukee
414/372-4567 **DA**
This is a world view indeed, as folks

learn about the vast differences between African and American nations. Taste Ashanti peanut stew, dress up to dance to rhythm and blues, or feel the spirit of the gospel choir. African craft booths maintain a steady stream of business. Held the first weekend of August.

ANNUAL HOLIDAY FOLK FAIR INTERNATIONAL
The Midwest Express Center
500 W. Kilbourn Ave., Milwaukee
414/225-6225 **DA**
This annual fair has been a Milwaukee cultural tie since its inception over 50 years ago. Produced by the International Institute of Wisconsin and more than 50 affiliated groups, the fair serves a wide variety of cultural cuisine. Food preparation demonstrations, entertainment, exhibits, and crafts make this three-day event a world tour. Entrance fee. Held in November.

ASIAN MOON FESTIVAL
Summerfest Grounds
200 N. Harbor Dr., Milwaukee
414/481-3628 **DA**
Colorful displays in a culture tent, daily presentations of Asian legends, and Chinese opera performed by the National Fu Hsing Dramatic Arts Academy of Taipei made the 1996 festival memorable. Asian food booths offer some American choices. Festival is traditionally held during the first full moon in June.

BASTILLE DAYS
Cathedral Square
802 N. Jackson St., Milwaukee
414/271-1416 **DA**
This popular French festival, held in a park between St. John's Cathedral and a number of the city's dining establishments, turns the park into an

outdoor cabaret. Four music stages allow ongoing performances of blues, jazz, and even French torch songs. French and American food is available, although outdoor seating is scarce. Held in July.

BAVARIAN VOLKFEST
Old Heidelberg Park
700 W. Lexington Blvd.
Milwaukee
414/462-9147 **NS**
This traditional, Old Munich–style festival features brass bands, Schuhplattler dancers, yodeling, singalongs, and beer garden *Gemütlichkeit*. Held in late June.

FESTA ITALIANA
Henry W. Maier Festival Park
200 N. Harbor Dr., Milwaukee
414/223-2180 or 800/223-2194 **DA**
One of the more popular ethnic festivals, attendance in 1996 surpassed 134,000. Colored lights give the appearance of an Italian street festival, while costumed ethnic dancers roam the grounds. The Pompeii Sacred Art Exhibit, brought to Milwaukee in 1996 as an annual event, emphasizes traditional Catholic conviction, as does the Sunday Holy Mass performed at the Marcus Amphitheater inside the festival grounds. Abundant Italian food. This festival is always scheduled for the third weekend in July.

FIRSTAR FIREWORKS
Lakefront, Milwaukee
414/765-4321 **DA**
Many revelers pack a lunch, grab a few blankets, and plan a daylong picnic along the lakefront to wait for these spectacular fireworks. This largest fireworks display in Milwaukee begins at 9 p.m. on July 3 and lasts about an hour.

GERMAN FEST
Henry W. Maier Festival Park
200 N. Harbor Dr., Milwaukee
414/464-9444 or 800/355-9067 **DA**
Sauerbraten and *rouladen;* pitchers of rich, foamy beer in beer gardens; yodeling and song—all create a

---

Travel with the Washington County Pioneer Wagon Train

History lovers can plan ahead to join the Washington County Tourism Association's pioneer wagon train. Interested individuals and groups will be required to wear nineteenth-century clothing and use vehicles from that era. The June 1998 reenactment, planned as part of the state's sesquicentennial anniversary, will follow one of Wisconsin's earliest settlement routes. The train will proceed north from the Illinois border at the beginning of June and travel along the historic Green Bay Indian Trail/Military Road. For more information, call 414/626-4278.

three-day Oktoberfest in Milwaukee the last weekend of July. German bands and folk dancing provide an authentic taste of the culture.

INDIAN SUMMER
Henry W. Maier Festival Park
200 N. Harbor Dr., Milwaukee
414/774-7119 **DA**
Traditionally held the first weekend in September, Indian summer emphasizes spirituality and heritage. Ethnic dress is worn everywhere and available at a seemingly unlimited supply of craft booths. Pow-wows are held daily. Historical reenactments take place throughout the festival. If you've never had Indian fry bread, you're in for a treat. Indian pizza is served with a spread of beans, onions, and tomatoes spooned over the fluffy, deep-fried delicacy. For dessert or a snack, a sprinkling of powdered sugar and cinnamon seasons the bread.

IRISH FEST
Henry W. Maier Festival Park
200 N. Harbor Dr., Milwaukee
414/476-3378 **DA**
Third in popularity only to Summer-fest and Festa Italiana, Irish Fest brings out the Irish in all its devotees. Irish music, culture, and arts are highlighted. The beer flows freely as arm-in-arm groups raise their voices in choruses of "When Irish Eyes Are Smiling." Held the third weekend of August.

JUNETEENTH DAY
Martin Luther King Drive
Milwaukee
414/372-3770 **DA**
This festive day begins with a parade from 19th Street and Atkinson Avenue, to Green Bay Avenue, to Martin Luther King Drive and Burleigh Street. Political and public dignitaries officially open the festival at 10 a.m. Exhibitions, food, and drink round out the day.

MARITIME DAYS
Veterans Park
Lakefront, Milwaukee
414/221-0200 **DA**

TOP
TEN

Top Ten Reasons to Attend a Lakefront Festival

1. To hear great music
2. To sample a variety of food
3. To meet people from all over the world
4. To dance
5. To people-watch
6. To learn about other cultures
7. To learn about your own culture
8. To purchase local crafts
9. To enjoy the day with your family
10. To have the time of your life

Antique tall ships wait offshore for tours, while five stages provide nationally known entertainment that has included Three Dog Night and Judy Collins. A photo exhibit educates visitors on the rich history of the Great Lakes. Demonstrations and activities. More than 36 galley cafés provide a variety of foods. Held the last weekend of August.

MEXICAN FIESTA
Henry W. Maier Festival Park
200 N. Harbor Dr., Milwaukee
414/383-7066 **DA**
An impressive line of nationally recognized traditional dance troops, including Ballet Folklorico de Mexico and Ballet Cinco de Mayo, perform from many stages. Strolling mariachi musicians perform for diners. The Jalapeño Pepper-Eating Contest usually draws a crowd. Mexican food and beer are plentiful. Usually held the third weekend of August.

MILWAUKEE À LA CARTE
Milwaukee County Zoo
10001 W. Blue Mound Rd.
Milwaukee
414/771-3040 **WS**
Come watch the animals and eat your own way through gourmet delights. More than 30 restaurants serving sample-size portions are scattered around the zoo grounds. Four entertainment stages combine music, food, and fun for this four-day August food festival.

OKTOBERFEST
Old Heidelberg Park
700 W. Lexington Blvd.,
Milwaukee
414/462-9147 **NS**
Like the Bavarian Volkfest in June, (also held in Old Heidelberg Park) and German Fest in July, this festival

has lots of traditional German music, dancing, and food. Held the first three weekends in October.

THE ONE AND ONLY WEEK OF THE GREAT CIRCUS PARADE
Downtown Milwaukee
608/356-0800 **DA**
This week-long event, held immediately after Summerfest, begins as the Baraboo circus train winds its way through Milwaukee. The train arrives about five days before the parade. A tent city rises, and folks are encouraged to look at circus life on the Great Circus Parade showgrounds. The morning before the parade dawns with the World's Greatest Circus Breakfast and concludes with "Circus in the Sky" fireworks. The Great Circus Parade ends the week on Sunday at 2 p.m. The parade, which really is spectacular, may lose its sponsors and many circus lovers fear it is in danger of extinction.

POLISH FEST
Henry W. Maier Festival Park
200 N. Harbor Dr., Milwaukee

Indian Summer Festival, page 86

DCD/David LaHaye

GREATER MILWAUKEE

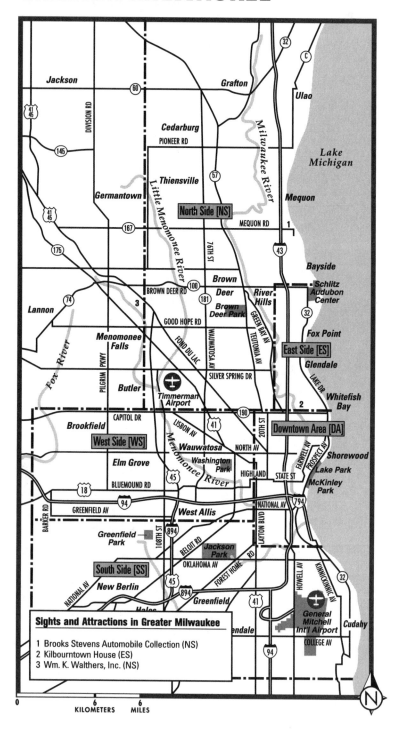

Sights and Attractions in Greater Milwaukee

1 Brooks Stevens Automobile Collection (NS)
2 Kilbourntown House (ES)
3 Wm. K. Walthers, Inc. (NS)

North Side [NS]
East Side [ES]
Downtown Area [DA]
West Side [WS]
South Side [SS]

0   6   6
   KILOMETERS   MILES

N

Top Ten City Monuments

1. *The Victorious Charge*, on West Wisconsin Avenue between 9th and 10th Streets

2. George Washington, on West Wisconsin Avenue between 9th and 10th Streets

3. Boerner Botanical Garden pool statue, in Whitnall Park, 5879 S. 92nd St.

4. *Spanish-American War Veteran*, on West Wisconsin Avenue between 9th and 10th Streets

5. Erastus B. Wolcott, in Lake Park near the lion bridges

6. General Thaddeus Kosciuszko, Kosciuszko Park, South 9th Place and West Lincoln Avenue

7. Frederick Von Steuben, West Lisbon, Lloyd and North Sherman Boulevard

8. Solomon Juneau, Juneau Park, opposite East Kilbourn Avenue

9. *Leif Ericson, The Discoverer*, Juneau Park, opposite East State Street

10. Henry Bergh, Wisconsin Humane Society, 4151 North Humboldt Blvd.

414/529-2140   **DA**
Bringing Milwaukee's infatuation with the Friday night fish fry to the lakefront, Polish Fest draws a fair number of people during its three-day run. The festival also supplies the community with a healthy sampling of Polish delicacies, from sauerkraut-filled *bigos* to Polish sausages. Held in June.

PRIDEFEST
Henry W. Maier Festival Park
200 N. Harbor Dr., Milwaukee
414/272-3378   **DA**
One of the newest additions to the summer festival lineup, Pridefest raises some eyebrows with its focus on gay lifestyles but has proven to provide an eclectic variety of music, from country to Spanish dancers. Held in June.

RAINBOW SUMMER
Marcus Center for the Performing Arts
929 N. Water St., Milwaukee
414/273-7206 or 800/472-2258   **DA**
Noon-hour and Tuesday evening entertainment at the Marcus Center riverfront features jazz, country, and rock. Rainbow Summer runs from the first week in June to the end of August. Most events are free.

SUMMERFEST
Henry W. Maier Festival Park
200 N. Harbor Dr., Milwaukee
414/273-FEST or 800/837-FEST   **DA**
Being billed as the mother of all festivals, Summerfest is currently celebrating its thirtieth "Big Gig." Six stages provide all varieties of music. Food booths keep the most hearty ap-

petite satisfied, while a steady flow of beer and wine have traditionally boistered spirits even during those seasons of torrential rains. Marcus Amphitheater, located on the grounds, nightly hosts internationally famous musicians and groups. Past performers have included Alabama, Jimmy Buffet, Boyz II Men, Bonnie Raitt, Paul Simon, and Sting. The ten-day festival is held from Thursday to Sunday, beginning the last Thursday in June and ending the Sunday after Independence Day.

WINTERFEST
Cathedral Square
802 N. Jackson St., Milwaukee
414/273-FEST or 800/837-FEST DA
Ice skating and music make winter warm in spirit, if not in fact. Figure-skating exhibitions, ice sculpting, and family activities add up to a festival worth attending. Held Dec–Jan.

WISCONSIN STATE FAIR
Wisconsin Exposition Center
8100 W. Greenfield Ave.
West Allis
414/266-7000 or 800/884-FAIR   SS
Attend the Wisconsin State Fair the first two weeks of August each year, or shop the ski sales in fall and the camper sales in spring. The annual State Fair combines agricultural traditions with the excitement of a contemporary urban environment. Top-name entertainment and fireworks cap off each evening. The grounds also offer year-round shopping, family events, and entertainment.

Discovery World

6

Rating education, day care, sports, culture, job opportunities, and other factors, Fortune *magazine recently ranked Milwaukee one of the best places to raise a family. Milwaukeeans weren't surprised. Where else can you find small-town friendliness in a city that offers top educational opportunities, theater, sports, and four seasons of fun? If your family loves great outdoor activities such as skiing, swimming, biking, and skating, head for the city's many parks. Indoor amusements such as theater, music, theme parks, and museums provide new ways of understanding the world we live in. Special kids' exhibits at many of the museums help make the city a window to our universe. All in all, Milwaukee brings the wonders of the world to kids, and, in the process, it becomes a delightful place for kids to be.*

ANIMALS AND THE GREAT OUTDOORS

THE APPLE WORKS ORCHARD
W179 N12536 Fond du Lac Ave.
Germantown
414/ 677-1888 or 800/306-8888   NS
This apple orchard offers scheduled school and day-care tours during August, September, and October. A tour guide explains about apples and beehives. A hay-wagon ride through the orchard culminates with a hands-on opportunity to pack apples and make cider. Each child receives a coloring book, two apples, and eight ounces of cider. Weekends from mid-September through mid-October, families are invited to pick their own apples and pumpkins. A free hay-wagon ride takes you to the orchard and pumpkin patch. When you get back, you pay only for whatever you've picked. The orchard is also a farm, with zoo pygmy goats, sheep, pot-belly pigs, geese, ducks, chickens, and turkeys. Kids really enjoy visiting with the animals, which are fenced. Picnic tables under a tent allow families who bring their

DOWNTOWN AREA

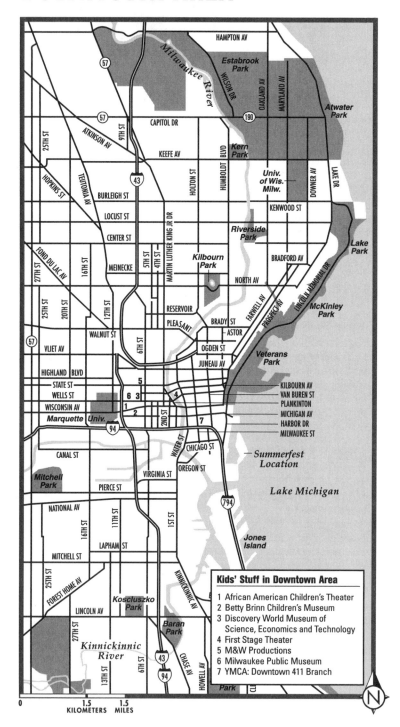

Kids' Stuff in Downtown Area

1 African American Children's Theater
2 Betty Brinn Children's Museum
3 Discovery World Museum of Science, Economics and Technology
4 First Stage Theater
5 M&W Productions
6 Milwaukee Public Museum
7 YMCA: Downtown 411 Branch

Things You Should Know about Organic Farming

According to Dennis Mackey, director of operations at Apple Works Orchard, organic product sales reached over $3 billion in 1996. The organic label is given only to foods that were farmed without chemical additives—no pesticides, no animal growth hormones, and no artificial preservatives. Most farmers, says Mackey, choose to farm organically because they believe it's a better way to treat the earth. Organic farming is considered one of the most modern farming methods in use today. Many organic farmers create balanced habitats in their fields and orchards by encouraging beneficial insects. Mackey says about one-half of the Apple Works orchards are currently organic. The rest of their apples are grown with "ecological" methods, meaning organic fertilizers, organic fungal control, no herbicides or weed sprays, and a balanced orchard habitat. Consumers can do their part to keep organic apples fresh and unblemished by storing them in a cool area. Cool, dry climates prevent decay and maintain juiciness and crispness. Apple Works Orchard decided to go into the children's education and entertainment business to spread the word about organic farming.

lunches to eat in the shade or be sheltered from foul weather. A visible beehive in the market area shows how the bees make honey. A farmer's market, complete with jams, apples, cider, and produce gifts, is open daily during apple season. The orchard grows over 150 varieties of apples, including antique and experimental types. The Wolf River, for instance, is an antique apple, a large baking apple not commercially available except through specialty orchards like this one. Experimental apples are hybridized at universities and grown here. The orchard is also 60 percent certified organic and within three years will be entirely so. Open daily Aug–Christmas Eve, 10–5:30. Call for current schedule of times. Group tours, $3.75 per person. Apple plus pumpkin tour, $5.50 per person.

CHILDREN'S PETTING ZOO
Milwaukee County Zoo
10001 W. Blue Mound Rd.
Milwaukee
414/771-3040   **WS**
Visit a working dairy farm and learn how many Wisconsin farmers provide the community's milk and dairy products. A hands-on exhibit teaches children about different domestic animals. An 1896 eight-sided barn stands in the middle of the farm area. Turn-of-the-century

EAST SIDE

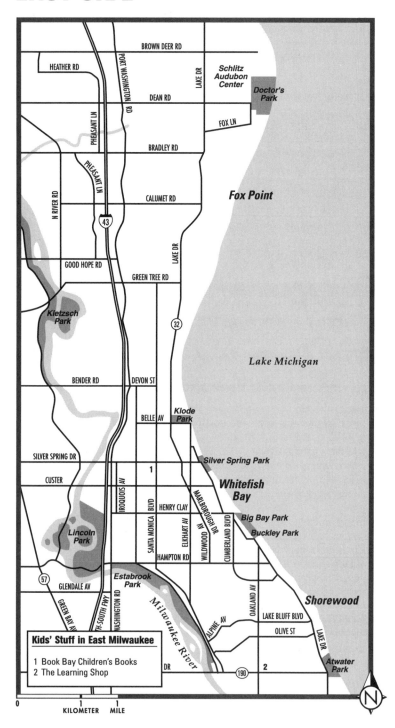

BROWN DEER RD

HEATHER RD

PORT WASHINGTON RD

LAKE DR

Schlitz
Audubon
Center

Doctor's
Park

DEAN RD

PHEASANT LN

FOX LN

BRADLEY RD

PHEASANT LN

N RIVER RD

CALUMET RD

Fox Point

43

GOOD HOPE RD

LAKE DR

GREEN TREE RD

32

Kletzsch
Park

Lake Michigan

BENDER RD

DEVON ST

BELLE AV

Klode
Park

SILVER SPRING DR

Silver Spring Park

1

CUSTER

Whitefish
Bay

IROQUOIS AV

SANTA MONICA BLVD

HENRY CLAY

MARLBOROUGH DR

ELKHART AV

WILDWOOD AV

CUMBERLAND BLVD

Big Bay Park

Buckley Park

Lincoln
Park

HAMPTON RD

57

GLENDALE AV

Estabrook
Park

OAKLAND AV

Shorewood

GREEN BAY AV

I-H-SOUTH FWY

WASHINGTON RD

Milwaukee River

ALPINE AV

LAKE BLUFF BLVD

OLIVE ST

LAKE DR

DR

190

2

Atwater
Park

Kids' Stuff in East Milwaukee

1 Book Bay Children's Books
2 The Learning Shop

0   1
KILOMETER   MILE

N

> Zoomobiles and train rides provide a relaxing respite from the long walking trails that wind around the Milwaukee County Zoo animal exhibits.

dairymen preferred this design because it accommodated more cattle. Milking demonstrations take place daily. Adults $7.50, children $5.50, 2 and under free April–Oct. In winter, adults $6, children $4. Parking $5.

JOY FARM
7007 N. 115st St., Milwaukee
414/353-9900   **NS**

As children, many Milwaukee adults rode their first horse at Joy Farm. Nowadays their kids saddle up and learn the basics of riding with an English saddle. The 30-minute riding sessions are geared toward beginning and intermediate riders. Groups of up to six beginners can practice their trot in the indoor ring or outside, weather permitting. The farm also boards horses. Adults and children, $12.50 for each 30-minute session. Open year-round.

LIVE WORLD
6904 N. 41st St., Milwaukee
414/228-6305   **NS**

Live World has the finest live-ectothermic-animal presentation in southeastern Wisconsin; in other words, they answer the question, "What's an amphibian?" The center has a globally diverse selection of frogs, toads, salamanders, lizards, and snakes. The longest member of their reptilian family is an 8-foot boa constrictor. A 3.5-foot alligator and 5-foot iguana remain the largest overall. These captive-bred animals have been raised since birth by the Live

World owners , so you can get as close as you like—you can even pet most of them. Planned presentations give a full rundown on each amphibian's current status in nature. For groups of ten kids or more, the animals can be transported—they have helped celebrate birthday parties, scouting events, and church socials. Smaller groups of kids are encouraged. Hours are 11 to 3 daily, by appointment. Daytime shows are preferred because many of the diurnal amphibians are difficult to wake at night. Cost of "road shows" is based on where you live but ranges from $120 to $140. A typical presentation runs 90 minutes to two hours. The smaller the group, the better, because each child gets more hands-on time. Group presentations for under ten people at the facility are about $85.

MUSEUMS AND LIBRARIES

BETTY BRINN CHILDREN'S MUSEUM
929 E. Wisconsin Ave.
Milwaukee
414/291-0888   **DA**

This museum features hands-on interdisciplinary exhibits and activities for children ages 1 through 10 and their families. Located at O'Donnell Park, the museum looks out on Milwaukee's lakefront. Culturally diverse fantasy and role-playing exhibits encourage learning experiences and ignite imaginations. Tue–Sun, noon–5; closed

Top Ten Most Interesting Exhibits at the Zoo

The following kids' list was compiled by Milwaukee-area kids, Stephanie Angel, 11, and Joe Angel, 12.

1. Monkey Island, home to an active group of Japanese macaques, or snow monkeys.

2. The Mahler Family Aviary, where hundreds of colorful birds fly overhead as visitors explore a tropical paradise.

3. Miller Brewing Company–sponsored "Oceans of Fun": sea lions entertain and teach; four shows a day, seven days a week.

4. Aquatic and Reptile Center (ARC), featuring a 28,000-gallon Pacific Coast marine aquarium.

5. The Small Mammal building, home to little furry survivors from all regions of the world.

6. Apes of Africa/Primates of the World, an exhibit of Western lowland gorillas, orangutans, simians, and spider monkeys.

7. Feline Building, where lions, hyenas, cheetahs, and tigers prowl in open outdoor yards.

8. Polar Bear underwater viewing area.

9. The Stackner Heritage Farm, formerly known as the Children's Zoo.

10. The miniature train that winds through the zoo grounds, carrying riders every day (weather permitting).

Mon. Ages 2 and up $3, under 2 free. Family memberships $45 per year.

DISCOVERY WORLD MUSEUM OF SCIENCE, ECONOMICS AND TECHNOLOGY
712 W. Wells St., Milwaukee
414/765-0777   DA
Interactive science and technology exhibits, live theater, and other memorable experiences await kids at Milwaukee's newest museum. The entrepreneurial village, a stock wall, and "Into Einstein's Brain" are just three exhibits that opened in 1996. Adults $4.25, children $2.25, under 6 free.

DISCOVERY ZONE
5008 S. 74th St., Greenfield
414/281-3220 or 800/282-4386   SS
This is a great place for the youngest set's birthday parties. Lots of things to climb and bounce on. Concessions available. Open Sun–Thur, 11–7, Fri and Sat, 10–9. Ages 3 and up, $5.99, 12 mos.–36 mos., $3.99. Socks are required for play.

HEIRLOOM DOLL SHOPPE, HOSPITAL & MUSEUM
416 E. Broadway, Waukesha
414/544-4739   WS
Most locals come across this museum

while attempting to repair a child's favorite doll. They usually discover a taste of their own childhood in its collection of over 2,000 dolls. Barbie dolls, baby dolls, ballerinas, and brides line the shelves, nap in carriages, and stand posed to perform their specific duties. The shop caters to collectors and doll lovers alike.

MADISON CHILDREN'S MUSEUM
100 State St., Madison
608/256-6445　　　　　　　WS
Exhibits change often at this wonderfully diverse museum, located an hour west of Milwaukee. Highlighted in 1997 was the "Light and Color" exhibit. Currently "Brazil: Beyond the Rainforest" helps audiences understand Brazil as a nation. Open Tue–Sun, 10–5. Adults and children $3, seniors $2. Economy times Tue–Fri from 3–5, $2 a person.

MILWAUKEE PUBLIC MUSEUM
800 W. Wells St., Milwaukee
414/278-2700 or
414/278-2702 for 24-hour recorded
events line　　　　　　　　　DA
The IMAX dome theater is the biggest news at the Milwaukee Public Museum, but kids still gravitate toward the dinosaur exhibit and its sound effects, and to the Indian village, which includes a modern-day powwow. Curiosity Zone, on the ground floor, is a hands-on interactive exhibit that shows how things work. Open daily 9–5. Adults $5.50, seniors $4.50, children $3.50, under age 3 free.

PERFORMING ARTS

AFRICAN AMERICAN CHILDREN'S THEATER
2821 N. 4th St., Milwaukee

414/283-9588　　　　　　　　DA
This small theater troupe is making a cultural impact with such productions as *How the Buffalo Was Taken by the Hunter*. Adult and child actors are emerging from this theater and making a difference in the city's cultural awareness. Shows are usually staged at the Avalon Theater, 2473 S. Kinickinnic Ave., a South Side location.

FIRST STAGE THEATER
Todd Wehr Theater
929 N. Water St., Milwaukee
414/273-2314 or 800/472-2258　DA
First Stage produces both classic children's stories and contemporary plays for children. Recent dramatizations of children's novels include *Caddie Woodlawn* and *Lyle, Lyle, the Crocodile*. *Caddie* proved so popular in 1995 that it was repeated in 1996. First Stage also offers year-round children's acting classes, casting many of these young thespians in company productions.

Rainforest Exhibit at the Milwaukee Public Museum

NORTH SIDE

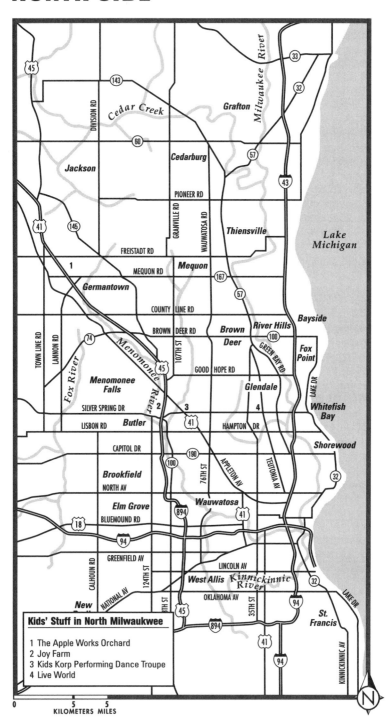

Kids' Stuff in North Milwaukkee

1 The Apple Works Orchard
2 Joy Farm
3 Kids Korp Performing Dance Troupe
4 Live World

0   5   5
KILOMETERS MILES

N

KIDS KORP INC.
5626 N. 91st St.,
Milwaukee
414/463-8530 **NS**
These kids, trained at Gayle's Dance Studio, perform jazz, tap, and contemporary ballet for private and civic occasions.

M &W PRODUCTIONS
Cooley Auditorium (on
Milwaukee Area Technical
College campus)
1015 N. 6th St., Milwaukee
414/272-7701 **DA**
This company, which uses the talents of professional adult and child actors, established itself in Milwaukee ten years ago. A full-service company based entirely in Milwaukee, it provides costuming, talent, and/or full production to such clients as Marshall Field & Co., Bergners, Boston Store-Carson Pirie Scott, the U.S. Navy, and Junior Miss of Wisconsin. As full-production presenters, the company stages three productions a year: fall, winter, and spring. Performances are scheduled for Oct, Dec, and May. No classes are offered currently. The May 1997 production is *The Wizard of Oz.* $7 per person (adult or child); group rates available to qualifying groups. Prices subject to change.

MILWAUKEE YOUTH THEATER
2479 S. Kinnickinnic Ave.
Bay View
414/390-3900 **SS**
Many productions by this "totally kids" theater company are written, produced, and performed by kids in the group's acting workshops and classes, under the guidance of some of Milwaukee's most talented acting teachers. Call for details.

Boatswain Chair at Discovery World, page 96

Discovery World

STORES KIDS LOVE

ARTIST & DISPLAY
9015 W. Burleigh St., Milwaukee
414/442-9100 or 800/722-7450 **WS**
Bringing out the artist in every child and adult, Artist & Display features imaginative store displays that explore all art media. The store is set up to encourage kids to explore the use of color and design in their daily lives. Single-day workshops and classes in drawing, clay jewelry, sculpture, and even doll design are offered on an ongoing basis.

BALL FOUR SPORTS MEMORABILIA
11712 W. North Ave.
Wauwatosa
414/443-0763 **SS**
Milwaukee's first baseball-card shop has been serving collectors since 1979. Autographed cards, memorabilia, and used equipment make this a field of dreams for baseball fans.

BOOK BAY CHILDREN'S BOOKS
415 E. Silver Spring Dr.

Whitefish Bay
414/962-3444 **ES**
Milwaukee's only bookstore just for children, the Book Bay has the largest selection of children's books, games, and book-related accessories of any local bookstore. This independent bookstore is recommended again and again by area teachers for its complete stock as well as for its knowledgeable sales associates.

FINCH'S NEST
18900 W. Blue Mound Rd.
Brookfield
414/796-0450 **WS**
Collectors' dolls as large as small children, with tiny fingernails and pierced ears, greet you as you enter the Finch's Nest. The shelves are stocked with Vander bears, Gund stuffed animals, and a complete line of Ginny, Carolle, and Madame Alexander dolls. Wicker carriages and bassinets are filled with sleeping babes. It's hard to keep curious hands off the taffeta-

and-lace outfits on these fine dolls, but be forewarned: on at least one occasion, staff has been heard to tell little girls not to touch the merchandise. A second store is at Mayfair in Wauwatosa.

GEPETTO'S TOY STORE
17155A W. Blue Mound Rd.
Brookfield
414/797-9588 **WS**
High-quality games, toys, and puzzles are sold in this delightful store, and one or two Brio wood trains are usually set up and ready to roll. Ravensburger puzzles line the shelves, and musical instruments fill floor bins. Science activities, infants' and babies' toys, stuffed animals, play-action figures, and building sets (including Lego and Playmobil) in a variety of themes are stocked here. Additionally dolls, tea sets, and much more vie for attention.

HARRY W. SCHWARTZ
BOOKSHOPS

Author book signing at the Book Bay, page 99

Book Bay

WEST SIDE

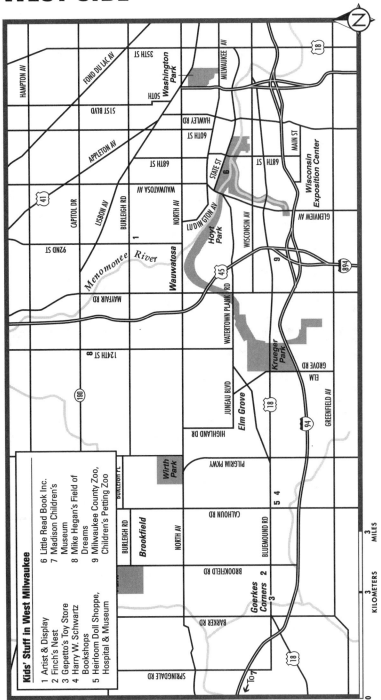

Kids' Stuff in West Milwaukee

1 Artist & Display
2 Finch's Nest
3 Gepetto's Toy Store
4 Harry W. Schwartz Bookshops
5 Heirloom Doll Shoppe, Hospital & Museum
6 Little Read Book Inc.
7 Madison Children's Museum
8 Mike Hegan's Field of Dreams
9 Milwaukee County Zoo, Children's Petting Zoo

Top Ten Things to Do with Kids While You're in Milwaukee

Sharon Hart Addy, a Milwaukee writer and author of *Kidding Around Milwaukee,* says the list of things you can do with kids here is endless. These are her very favorites.

1. Visit Milwaukee County Zoo—worth seeing with or without the Dino-Mation exhibit.

2. Play at McKinley or Doctor's Park Beach, where you can build sand castles or watch the waves.

3. Spend some time at any Milwaukee nature center, but especially Schlitz Audubon Nature Preserve.

4. Explore the parks—especially Lake Park and Whitnall Park.

5. Visit Discover World—stop at the R & D (that's Research & Discover) Café, where you can select from a menu of experiments and projects to complete.

6. Enjoy everything about Betty Brinn Children's Museum.

7. Take in the Milwaukee Public Museum—view the great (and small) beasts at "3rd World Dinosaur Hall" or the mummies at "Temple, Tells and Tombs."

8. Visit the Milwaukee Public Museum's IMAX Theater and get all wrapped up in the wonders on a 360-degree screen.

9. Tour the Milwaukee Maritime Center to see the tall ship being built there.

10. Find a park with a playground, have a picnic, and listen to each other's dreams.

17145 W. Blue Mound Rd.
Brookfield
414/797-6140   **WS**

This locally owned bookshop also has branches dowtown and on the East Side (Shorewood). The Brookfield store has a children's section stocked to the brim with best-loved titles in hardcover and paperback. Trained booksellers can really talk books here—they know what appeals to kids, what's quality, and what's just a plain good title for specific age groups. Nationally known children's authors often appear here to read and sign books.

THE LEARNING SHOP
4060 N. Oakland Ave., Shorewood
414/962-1491   **ES**

With additional stores in Wauwatosa, Brookfield, Greenfield, Mequon, and West Allis, the Learning Shop has become synonymous with a great place to purchase educational gifts for children of all ages. Kids love the store, which sells just about every kind of sticker imaginable, art supplies, craft kits, felt-board items, dolls and dress-up costumes, science and math games, and reading materials. The store was originally created as a source of educational materials for teachers, but kids also love it once they discover all the neat items in the nooks and crannies.

LITTLE READ BOOK, INC.
7603 W. State St., Wauwatosa
414/774-2665 **WS**
Moms and dads love this store because of the puzzle table, where kids can work on puzzles while their parents browse shelves of hardcovers and paperbacks. Kids also love the special children's book room, stuffed with picture books and book-related gifts. One of the store's most special features is the many shelves hung at children's eye level, so kids can browse the merchandise without having to rely on adults' assistance.

RECREATION

CHUCK E. CHEESE
2701 S. Chase Ave., Milwaukee
414/483-8655 **SS**
The pizza's OK, but kids really come here to play the video games, take a tot ride, or jump around in the Styrofoam ball room. Bring lots of cash, which you can readily change for Chuck E. Cheese tokens at any number of token machines. This pizza parlor/video arcade is a birthday-party haven and noisy as all get-out. Is it any surprise, then, that beer and wine are served for weary parents? A second South Side site and a Brookfield location make this arcade accessible no matter what part of town you're coming from.

FUN WORLD
620 N. Elizabeth Ct., Brookfield
414/789-5370 **SS**
Southeastern Wisconsin's largest indoor entertainment center has 25,000 square feet of space. Its 24-foot-high indoor Ferris wheel, laser-tag arena, motion simulator, game arena, and 18-hole miniature indoor golf course have been known to keep many local kids happy during the gloomy midwinter Milwaukee slump.

MIKE HEGAN'S FIELD OF DREAMS
12540 W. Townsend Ave.
Brookfield
414/781-7526 **WS**
This indoor sports center has gained a reputation for training budding ballplayers. Year-round coaching and group instruction are available. Many of the coaches are professional and semi-pro ballplayers themselves. Kids love the opportunity to spot a famous face here, and they often wile away a Saturday or Sunday in the soft-pitch or hardball batting cages. Two basketball courts in the back of this old warehouse also provide the opportunity to improve basketball skills. A number of video games keep kids busy while they wait their turns. A concession stand sells food and beverages. Birthday parties can also be held here.

T I P

Maier Festival Park provides a free children's play area surrounded by benches, a great stopping place for weary parents with energetic kids.

SOUTH SIDE

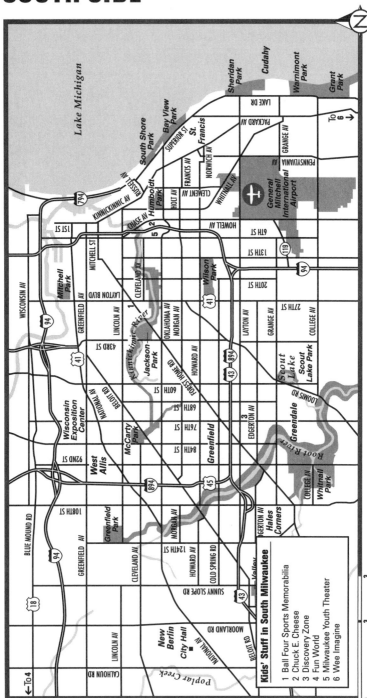

Kids' Stuff in South Milwaukee
1 Ball Four Sports Memorabilia
2 Chuck E. Cheese
3 Discovery Zone
4 Fun World
5 Milwaukee Youth Theater
6 Wee Imagine

STORM'S GOLF RANGES
16120 W. Blue Mound Rd.
Brookfield
414/782-4010   **WS**
One of Milwaukee's first miniature golf ranges, Storm's now has locations in New Berlin and Oconomowoc. Kids of all ages can golf the outdoor range, take lessons, or practice their drives and putting.

WEE IMAGINE
8624 S. Marketplace, Oak Creek
414/764-9120   **SS**
Set in an 1800s village, inside a little red schoolhouse, Wee Imagine is a unique party center. This is the place to have a tea party with special pals. Treasure hunts, led by Captain Merryweather and complete with pirates and tattoos, are available for boys, who always end up finding a treasure chest. Some special events—such as playtime, where kids are welcome to come in, dress up, and play "pretend"—are offered period-ically. Birthday parties are a Wee Imagine specialty. Adults' and children's costumes are also available for rental. Wee Imagine has recently taken over a ballroom in a building across from the schoolhouse and has decorated it as an enchanted forest. This room is available for adults' as well as children's parties. A 1950s ice-cream parlor has also been decked out for parties. Located on the corner of Highway 32 and Putz Road. Party packages for four are $55, and $10 for each additional child.

YMCA: DOWNTOWN 411 BRANCH
411 E. Wisconsin, Suite 600
Milwaukee
414/291-9622   **DA**
If you belong to a YMCA, you can come to area Ys free for up to 12 visits a year. Take advantage of water and gym sports. Relax and refresh yourself with a multitude of classes for kids and adults.

7

MUSEUMS AND GALLERIES

Milwaukee has an undeserved reputation as a typically dowdy Midwestern community, but a look at the city's art galleries and museums proves that nothing could be further from the truth. Rather, it's a community that's alive with fine arts and eclectic opportunities to explore creative expression. Visit the area's galleries and you'll find expressive examples of wearable art, whimsical furniture, watercolors, mixed media, art-metal sculptures, and jewelry, all of which excite the imagination. The wealth of museums brings history into the present with visually stimulating displays. Walk Milwaukee's streets and you'll discover that they, too, are filled with historic and contemporary monuments, sculpture, and architectural treasures. Experience the cultural vitality of this city that's brimming with creativity.

Many galleries are located in little Soho-type communities in downtown Milwaukee, but pockets of each suburb and many side streets have storefronts filled with pottery and new-wave art. Many of these galleries are new; some are yet to be discovered. They're all worth a stop. Take some time to browse Milwaukee's art scene.

MUSEUMS

AMERICA'S BLACK HOLOCAUST MUSEUM
2233 N. 4th St., Milwaukee
414/264-2500   DA
Museum curator James Cameron dedicated his life to the creation of this museum, after narrowly escaping his own lynching in Indiana in 1930.

The museum traces the history of slavery, Jim Crow laws, the struggle to obtain civil rights, and the country's efforts at integration. Open Mon–Sat, 9 a.m.–5 p.m.; adults $5, children under 12, $2.50.

CHARLES ALLIS ART MUSEUM
1801 N. Prospect Ave., Milwaukee
414/278-8295   DA

DOWNTOWN AREA

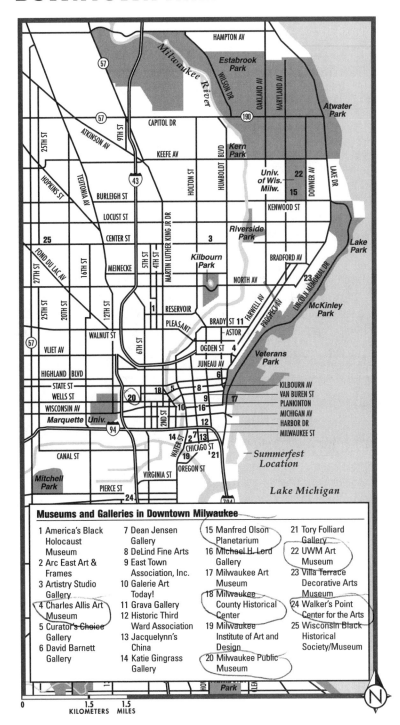

HAMPTON AV

Estabrook Park

Atwater Park

CAPITOL DR

KEEFE AV

Kern Park

Univ. of Wis. Milw. 22 15

KENWOOD ST

Riverside Park

Lake Park

BRADFORD AV

Kilbourn Park

NORTH AV

McKinley Park

RESERVOIR

PLEASANT

BRADY ST 11

ASTOR

Veterans Park

OGDEN ST 4

JUNEAU AV

6

KILBOURN AV
VAN BUREN ST
PLANKINTON
MICHIGAN AV
HARBOR DR
MILWAUKEE ST

Marquette Univ.

Summerfest Location

CANAL ST

VIRGINIA ST

OREGON ST

Mitchell Park

PIERCE ST

Lake Michigan

Museums and Galleries in Downtown Milwaukee

1 America's Black Holocaust Museum
2 Arc East Art & Frames
3 Artistry Studio Gallery
4 Charles Allis Art Museum
5 Curator's Choice Gallery
6 David Barnett Gallery
7 Dean Jensen Gallery
8 DeLind Fine Arts
9 East Town Association, Inc.
10 Galerie Art Today!
11 Grava Gallery
12 Historic Third Ward Association
13 Jacquelynn's China
14 Katie Gingrass Gallery
15 Manfred Olson Planetarium
16 Michael H. Lord Gallery
17 Milwaukee Art Museum
18 Milwaukee County Historical Center
19 Milwaukee Institute of Art and Design
20 Milwaukee Public Museum
21 Tory Folliard Gallery
22 UWM Art Museum
23 Villa Terrace Decorative Arts Museum
24 Walker's Point Center for the Arts
25 Wisconsin Black Historical Society/Museum

0   1.5   1.5
   KILOMETERS MILES

N

Expansion Plans for the Milwaukee Art Museum

A Milwaukee Art Museum expansion, planned for year-2000 comple-tion, will also be the museum's contribution to the city's architec-tural sculpture. A grand, translucent pavilion enclosed by light- and temperature-control louvers that can be raised or lowered creates a "sculpture" that has been likened to a bird by the architect. The pro-ject also includes a single-story galleria containing exhibition space and a lecture hall, and a suspended pedestrian bridge with a 100-foot-tall angled mast and cables that reflect the architect's experi-ence in bridge design.

A $35-million fund-raising campaign will provide $27 million for expansion and construction costs plus an $8-million endowment for operation. The expansion on the Lake Michigan shore will stretch southward from the existing landmark museum building, which was designed by architect Eero Saarinen and opened in 1957.

A major 1975 addition was designed by David Kahler of the Milwaukee firm Kahler Slater, also the architect of record for the new project.

Home of the annual Morning Glory Art Fair, this 1910 Tudor mansion houses a global collection that spans 2,000 years. The museum fea-tures art openings, classes, work-shops, classic feature films, and other programs. Wed–Sun 1–5 and Wed evenings 7–9. General admis-sion $2, free to members and chil-dren 13 and under.

MANFRED OLSON PLANETARIUM
1900 E. Kenwood Blvd.
Milwaukee
414/229-4961　　　　　　　**DA**
Located in the University of Wiscon-sin's physics building, this planetar-ium brings Milwaukee's night sky into

focus. "The Universe of Dr. Einstein" is the current planetarium star show, open to the public Friday evening. $1 general admission tickets are sold 30 minutes before each show. Children under 6 not admitted. School groups for grades 3 and above often visit the planetarium to learn about the stars and sky. For $25, groups can sched-ule private shows Mon–Fri during the day or Mon–Thur evening. Call to make arrangements.

MILWAUKEE ART MUSEUM
750 N. Lincoln Memorial Dr.
Milwaukee
414/224-3200　　　　　　　**DA**
A latex janitor, so real that regular

visitors get a kick out of suggesting their friends ask him the time, always grabs attention at this museum. Visitors may talk about the janitor, but they'll never forget the outstanding collections of German period art from the nineteenth and twentieth centuries. Rene von Schleinitz's collection of nineteenth-century German genre art, depicting scenes of German life, was donated to the museum so that German descendants could get a sense of their culture through both the artwork and a rather impressive stein collection. Twentieth-century German expressionist art also keeps viewers interested. Gabriele Munter, a contemporary German female artist, is also represented in this collection. In addition, the museum maintains the Bradley Collection, a strong compilation of American and European modern and contempary art, including works by Georgia O'Keeffe, Picasso, Chagall, and Andy Warhol.

"Exhibits Come Alive" at the Milwaukee County Historical Center

Milwaukee County Historical Society

The museum has made an effort to acquire the work of women and minorities. Its Haitian collection is one of the finest outside of Haiti. In late 1997, traveling exhibits include a Parisian collection of African American art from 1945 through 1965. Closed Mon. Open Tue, Wed, Fri, Sat 10–5; Thur noon–9; Sun noon–5. Adults $5, students and seniors $3, accompanied children free.

MILWAUKEE COUNTY HISTORICAL CENTER
910 N. Old World Third St.
Milwaukee
414/273-8288 DA
The center maintains an impressive file of Milwaukee County's historical documents, including photographs, newspaper clippings, and some county records. Its museum includes

exhibits on a number of Milwaukee topics. Fire-fighting equipment from the past to the present honors area firefights. A cooper's (barrelmaker's) shop is set up alongside a pharmacy that allows visitors to glimpse yesteryear's drugstore. An exhibit on the importance of the Milwaukee River illustrates the river's history. "Children's World," a look at yesterday's children, and a display about Milwaukee's founding settlers draw special interest. No fee for the museum, but a donation box is near the door. The library requires a $1/day user's fee for nonmembers. Library: Mon–Fri 9:30–noon and 1–4:30, Sat 10–noon and 1–4:30. Closed Sun. Museum: Mon–Fri 9:30–5, Sat 10–5, Sun 1–5.

MILWAUKEE INSTITUTE OF ART AND DESIGN
273 E. Erie St., Milwaukee
414/276-7889 DA
Located in a renovated warehouse in the Historic Third Ward, the institute

proudly bears a reputation as one the country's leading visual arts colleges. MIAD offers free access to changing exhibitions in its Fine Arts Gallery and the Brooks Stevens Gallery of Industrial Design.

MILWAUKEE PUBLIC MUSEUM
800 W. Wells St., Milwaukee
414/278-2700   **DA**
You can stroll the streets of old Milwaukee, tour a Pueblo village, take in the details of the Mayan culture, and visit primitive tribes. Find a mummy. Learn how shrunken heads are made. There's enough to see to exhaust even the most energetic visitors. One of the most impressive exhibits here is the rainforest: An elevated walkway takes you through the layers of forest canopy. Hands-on exhibits help you identify the insects, birds, trees, and vines found here. Audiovisual presentations create an understanding of the many uses of the rainforest's resources, and rainforest preservation tactics are discussed. Daily 9–5. Adults $5.50; seniors over 60, $4.50; students and children over 4, $3.50; 3 and under, free.

OLD FALLS VILLAGE MUSEUM
N96 W15791 County Line Rd.
Menomonee Falls
414/255-8346   **NS**
Eight buildings furnished with antiques and artifacts from this area's earliest settlers can be viewed here. The museum is maintained by the Menomonee Falls Historical Society. Guided tours are available. A gazebo can be rented for weddings (call 251-1202 to make arrangements). Special events and historical exhibits are held throughout the summer. Groups of ten or more can schedule private tours by calling 414/251-2888. Adults

Top Ten Reasons to Visit an Area Museum or Art Gallery
Courtesy of the West Bend and Milwaukee Art Museums

1. To take one of the many art classes offered by museum faculty
2. To view changing exhibits
3. To attend receptions for visiting artists
4. To view the Bradley collection of contemporary art at the Milwaukee Art Museum
5. To view the Carl von Marr collection at the West Bend Art Museum
6. To see a real Georgia O'Keeffe or Andy Warhol
7. To appreciate the history of art
8. To appreciate local contributions to the world's art
9. To visit museum gift shops
10. To contribute to the art scene by attending a museum-sponsored special event, planned throughout the year

GREATER MILWAUKEE

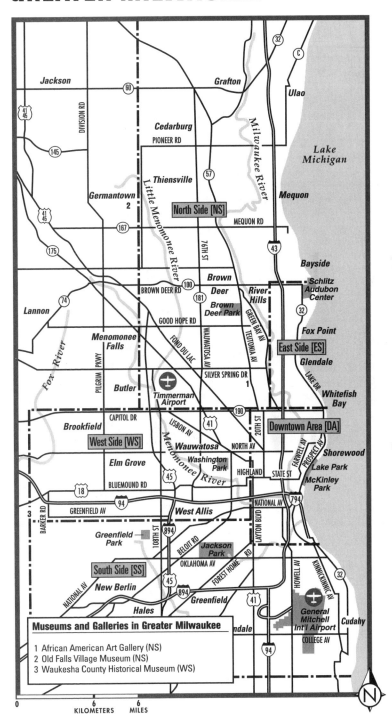

Jackson

Grafton

Ulao

32

C

41
45

DIVISION RD

60

Cedarburg

PIONEER RD

Milwaukee River

Lake Michigan

145

Thiensville

57

Mequon

Germantown
2

North Side [NS]

MEQUON RD

167

43

41
45

Bayside

175

Little Menomonee River

76TH ST

Brown
Deer

Schlitz Audubon Center

100

BROWN DEER RD

181

River
Hills

32

Lannon

74

Brown
Deer Park

GOOD HOPE RD

GREEN BAY AV

TEUTONIA AV

Fox Point

East Side [ES]

Menomonee
Falls

Fox River

FOND DU LAC

WAUWATOSA AV

Glendale

PILGRIM PKWY

SILVER SPRING DR
1

LAKE DR

Whitefish
Bay

Butler

Timmerman
Airport

CAPITOL DR

LISBON AV

41

190

20TH ST

Downtown Area [DA]

Brookfield

West Side [WS]

Wauwatosa

NORTH AV

FARWELL AV

PROSPECT AV

Shorewood

Elm Grove

Washington
Park

45

HIGHLAND

STATE ST

Lake Park

McKinley
Park

Menomonee River

18

BLUEMOUND RD

94

NATIONAL AV

794

BARKER RD

GREENFIELD AV

West Allis

3

Greenfield
Park

894

108TH ST

BELOIT RD

Jackson
Park

LAYTON BLVD

HOWELL AV

KINNICKINNIC AV

32

South Side [SS]

45

OKLAHOMA AV

FOREST HOME RD

New Berlin

NATIONAL AV

894

Greenfield

41

General
Mitchell
Int'l Airport

Cudahy

Hales

ndale

COLLEGE AV

94

Museums and Galleries in Greater Milwaukee

1 African American Art Gallery (NS)
2 Old Falls Village Museum (NS)
3 Waukesha County Historical Museum (WS)

0   6   6
      KILOMETERS   MILES

N

While touring Milwaukee art galleries and shops, be prepared to participate in spontaneous art events. Many gallery owners are also performers and teachers who love to share their passion for art with the uninitiated.

$3; children 6–16, $1; under 6 free. May–Sept, Sun 1–4.

UWM ART MUSEUM
UWM Campus
3253 N. Downer Ave., Milwaukee
414/229-5070   DA
Shown in three UWM campus locations, these historical collections and contemporary art displays can be viewed during the campus walking tour. Collections include work of European, African, and Russian artists; some student work is also exhibited. Free.

VILLA TERRACE DECORATIVE ARTS MUSEUM
2220 N. Terrace Ave., Milwaukee
414/271-3656   DA
This Italian-style villa overlooking Lake Michigan, originally built as a private home, is now a museum dedicated to the decorative arts. Self-guided tours are open to the public; guided tours may be scheduled. Wed–Sun 12–5. Admission $2. Members free.

WAUKESHA COUNTY HISTORICAL MUSEUM
101 W. Main St., Waukesha
414/548-7186   WS
Located next to a Native American burial mound, the museum offers services providing answers to genealogical and historical questions. Educational kits that have Native American and pioneer themes are provided for groups. The kits contain boxed artifacts and explanatory text geared for school curricula. The museum is free; research center is $2.25 per person per day. Tue–Sat 9–4:30. Closed on major holidays.

WISCONSIN BLACK HISTORICAL SOCIETY/MUSEUM
2620 W. Center St., Milwaukee
414/372-7677   DA
From the 1930s to the 1950s, one Milwaukee area was known as Bronzeville. It's captured here with photos and artifacts. A 14-panel mural traces African Americans from Egypt to Milwaukee. This museum offers a personal look at the life of African Americans. By reservation.

ART GALLERIES

AFRICAN AMERICAN ART GALLERY
3528 W. Villard Ave., Milwaukee
414/536-6440   NS
Local African American artists who portray the community are exhibited here. To bring African American art to the forefront, prints and originals are sometimes displayed by the gallery throughout the metro Milwaukee area. A custom framing service is also available here.

ARC EAST ART & FRAMES
217 N. Broadway, Milwaukee
414/277-9494   DA
Located in the Historic Third Ward, Arc provides an outlet for local

artists. Recent work included paintings by Garry Pisarek, whose abstracts explore vibrant color, line, and shape. Prints, posters, and fine custom framing are also available.

ARTISTRY STUDIO GALLERY
833 E. Center St., Milwaukee
414/372-3372   DA
This eclectic studio, located in an old bakery, exhibits only Milwaukee artists. Taffnie, who makes porcelain bedside lamps with handmade shades, and Susan Alexander, who has a following for her whimsical porcelain houses, also produce custom clay tiles. The partners exhibit three or four shows a year, usually with seasonal themes. Spring garden and fall paintings adorn the walls. This studio-gallery also offers ongoing pottery classes. Tue–Fri 2–6, Sat 11–5, and by appointment.

CURATOR'S CHOICE GALLERY
6222 N. Water St., Milwaukee
414/271-3715   DA
This gallery in the Bank One Plaza exhibits contemporary cityscapes and prints.

TRIVIA

Each December, artists bring unique gift-giving opportunities to the community with their combined efforts to host the annual Studio Art Crawl. Located in a historic Walker's Point warehouse building (133 W. Pittsburgh Ave., Milwaukee), over 35 artists representing a variety of media open their studios to the public.

DAVID BARNETT GALLERY
1024 E. State St., Milwaukee
414/271-5058   DA
From modernists to surrealists, the artists shown at the Barnett see magic in ordinary events. The gallery provides visitors with an impressive rotating exhibit of paintings, watercolors, and drawings. Barnett opened this gallery over 30 years ago, when he was an art history student at the University of Wisconsin-Milwaukee. For the first time in 30 years, Barnett recently displayed a collection of his own work and was pleased that it received a strong critical response.

DEAN JENSEN GALLERY
165 N. Broadway, Milwaukee
414/278-7100   DA
Gallery owner Dean Jensen gained his artistic credibility as an art critic for the *Milwaukee Journal Sentinel*, Milwaukee's morning daily. No slouch, Jensen enjoys exhibiting work that provokes viewer response. Abstract and expressive works sometimes depict bleak philosophical perspectives, but viewers are never disappointed if they want to see works that make them pause and reflect. Tue–Fri 10–6, Sat 10–4.

DELIND FINE ARTS
811 N. Jefferson St., Milwaukee
414/271-8525   DA
DeLind represents U.S. and Canadian artists with over 200 classic and antique posters, paintings, mobiles, and jewelry.

EAST TOWN ASSOCIATION, INC.
770 N. Jefferson St., Milwaukee
414/271-1416   DA
Milwaukee's artists have long been key players in revitalizing the downtown area. Their efforts are most ev-

Artist's rendition of the Milwaukee Public Museum, page 110

ident in such unifying forces as the East Town Association. Organized attempts have brought artists, art schools, and the community together in studio crawls and gallery nights. Call for updated brochures and information.

GALERIE ART TODAY!
218 N. Water St., Milwaukee
414/278-1211   DA
Galerie Art Today! shows contemporary collections from Europe and the United States. Exhibitions change frequently. Call for latest exhibits.

GRAVA GALLERY
1209 E. Brady St., Milwaukee
414/277-8228   DA
This gallery, in an old storefront with handpainted wood floors, makes you feel like you're in Soho. Displaying a variety of media, Grava usually exhibits such Milwaukee artists as Sally Gauger Jensen, Mark Winter, Richard Waswo, and Randy James.

HISTORIC THIRD WARD ASSOCIATION

219 N. Milwaukee St., Milwaukee
414/273-1173   DA
This association is the historical backbone and marketing wizard for Third Ward businesses and historical warehouses. The group, which makes sure the media are keeping the rest of Milwaukee informed about what's new and what's hot in the Ward, has helped the area gain its reputation as the Soho of Milwaukee. In addition, it offers an impressive assortment of walking tours. To be sure not to miss any Third Ward art galleries or antique shops, contact the association for information about special gallery nights and antique sales. A walking tour of area warehouses also brings Milwaukee's manufacturing and shipping history to life. This is a must for serious history buffs.

JACQUELYNN'S CHINA
219 N. Milwaukee St., Milwaukee
414/272-8880   DA
Vintage English and American porcelains as well as mixed media arts are represented here. Summer 1996

Milwaukee Institute of Art and Design

Milwaukee Institute of Art and Design, page 109

included a show of artist Eugene Mecikalski's prints.

KATIE GINGRASS GALLERY
241 N. Broadway, Milwaukee
414/289-0855 DA

An incredible assortment of wearable art, handpainted furniture, and jewelry is displayed in this Historic Third Ward gallery. Practically every inch of floor and wall space is covered with prints, pots, jewelry cases, and weavings. Prices are Chicago, but the work is exquisite.

MICHAEL H. LORD GALLERY
420 E. Wisconsin Ave.
Milwaukee
414/272-1007 DA

Michael Lord Gallery, in operation for over 20 years, is located off the lobby of the Pfister Hotel. Prints, photographs, paintings, and sculpture by local, regional, and international artists reflect the contemporary art scene.

TORY FOLLIARD GALLERY
233 N. Milwaukee St., Milwaukee
414/273-7311 DA

Fine oils, acrylics, and porcelain sculpture shown here represent Milwaukee's upscale tastes and features artists' new work. Summer 1996 Gallery Night included Ed Larson's folk paintings and wooden fish painted in rainbow colors. Prices reflect the high reputation of the work.

WALKER'S POINT CENTER FOR THE ARTS
911 W. National Ave., Milwaukee
414/672-2787 DA

This artists' co-op offers a variety of mixed-media exhibits and offers new and student artists the opportunity to show the community their work. Seasonal shows continue to attract the area's fiber, enamel, metal, wood, and glass artists.

8

PARKS AND GARDENS

Milwaukee's four seasons inspire wonder in every visitor to the county and its state parks, which wind around Lake Michigan's shores, meander along rivers and streams, and roll over hills and valleys. Long before the snow melts, miniature crocus, trillium, and May apples push their green stalks through the icy earth. Summer blooms with all manner of wild berries and flowers. Wood violets, buttercups, and wild geraniums spill out along walking paths and across meadows, while the trees form cool canopies for those enjoying summer sports and picnics. Autumn brings a symphony of color to oak, maple, and elm trees, while the grandeur of snow-covered pines captures the essence of winter. Depending on your mood and the season, you can trace glacial freezes and melts along the Ice Age Trail, bike almost 90 miles on the county's Bicentennial 76 Bike Trail, or choose between swimming in Lake Michigan's frigid water or the warmer, sand-bottomed lakes. County and state parks offer the chance to explore the environment with hands-on educational opportunities, outdoor floral gardens with a variety of wild and cultivated flowers and shrubs, and indoor botanical gardens that help soften Wisconsin's winters with tropical gardens and flower shows. Unless otherwise stated, parks are open year-round from dawn until dusk.

ALFRED L. BOERNER BOTANICAL GARDENS AND ARBORETUM
Charles B. Whitnall Park
5879 S. 92nd St., Hales Corners
414/425-1130   SS
This outdoor delight provides over 40 acres of perennials, annuals, wildflowers, crab apple trees, and rock gardens. The landscaped gardens, in the tradition of English country gardens, include an herb garden, a bog, formal arrays of spring bulbs in the Tulip Garden, a shade garden, and much more. Boerner Botanical Gardens were created in 1932 by New Deal agen-

DOWNTOWN AREA

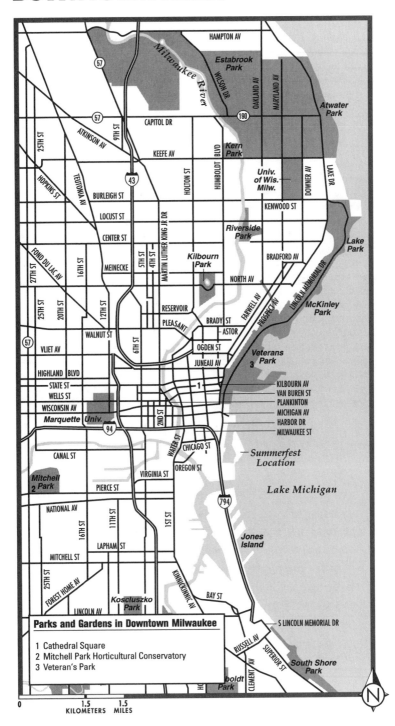

Parks and Gardens in Downtown Milwaukee

1 Cathedral Square
2 Mitchell Park Horticultural Conservatory
3 Veteran's Park

0   1.5   1.5
    KILOMETERS   MILES

cies and Milwaukee County Relief workers. Professional horticulturists teach classes here year-round. The nine-day Annual Rose Festival brings outdoor concerts, workshops, demonstrations, and entertainment to the gardens each June. Gardens are open early April–Oct 31, 8 a.m.–sunset. The Garden House is open 8–4 all year. Free, with a parking fee Sat, Sun, holidays, and for special events.

CATHEDRAL SQUARE
802 N. Jackson St., Milwaukee
414/962-8809 DA
This square, located in front of St. John's Cathedral in the heart of downtown, is a favorite stopping spot for downtown employees. Weekends, the square's wooden benches fill with people-watching city dwellers, many of whom feed the squirrels and pigeons. This is also the site for the annual Winterfest. Summer or winter, the square remains a beautiful resting place in the bustling downtown area.

CHARLES C. JACOBUS PARK
6501 Hillside Ln., Wauwatosa
414/257-9404 WS
A 30-acre nature trail, a lagoon, two picnic areas, softball fields, and a kids' wading pool and play area are nestled in the Menomonee River Valley. In spring, Vanishing Creek rushes with winter's runoff. Summers, the trails are lined with native flora and fauna, including jack-in-the-pulpit and trillium. Winters, the area becomes a living Currier & Ives postcard, with families ice-skating on the lagoon, parents pulling toddlers on sleds across the ice, and kids playing crack-the-whip or practicing their hockey skills. A warming area inside Jacobus Park Lodge has an inviting fireplace. Surely this is one of the prettiest Milwaukee County parks.

COOPER PARK
8701 W. Chambers St., Milwaukee
414/871-1780 WS
A wading pool, softball fields, basketball courts, and playground equipment bring lots of activity to this

---

The Beginning of the State Park System

Wisconsin was one of the first states to establish a park system. In 1878, the legislature set aside a tract of 50,000 acres in what was then Lincoln County. This noble act was reversed in 1879, however, when that land was sold to lumber companies. The first dedicated park was actually created in 1900, when commissions from Wisconsin and Minnesota dedicated lands on each side of the St. Croix River as Interstate State Park. It wasn't until 1907 that nationally known landscape architect John Nolan began to plan the state's park system. Today, Wisconsin state parks number more than 50. Nine state forests, three state recreation areas, and 13 state trails are incorporated into this system.

EAST SIDE

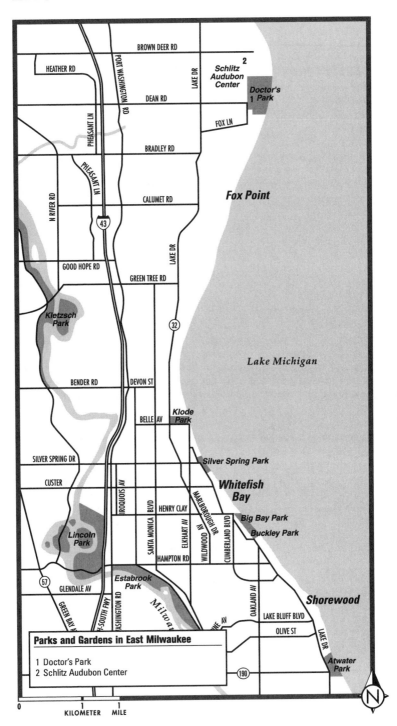

BROWN DEER RD
HEATHER RD
PORT WASHINGTON RD
LAKE DR
Schlitz Audubon Center 2
Doctor's Park 1
DEAN RD
FOX LN
PHEASANT LN
BRADLEY RD
PHEASANT LN
N RIVER RD
CALUMET RD
Fox Point
43
LAKE DR
GOOD HOPE RD
GREEN TREE RD
Kletzsch Park
32
Lake Michigan
BENDER RD
DEVON ST
BELLE AV
Klode Park
SILVER SPRING DR
Silver Spring Park
CUSTER
Whitefish Bay
IROQUOIS AV
SANTA MONICA BLVD
HENRY CLAY
MARLBOROUGH DR
Big Bay Park
ELKHART AV
WILDWOOD AV
CUMBERLAND BLVD
Buckley Park
Lincoln Park
HAMPTON RD
57
GLENDALE AV
Estabrook Park
GREEN BAY RD
N-SOUTH FWY
WASHINGTON RD
Milwa
OAKLAND AV
Shorewood
NE AV
LAKE BLUFF BLVD
LAKE DR
OLIVE ST
Atwater Park
190

Parks and Gardens in East Milwaukee

1 Doctor's Park
2 Schlitz Audubon Center

0   1   1
   KILOMETER MILE

N

8-acre county park. This is one of the quieter park settings in the Milwaukee area. Cooper Park Pavilion can be rented for gatherings of up to 60 people.

DOCTOR'S PARK
1870 East Fox Lane, Fox Pointe
414/352-7502 ES
Located at the east end of Dean Road in Bayside and Fox Point, on the southeastern corner of the Schlitz Audubon Center, this nature preserve provides a quiet wooded setting and a sandy beach with wild oats and peas growing among the dunes. The park has a picnic area, a softball diamond, and hiking trails. One of the most attractive places to spend some solitary moments gazing at Lake Michigan's ever-changing waves.

FALK PARK
2013 W. Rawson Ave., Oak Creek
414/761-1152 SS
These 216 acres of undeveloped woodland, home to the Milwaukee County Horticulture and Nature Center, support a variety of flora and fauna. Nature trails lead hikers through the park and to Falk Park Pavilion, a stone and brick building that contains a stage. The park is near I-94 and the airport.

FRANK CANNON PARK
303 N. 95th St., Milwaukee
414/453-5210 WS
Located just east of the Milwaukee County Zoo, this 9-acre site encompasses a wading pool, soccer field,

Havenwoods State Forest

Havenwoods State Forest, page 121

playground equipment, and tot lot. The Cannon Park Pavilion can be rented for parties, meetings, weddings, and other groups of up to 50 people.

GEORGE HANSEN PARK
9800 Underwood Pkwy.
Wauwatosa
414/453-4454 WS
This county park is a golfer's and runner's delight. The 18-hole course offers satisfying challenges for all levels, while Hansen Parkway provides an enjoyable distance run. A pavilion, located in the middle of the park, serves concessions and offers relief from the sun or foul weather. Hoyt Park, an adjacent park with an outdoor swimming pool complete with water slides, is within walking distance. A steep hill in the southwest section

To learn more about the Ice Age Trail—the longest trail in the state park system—read *On The Trail of the Ice Age* by Henry S. Reuss (Sheboygan, WI: Ice Age and Trail Foundation, Inc., 1990).

Visitors interested in learning more about the many state parks within the metropolitan area and throughout Wisconsin should obtain a copy of *A Traveler's Guide to Wisconsin State Parks and Forests* by Don Davenport. The guide can be ordered from the Bureau of Parks and Recreation, Wisconsin Department of Natural Resources, P.O. Box 7921, Madison, WI 53707. The cost, with shipping, is $10.95.

of the parkway provides great sledding and toboggan runs in winter.

GRANT PARK BEACH AND BOAT LAUNCH
100 E. Hawthorne Ave.
South Milwaukee
414/762-8417   SS
This lakefront park has changing rooms and restrooms for swimmers, and a boat launch allows access to Lake Michigan. If you're using the boat launch, make sure to check bulletin boards and radio stations for small-craft warning advisories. Because of an extensive breakwater, the lake's fury can appear deceptively calm from shore. Once you pass the breakwater, rough waters can make the heartiest sailor seasick and can be exceedingly dangerous.

HAVENWOODS STATE FOREST
6141 N. Hopkins St., Milwaukee
414/527-0232   NS
Just off West Silver Spring Road on the site of a former Nike missile installation, this 235-acre green space sits squarely in one of the city's most densely populated areas. It is dedicated to environmental education for teachers, adults, and children. A self-guided nature trail and 3 miles of cross-country ski trails make this a year-round attraction. When the area was restored, Milwaukee-area school children assisted center operators with a land restoration plan to turn this preserve into an outdoor school. A variety of native animals now populate this area, including skunk, red fox, opossum, woodchuck, deer, and many species of birds. Havenwoods Environmental Awareness Center, relying on passive solar energy for heat, has an auditorium and classrooms and offers exhibits and displays on natural history and related issues.

HOYT PARK
1800 Swan Blvd., Wauwatosa
414/476-0712   WS
This park has one of the first outdoor pools to be built in Milwaukee County. The Menomonee River Parkway winds through this park; after a parkway cross-country fitness course, you can finish up with a swim. The pool opens on the last day of the public school year and remains open daily until school resumes. Weekend swims until Labor Day. Adults $1.50, children 50¢.

LIME KILN PARK
Access from Mill Street parking lot Menomonee Falls   NS
414/255-8300
This hiking and biking trail leads around historic lime kilns that once fired the lannon stones used throughout the area to accent brick homes, build retaining walls, and set into walkways. The kilns are giant red-brick ovens, each the size

of a garage with cast-iron doors that are sealed shut. Pleasant, wooded walks tie into Menomonee River trails, which lead you west into Wauwatosa or north into Mequon. Although the kilns are no longer functioning, lannon stone quarries continue to produce an abundant harvest of lime and stone.

MEDICINE HAWK WILDERNESS SKILLS
P.O. Box 07482, Milwaukee 53207
414/482-8722   SS
Medicine Hawk is not an outdoor facility; rather, it is a teaching center that specializes in wilderness skills workshops and classes. Workshop participants travel to different wilderness sites throughout the state—and sometimes as far away as Alaska—to learn animal tracking, identifying edible plants, winter-shelter building, and forensic tracking. Tom Hanratty, the center's director and author of *The Art and Science of Tracking Man*, has taught deputy sheriffs and FBI agents in workshops centering on crime-scene forensics. The center also offers classes through universities and colleges, and even caters to students who dislike the cold and snow by holding classes at the Bear Paw Inn, a northern Wisconsin bed and breakfast with an attached wilderness center. Here, the center's students learn tracking along the Wolf River during the day and return to the luxury of the bed and breakfast at night. Classes are in session year-round, with spring and fall the busiest seasons. Call for prices and class schedules.

MILWAUKEE COUNTY PARK SYSTEM
414/257-6100
Milwaukee County owns and operates more than 30 parks scattered throughout the area. Each facility offers different sports and recreational opportunities. Many parks contain pavilions which can be rented for large and small gatherings. To locate

---

A Look at Milwaukee County Parks

The Milwaukee County Park System offers over 150 parks and parkways, encompassing nearly 15,000 acres of recreational enjoyment. That's about 1 acre for every 60 residents. Park facilities open in spring, summer, and fall include 16 golf courses, 10 senior and community recreation centers, 23 pavilions, 13 outdoor pools, 200 athletic fields, 122 tennis courts, 655 boat slips, six archery ranges, 180 picnic areas, 46 wading pools, and 22 sand volleyball courts. Activity continues through winter with 13 sledding hills, three indoor pools, one toboggan run, 16 groomed ice rinks, the community and senior centers, five groomed cross-country ski trails, and the year-round Wilson Park ice arena.

NORTH SIDE

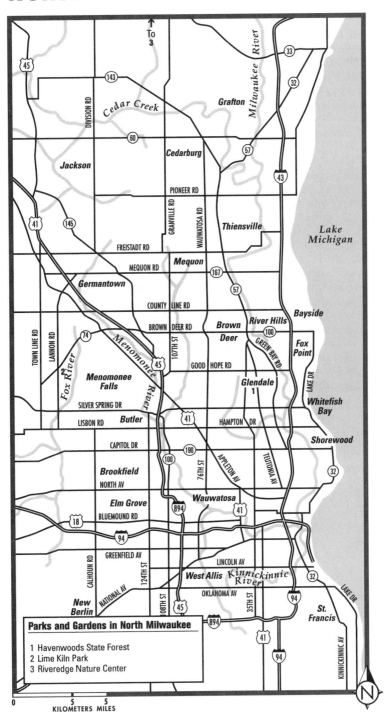

To 3

US 45

143

Division Rd

Cedar Creek

Grafton

Milwaukee River

33

32

60

Cedarburg

Jackson

57

I-43

Pioneer Rd

Granville Rd

Wauwatosa Rd

Thiensville

Lake Michigan

41

145

Freistadt Rd

Mequon Rd

Mequon

167

57

Germantown

County Line Rd

Brown Deer Rd

Brown Deer

River Hills

Bayside

Town Line Rd

Lannon Rd

74

Menomonee River

Fox River

107th St

Good Hope Rd

Green Bay Rd

100

Fox Point

45

Menomonee Falls

Glendale

1

Whitefish Bay

Silver Spring Dr

Lake Dr

Lisbon Rd

Butler

41

Hampton Dr

Shorewood

Capitol Dr

190

100

76th St

Appleton Av

Teutonia Av

32

Brookfield

North Av

Elm Grove

894

Wauwatosa

41

18

Bluemound Rd

I-94

Calhoun Rd

Greenfield Av

124th St

Lincoln Av

West Allis

Kinnickinnic River

32

National Av

108th St

45

Oklahoma Av

35th St

94

Lake Dr

New Berlin

894

St. Francis

41

94

Kinnickinnic Av

Parks and Gardens in North Milwaukee

1 Havenwoods State Forest
2 Lime Kiln Park
3 Riveredge Nature Center

0   5   5
KILOMETERS MILES

N

a park or pavilion that meets your needs, call the above number.

MITCHELL PARK HORTICULTURAL CONSERVATORY (THE DOMES)
524 S. Layton Blvd., Milwaukee
414/649-9800   DA

From the outside, as you travel I-94 to or from downtown Milwaukee, the Domes appear to be weird architecture. Once you get inside them, you find an exotic world of fragrance and flowers. Mitchell Park Conservatory offers a unique opportunity for year-round relaxation. Three massive glass domes, each seven stories high, are planted with tropical, arid, and seasonal displays. The arid and tropical displays are especially appreciated in late January and early February, when Milwaukee is pounded with snow and cold. The Show Dome features six theme shows per year, including the Christmas and Easter floral extravaganzas. The Arid and Tropical Domes are planted with thousands of species from around the world. Daily 9–5. Adults $3.25, children and seniors $1.25, Milwaukee County residents free 9–10:30 a.m. weekdays.

PIONEER CEMETERY
Pilgrim Road and North Avenue, Brookfield   WS
414/796-6675

This cemetery made headlines a few years ago when a retired couple suddenly appeared and cleaned it, repaired gravestones, and began building a split-log fence. Before long, area residents noticed their work, and so many made donations to the cleanup efforts that the retired couple made a profit on their volunteer project and promised to return every year to keep the cemetery

in repair. This incident illustrates the local residents' commitment to Brookfield's history: the cemetery is the final stop for many of the area's first settlers. Whole families are buried here, and visitors can trace the early village's efforts to survive flu epidemics and war by reading the brief messages carved in the stones.

RIVEREDGE NATURE CENTER
4458 W. Hawthorne Ave.
Newburg
414/375-2715   NS

This 350-acre nature preserve, about 35 miles north in Cedarburg, hosts classes and special events, including Maple Sugar'n' Breakfast, Harvest Fest, Haunted Hike, and Night Skis. The sanctuary is home to cross-country skiing and hiking trails that meander through forests and meadows, along riverbanks and ponds. Classrooms provide learning activities and meeting space for groups and students. Trails are open daily, year-round, dawn until dusk. Building: 8–5 Mon–Fri, noon–4 weekends. Trails close during deer-hunting season because neighboring properties allow hunting. Adults $1.50, children $1; members hike for free.

SCHLITZ AUDUBON CENTER
1111 E. Brown Deer Rd., Milwaukee
414/352-2880   ES

Located on the northeastern end of Milwaukee County, this nature preserve is a mix of terrains, including prairie, grassland, pond, and wetlands, and heavily wooded areas that lead to Lake Michigan. The preserve has marked trails for self-guided tours. An observation tower offers a panoramic view of the surrounding countryside. An amphitheater hosts outdoor programs and concerts.

WEST SIDE

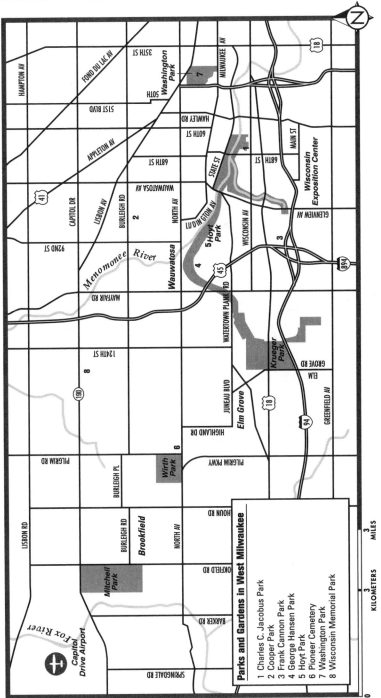

Parks and Gardens in West Milwaukee

1 Charles C. Jacobus Park
2 Cooper Park
3 Frank Cannon Park
4 George Hansen Park
5 Hoyt Park
6 Pioneer Cemetery
7 Washington Park
8 Wisconsin Memorial Park

Seasonal activities include cross-country skiing, maple sugaring in March, and a nature-related craft fair the first Saturday in June. Education is a primary function at the preserve. A book and gift store on-site provides a wide assortment of educational materials and gifts. The property, originally owned by the Schlitz Brewing Company, has been set aside primarily as a sanctuary, so no collecting or swimming is allowed, and smoking and pets are forbidden. Open Tue–Sun 9–5. Trail-use fees: adults $2, children $1.

SCOUT LAKE PARK
5901 W. Loomis Rd., Greendale
414/282-6610 SS
Scout Lake is the only natural inland lake in the Milwaukee County Park System. The park has an extensive trail system, paddle boats, and a picnic area. A variety of birds and thick woods surrounding a duck-filled lake make this park an enchanting surprise in such an urban area. County Parks directors have chosen this park as a pollution and habitat education area. Groups can call ahead

and have volunteers teach them about the small life forms found on the lake and about the negative effects of city pollution on the environment. The pavilion is open April–Dec.

SOUTH SHORE PARK BEACH
2900 South Shore Dr., Milwaukee
414/747-0514 SS
This Lake Michigan public beach is easily accessible from downtown and provides boat-launch facilities as well as a swimming beach and fishing. South Shore Yacht Club, located right next door, makes this one of the most scenic beaches. A picnic area with fireplaces allows for cookouts. Volleyball and softball areas, horseshoe courts, and a children's play area make this an ideal place to wile away a long weekend afternoon. A pavilion provides a complete line of concessions as well as indoor facilities. The Bicentennial 76 Bike Trail follows the shoreline through this park.

TODD WEHR NATURE CENTER
Whitnall Park
9701 W. College Ave., Franklin
414/425-8550 SS

Boerner Botanical Gardens, page 116

Milwaukee Covention and Vistitors Bureau

SOUTH SIDE

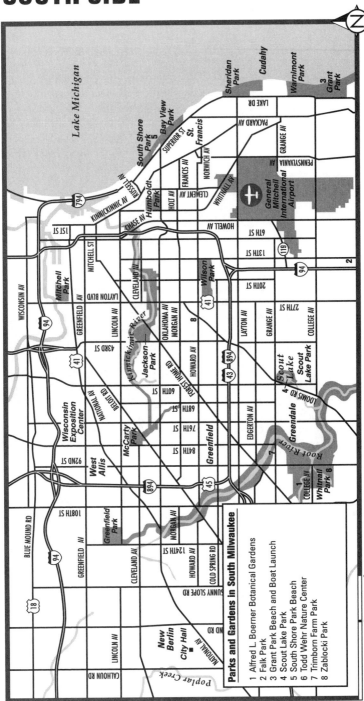

Lake Michigan

Parks and Gardens in South Milwaukee

1 Alfred L. Boerner Botanical Gardens
2 Falk Park
3 Grant Park Beach and Boat Launch
4 Scout Lake Park
5 South Shore Park Beach
6 Todd Wehr Nature Center
7 Trimborn Farm Park
8 Zablocki Park

0   3   KILOMETERS

0   3   MILES

Veteran's Park Lagoon

Promoting environmental awareness, this nature center features prairies, savannas, oaks, woodlands, wetlands, and a 20-acre lake. School tours through this center's varied habitats are part of almost every Milwaukeean's memory. Wehr Nature Center was one of the first park centers committed to educating people about the environment. Individuals are welcome to join one of the many tours, lectures, and demonstrations. Open year-round 9–4:30, except major holidays.

TRIMBORN FARM PARK
8881 W. Grange Ave., Franklin
414/529-7744 SS
This Milwaukee County park has a historic theme, containing a variety of mid-1800 to early 1900 structures. A stone barn, a wood barn, a farmhouse, kilns, sheds, and the Jeremiah Curtin House are found here. The circa 1847 Curtin House, a cottage, is made of limestone from the quarry directly across the road. July–Aug 8–5, winter 9–1. Free.

VETERAN'S PARK
East side of Lincoln Memorial Drive, Milwaukee
414/481-9937 DA
Located between the War Memorial Center and the Milwaukee Yacht Club, Veterans Park features bike, skate, and other recreational rentals and concessions. It hosts many major summer events, including the Maritime Festival, the Circus Parade Tent Show, and a number of marathon runs. In-line skaters, bikers, and joggers flock to this activity-filled park from dawn to dusk. Amenities include picnic areas, bathrooms, and running water.

WASHINGTON PARK
1859 N. 40th St., Milwaukee
414/342-0215 WS
Only ten minutes from the center of downtown Milwaukee, this county park provides diverse activities and entertainment. Baseball fields, lighted tennis and basketball courts, soccer fields, boat rentals, lily ponds, bike paths, walking trails, and wildlife all converge here. The Washington Park Community Recreational Building is the center of many county-wide senior citizen recreation activities. The band shell hosts many summer-evening free concerts. The outdoor pool is open from Memorial Day through Labor Day. Be forewarned, though: muggings are not uncommon in this park. This is one area where you'll want to remain in the company of friends.

WISCONSIN MEMORIAL PARK
13235 W. Capitol Dr., Brookfield
414/781-7474 WS
Veterans Day and other holiday celebrations are open to the public at this nonsectarian, not-for-profit memorial park. One of the most beautiful ceme-

teries in the city, the park is included here for its many family-centered ceremonies in observation of civic holidays.

ZABLOCKI PARK
3717 W. Howard Ave., Greenfield
414/282-1370   SS
This county park in the city of Greenfield provides neighbors with a place to picnic or learn to golf. A nine-hole par-three golf course, tennis courts, a soccer field, and baseball diamonds make this the ideal setting for family activities. A pavilion can be rented for gatherings of up to 150 people.

Milwaukee Covention and Vistitors Bureau

9

SHOPPING

Milwaukee shopping once consisted of a few elite shops that specialized in women's formal wear, one or two quality children's and men's clothing stores, a few designer furniture stores, and what seemed like hundreds of "country kitsch" outlets. Efforts to revitalize different areas, especially downtown Milwaukee, have changed the shopping scene dramatically. New arty shops, contemporary furniture stores, and high-quality clothing stores have made their way to the Historic Third Ward and Riverwest neighborhoods downtown, while Mequon and Brookfield have boomed with specialty clothing and gift shops. Although "country primitive" still seems to dominate gift and home-decorator stores, a few outstanding shops that carry the unusual and the classically elegant have opened in outlying areas.

SHOPPING DISTRICTS

Downtown Shopping

Milwaukee's downtown Grand Avenue Mall is connected to offices and parking with a skywalk, making it a convenient place to browse regardless of the weather. Renovated neighborhoods can make downtown shopping an eclectic experience, where you can pick up a Mexican corner cabinet at Phoenix Design, acquire a wearable art coat from Katie Gingrass Gallery, purchase a kachina doll at White Thunder Trading Post, stock up on a teen's favorite Gap or Banana Republic T-shirt, or pierce a body part at Betty's Bead Bank before lunchtime. Whatever your shopping needs and desires, the downtown area is sure to fulfill them.

ARTISTRY STUDIO-GALLERY
833 E. Center St., Milwaukee
414/372-3372 **DA**
Constantly changing inventory at this studio-gallery makes it possible to pick up a wide range of crafts and artwork. This is an especially good place

DOWNTOWN AREA

Shopping in Downtown Milwaukee

1 Grand Avenue Mall
2 Old World Third Street
  Shopping District

to find a unique and tasteful pottery gift. Pottery classes are offered.

BETTY'S BEAD BANK
300 W. Juneau Ave., Milwaukee
414/276-8996   DA
Located 1 block north of the Old World Third Street shopping district, Betty's provides over 1,000 different beads and ideas for area crafters. Some of the most exquisite hand-crafted costume jewelry is also for sale here, and a jewelry repair service is available.

BREW CITY BEER GEAR
275 W. Wisconsin Ave.
Milwaukee
414/347-1811   DA
Owners of this store design and produce their own product line relating to Milwaukee and everything that goes on here, from beer to sports to parades. The store sells its own licensed products for the breweries. One of the biggest early 1997 sellers was custom-designed "Air Attack" T-shirts that depicted the Green Bay Packers' "Lambeau Leap"—the Pack's relatively new (1995) tradition of jumping into the Lambeau Field stands after a touchdown. Everything in the store is a unique custom design. Winter 1996–97 brought New Miller Park–logoed T-shirts to the store. Brew City has two other locations: one at Grand Avenue and the second, called Milwaukee Traditions, at Southridge Mall.

THE CHOCOLATE TREE
1048 N. Old World Third St.
Milwaukee
414/271-5774   DA
Homemade fudge in eight flavors, made fresh each day, makes this a repeat stop for visitors to the downtown area. Ambrosia offers the largest selection of chocolates in Wisconsin. Overflowing bins, stocked with gift packs and candies, satisfy even the hugest chocolate cravings.

D & R INTERNATIONAL ANTIQUES
137 E. Wells St., Milwaukee
414/276-9395   DA
Only the finest and most perfect antique furniture and home-decorating items from Europe and the United States are displayed here. All the furniture in this shop retains the original finish. Quality pieces have been maintained to such a degree that even other antique dealers shop here.

GEORGE WATTS & SONS
761 N. Jefferson St., Milwaukee
414/291-5120 or 800/747-WATTS DA
Milwaukee's premier fine china, silver, and crystal shop gained a reputation among Milwaukee brides for being the ultimate place to select dining necessities as well as luxuries. The shop has been on the same corner for over 125 years. Royal Doulton, Gorham, Noritake, and Lexington are just a few of the fine name brands that Watts carries. Staff are trained to mix and match tableware in setting a fine table and to help in gift selections. Watts is in its fourth generation of owner-operated service to Milwaukee.

HARRY W. SCHWARTZ BOOK STORES
209 E. Wisconsin Ave.
Milwaukee
414/332-1182   DA
The Schwartz bookstores have established a commitment to Milwaukee's literary scene. At this main branch, a large selection of best-sellers, magazines, paperbacks, and hardcover books on subjects ranging from self-help to fine art, geography,

travel, fiction, and biography is found on the floor-to-ceiling shelves that seem to continue forever. This is one bookstore where you'll be free to browse to your heart's content. But if you're looking for a particular title, a helpful employee will locate it on the shelves or special order it. This locally owned and operated bookstore regularly invites nationally known children's and adult authors to read and hold workshops. Book talks, workshops, and children's story hours are all part of the package at this wonderfully warm place. Additional stores are located in Shorewood, Brookfield, and Mequon.

Mayfair Mall, page 145

LAACKE & JOYS
1433 N. Water St., Milwaukee
414/271-7878   **DA**

Milwaukee's first and only original outdoor supply store still maintains headquarters in the downtown area. Tents, camping and hiking clothing, downhill and cross-country skis, and outerwear are all available here. This is the outdoor person's dream store. You can replace broken and lost tent stakes here, select the best insect repellent, purchase a unique fishing fly, and investigate trail mix and dehydrated meal plans. Tent repair is also available. A second outlet is located on Blue Mound Road in Brookfield.

MADERS ART GALLERY
1025 N. Old World Third St.
Milwaukee
414/278-0088   **DA**

Maders carries original paintings and limited-edition prints, nature landscapes, and more. The gallery is next door to the restaurant of the same name.

MILITARY RELICS SHOP
6910 W. North Ave., Milwaukee

414/771-4014   **DA**

Military collectibles from the Civil War through the Vietnam War include caps, daggers, badges, and uniforms from all countries. The store has been in business since 1981 and caters to serious military collectors as well as others looking for war memorabilia.

ROGER STEVENS
428 E. Wisconsin Ave.
Milwaukee
414/277-9010   **DA**

Impeccable menswear can be purchased at this shop in the historic Pfister Hotel. A full-service tailor shop guarantees made-to-order clothing. The store features Southwick, Hickey-Freeman, and Robert Talbott clothing.

THE SPICE HOUSE
1031 N. Old World Third St.
Milwaukee
414/272-0977   **DA**

This shop's reputation for carrying high quality, hard-to-find spices has been enhanced by mentions in *Bon Appetit, Good Housekeeping,* and *Martha Stewart Living.* Bags and jars of spices, each with a paragraph describing its flavor and uses, line rustic wood shelves. A variety of house specialties has been tested by area chefs and gourmet cooks. Look for Wauwatosa Village Seasoning or Walker's Point Seasoning. Gift boxes available.

TIE ME DOWN
1419 E. Brady St., Milwaukee
414/272-3696   DA
If you're into the "biker" or "biker's chick" look or the tie-died hippie look, this is the shop for you. Located in the heart of the original counter-culture hangout of the 1970s and '80s, this store trades in alternative clothing for men and women. Body piercing is also available here.

USINGER SAUSAGE COMPANY
1030 N. Old World Third St.
Milwaukee
414/276-9100   DA
Made from family recipes that have remained the same for over 100 years, Usinger's products can be mailed anywhere in the world. This charming sausage shop delights tourists and regulars with sausages, bratwurst, and gift packages. U.S. presidents traveling through Wisconsin make Usinger's a regular stop. The retail store is decorated with oil murals, commissioned by Fred Usinger in 1906, that depict various Old World methods of sausage-making.

WHITE THUNDER WOLF TRADING COMPANY
320 E. Clybourn St., Milwaukee
414/278-7424   DA
The running-wolf logo is visible from I-94. Handmade Native American drums, recorded music, jewelry, and craft items that can't be found anywhere else in the city are available

here. How-to craft books help novices begin projects.

WISCONSIN CHEESE MART
215 W. Highland Ave., Milwaukee
414/272-3544   DA
More than 100 Wisconsin-made cheeses, including cheddar, Colby, Swiss, and brick, fill a long row of deli cases to provide a variety of gift selections. Cheese logs and pepper- and caraway-flavored assortments can be shipped worldwide. The cheese mart also carries crackers, mustards, jellies, cookies, and other gourmet items. A meat deli and a bakery case make the Cheese Mart a perfect spot for satisfying lunchtime hunger.

WOODLAND PATTERN, INC.
720 E. Locust St., Milwaukee
414/263-5001   DA
If you're looking for a book center that caters to small publishers or self-published authors, Woodland Pattern is the place to go. Readings and performance-art productions are standard fare at this unique store, which provides Milwaukee with a truly thorough offering of hard-to-find and specialized books.

ZITA OF MILWAUKEE
1122 N. Astor St., Milwaukee
414/276-6827
Bridal Salon 414/276-1979   DA
This is the ultimate place for women's designer wear. Specializing in evening and wedding attire, Zita has a reputation for carrying the most updated and highest quality fashions for women. Designer trunk shows, by invitation, are common here. Certainly this is where Milwaukee's most elegantly dressed women can be seen purchasing holiday and special-occasion dresses as well as

sophisticated suits and leisure wear. The store also carries a complete line of formal gloves, purses, and costume jewelry to complement the clothing.

Historic Third Ward Shopping

This area is nicknamed the Soho of Wisconsin, and for good reason. Warehouses, shops, and galleries make it hard to keep your wallet in your pocket. A wealth of interesting products, from furniture to gift paper, handwoven coats, and quirky knick-knacks, can be found in store after store in this area. This is certainly the center of Milwaukee's aspiring artistic community. You can watch many local artists produce their work, ramble through antique and second-hand clothing shops, and purchase some of the most versatile and practical art pieces in the city.

BROADWAY PAPER
181 N. Broadway, Milwaukee
414/277-7699 DA
This is the place to get one-of-a-kind wrapping paper, ribbon, greeting cards, paper plates, and handmade paper items. Paper moons and cardboard gift boxes—some already decorated, others waiting for your creative touch—line the shelves here. Many of the recycled products are actually made by Broadway Paper employees; still others are imported. Broadway Paper also offers

workshops and classes on creative gift-wrapping and paper-making.

ECCOLA
237 N. Broadway, Milwaukee
414/273-3727 DA
Unusual tables made of brushed metal heating grates, wooden picture frames carved with tiny abstract designs, wall mirrors that focus attention on the mirror rather than the reflection, and more unusual and one-of-a-kind pieces occupy every available space. Under the theme "Great Stuff That Makes a Room Happen," this shop is a feast for the eyes and souls of customers who cherish out-of-the-ordinary gifts and furniture.

GREAT LAKES FUTONS
309 N. Water St., Milwaukee
414/272-3324 DA
Need a bed or a living room couch? If casual and contemporary is your choice, Great Lakes Futons can outfit an entire bedroom, great room, or living room. Combining manufacturing with sales, owner-operator Jaffy Ryder learned the art of futon-making in Japan, returned to Milwaukee, and opened this factory in 1979. Beds, chairs, pillows, and a variety of accent items such as kites and artworks decorate this store. Many of the futons are all-cotton, others are recycled foam substitutes.

KATIE GINGRASS GALLERY
241 N. Broadway, Milwaukee

T I P Milwaukee seems to have a bounty of women's specialty stores scattered in odd and out-of-the-way locations: some in strip malls, others in old warehouse sections. When shopping for out-of-the-ordinary women's clothing, don't be afraid to look up these specialty stores. You'll most likely come away with great buys that you could otherwise find only in New York's Soho district.

Canvasbacks: Visually Innovative Women's Apparel, Made in Milwaukee

Virtually hidden in an ethnic South Side neighborhood, Canvasbacks designs and manufactures some of the most visually imaginative apparel in the marketplace. Known for its innovative blend of different patterns, prints, fabrics, and textures—all within a common color palette—Canvasbacks creates five collections a year. Although the collection are sportswear coordinates, the cornerstones of each design group are the artfully decorated jackets, vests, and coats. This mix of beautiful fabrics is sold to better specialty stores throughout the United States. Two separate divisions feature two different approaches to fashion: Canvasbacks' core collection is one of more tailored and structured dressy sportswear; the BETS collection is a grouping of soft, unconstructed clothing presented in both spring and fall.

This national award–winning company is located in the historic Walker's Point district, but its novelty clothing can be found in such Milwaukee-area fine stores as Zita's, Craig's, and Pam Kozlow Petites. Sizes range from 2 to 16 in both the misses and petite collections.

414/289-0855   **DA**
Although Katie Gingrass is a gallery, it can also be listed as one of the best stores in the area for purchasing high-quality artist-rendered jackets, dresses, coats, rings, necklaces, and earrings. Some of the city's best wearable art can be purchased here. Although both the jewelry and clothing are costly, they are exquisite and characteristic of this district's creative energy.

MILWAUKEE ANTIQUE CENTER
341 N. Milwaukee St., Milwaukee
414/276-0605   **DA**

It would take more than a full day to investigate all the nooks and crannies in this three-story antique mall housed in an old factory. Bikes, books, furniture, dolls, and colored glass await both the curiosity seeker and the serious collector. Over 75 dealers display their wares in more than 6,000 square feet of space.

PHOENIX DESIGN, LTD.
408 E. Chicago St., Milwaukee
414/271-6996   **DA**
This furniture store provides a refreshing alternative to traditional, colonial, and Early American home furnishings.

WEST SIDE

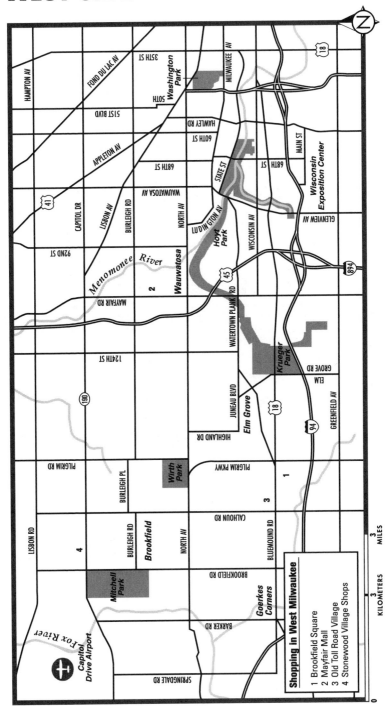

Shopping in West Milwaukee

1 Brookfield Square
2 Mayfair Mall
3 Old Toll Road Village
4 Stonewood Village Shops

Many wood pieces have a South-western or Mexican flavor. Unusual corner cabinets, missionary-style chairs, dining room tables made to order, and contemporary sofas and chairs that feature overstuffed pillows and abstract designs are displayed for customers who crave something different.

TADYCH FURNITURE
2974 S. 13th St., Milwaukee
414/672-4909 **DA**
This Amish furniture store has been operating since 1910. Whether you're in the market for a sofa or table, Tadych handcrafted furniture is beautiful and built to be passed from one generation to the next.

East Side Shopping

Shopping on this side of town is spread over a wide geographical area, but it's well worth a day trip to visit its many unique specialty shops.

AUDUBON COURT BOOKS
383 W. Brown Deer Rd., Bayside
414/351-9140 **ES**
Listing itself as Milwaukee's premier community bookstore, Audubon Books carries *New York Times* bestsellers at a discount and a large children's selection, and it willingly special orders books that aren't on the shelves. An espresso bar allows you to sip a cup of coffee while leafing through your purchases. The bookstore hosts many author readings, some with national as well as local reputations. Live music on Friday and Saturday nights means this bookstore stays open until 11 p.m. weeknights and till midnight on weekends.

GIRAFFE LTD.
527 E. Silver Spring Dr.

Whitefish Bay
414/332-8900 **ES**
The associates at Giraffe can do just about anything in the way of invitations and gift items. A wide selection of in-stock papers and fonts make it possible to design wedding and party invitations while you wait. Because customers seem to prefer traditional invitations, the gift boutique uses a calligrapher to print wedding programs, place cards, and addresses.

LES MOISE
151 E. Silver Spring Rd.
Whitefish Bay
414/964-5330 **ES**
This ski shop has been in business for well over 25 years, featuring a complete line of ski and tennis clothing and equipment for the whole family. The store's repair and service features include stone grinding, knee alignment, beveling, and custom ski balancing. A second store is in Brookfield on Blue Mound Road.

NAPOLEANS
3948 N. Maryland Ave.
Shorewood
414/962-6730 **ES**
Miniature-soldier collectors and science-fiction game buffs have been regular visitors here for years. This hobby store carries a complete line of military strategy, fantasy, and science-fiction games; chess and backgammon sets; and truly hard-to-find and unusual games.

OUTPOST NATURAL FOODS
100 E. Capitol Dr., Shorewood
414/961-2597 **ES**
One of the largest natural-food stores in Milwaukee, the Outpost has an enormous selection of organic foods. This full-service grocery includes a bakery, deli, and espresso bar.

West Side Shopping

Many of the stores in this broad area are high-end boutiques selling one-of-a-kind items. Explore the tiny corner shops in Elm Grove and Wauwatosa. If you're in the mood for more mainstream shopping, check out the many malls and decorator buildings that stretch for miles down Blue Mound Road in Brookfield.

CHOCOLATE SWAN
890 Elm Grove Rd., Elm Grove
414/784-7926   **WS**

This Elm Grove shop carries a variety of exceptional chocolates and desserts. Yule logs and tortes can be ordered and delivered to your address. The candy case features pecan turtles and creams, chocolate covered pretzels, and solid chocolate delights. Tiny chocolate mice, dragons, and frogs are filled with peanut butter. Ice-cream desserts smothered in chocolate fudge and creamy tortes can be purchased by the slice and served in the Swan's tearoom.

DIAMOND DESIGNS
17440-C W. Blue Mound Rd.
Brookfield
414/789-0801   **WS**

Customers can find anything in their price ranges here, from designer bands to Kladuagh rings (Celtic rings bearing a design of two hands holding a heart). Couples can also design their own wedding bands, choosing from a selection of widths, braided designs, and white or yellow gold or platinum. Although the jewelers will special order a piece, Diamond Designs only carries one of each setting at a time, so couples won't see their friends wearing the same designs.

DUNHAMS SPORTING GOODS
17300 W. Blue Mound Rd.
Brookfield
414/797-9100   **WS**

Basketball jerseys, specialty sports shoes, wristbands, clothing, balls, bats, weights, games, and just about anything else that's sports-related can usually be found on the floor-to-ceiling shelves and displays at this discount sporting-goods store.

EXPRESSIONS CUSTOM FURNITURE
18000 W. Blue Mound Rd.
Brookfield
414/792-9100   **WS**

This contemporary furniture store is gaining a reputation for quality con-

TRIVIA

Mount Mary College, at 2200 N. Menomonee River Pkwy. on Milwaukee's West Side, offers fashion and interior design programs that regularly graduate new designer and merchandising professionals. The talented and diverse graduates have found careers locally at such establishments as Harley-Davidson as well as in New York's garment district, in Los Angeles theaters, and in their own design studios. The Fashion Design Department provides the city with an outstanding historical costume collection. The clothing, which is usually displayed according to themes, can be seen at Mount Mary. Call 414/258-4810 to learn more about the costume collection currently on display.

Artistry Studio Gallery, page 130

struction. A wide selection of fabric choices, organized into compatible groups to provide easy options, and quick order turnaround help keep customers satisfied.

GRASCH FOODS, INC.
13950 W. North Ave., Brookfield
414/782-9330   WS
Once a corner grocery and butcher, this has grown to be one of the largest quality grocers and butchers in town. Staff members at this family-owned grocery store hand-pick flowers for sale every day. The butcher cases are packed with tasty seasoned meats, stuffed poultry, and seafood. Ask Bill Grasch about a wine to accompany your main dish and he'll be right-on every time.

HIXONS
10558 W. Blue Mound Rd.
Brookfield
414/241-1001   WS
This specialty women's clothier has outfitted Milwaukee women for generations. Highest quality fashions include coats, dresses, suits, and more.

LITTLE READ BOOK STORE AND GIFT SHOP
7603 W. State St., Wauwatosa
414/774-BOOK   WS
This is one of those cozy, friendly, neighborhood bookstores that encourage you to pick up a book and read a bit before making a purchase. A puzzle table allows children to play while their parents browse. Specialized sections indicate that this is a bookstore catering to serious readers and writers. Although the store tends to carry only one or two copies of each selection, they have a good variety of books for adults and children, and the friendly sales staff will willingly special order anything that might not show up on a shelf.

M E LOU
Mayfair
17115-BW. Blue Mound Rd.,
Brookfield
414/782-1212   WS
Specializing in casual designer wear, M E Lou carries Femini screen-printed and thermal knit T-shirts and

GREATER MILWAUKEE

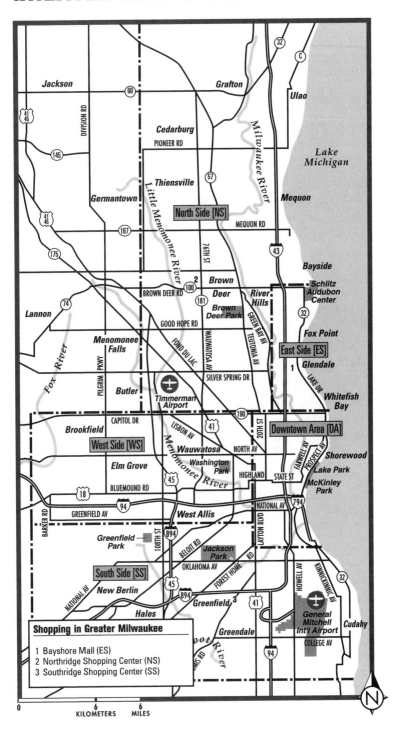

Jackson
Grafton
Ulao
60
32
C
DIVISION RD
41
45
Cedarburg
PIONEER RD
145
Milwaukee River
Lake Michigan
Thiensville
57
North Side [NS]
Germantown
Little Menomonee River
MEQUON RD
Mequon
167
41
45
175
76TH ST
43
Bayside
Brown
Schlitz Audubon Center
2
100
Deer
River Hills
32
Lannon
74
BROWN DEER RD
181
Brown Deer Park
GREEN BAY AV
TEUTONIA AV
Fox Point
Fox River
GOOD HOPE RD
East Side [ES]
Menomonee Falls
FOND DU LAC
WAUWATOSA AV
Glendale
1
PILGRIM PKWY
Butler
SILVER SPRING DR
LAKE DR
Whitefish Bay
Timmerman Airport
190
CAPITOL DR
20TH ST
Downtown Area [DA]
Brookfield
LISBON AV
41
FARWELL AV
PROSPECT AV
Shorewood
West Side [WS]
Wauwatosa
NORTH AV
Lake Park
Elm Grove
Washington Park
HIGHLAND
STATE ST
McKinley Park
Menomonee River
45
BLUEMOUND RD
18
NATIONAL AV
794
94
GREENFIELD AV
West Allis
BARKER RD
Greenfield Park
108TH ST
894
BELOIT RD
Jackson Park
LAYTON BLVD
HOWELL AV
KINNICKINNIC AV
South Side [SS]
OKLAHOMA AV
FOREST HOME RD
32
NATIONAL AV
New Berlin
45
894
Greenfield
3
41
General Mitchell Int'l Airport
Cudahy
Hales
COLLEGE AV
Greendale
94
Root River

Shopping in Greater Milwaukee

1 Bayshore Mall (ES)
2 Northridge Shopping Center (NS)
3 Southridge Shopping Center (SS)

0   6   6
KILOMETERS   MILES

N

cotton dresses, and Flax and Kiko burlap and corduroy pants and vests. River Road velours and Chin Chin silk pants and skirt outfits provide formal alternatives for dressy events. A wide selection of costume jewelry is also available.

MILEAGERS
2500 N. Mayfair Rd., Wauwatosa
414/476-1541   WS
This home and garden store carries a wide selection of potting and garden supplies and furniture as well as sun-room furniture, women's "country" clothing, seasonal sweaters and afghans, and a few collector-quality lines of stoneware dishes. This is the only Milwaukee-area store to offer Hadley pottery, a Kentucky-made stoneware dish that features blue, green, rose, and gray fingerpainted designs. Because Wisconsin is farm country, the biggest Hadley seller is the farm collection. Holidays are celebrated enthusiastically here, beginning with Halloween, continuing into Christmas, and ending with a full array of Easter and spring decorations.

OLD TOLL ROAD VILLAGE
16460 W. Blue Mound Rd.
Brookfield
414/782-8000   WS
Carrying a complete selection of Pennsylvania House and Lexington furnishings, this New England– and country-style furniture store caters to suburban clients with traditional tastes. Wallpapers, fabrics, dishes, and floor coverings, as well as gifts and accessories, can also be purchased here.

PAPER PERFECT
7471 Harwood Ave., Wauwatosa
414/476-7777   WS
This paper and gift company carries

Canvasbacks

Canvasbacks, women's apparel, page 136

a range of invitations, from traditional to calligraphic design, that can be applied to over 300 kinds of in-stock paper, some with patterns. A second store is at 10530 N. Port Washington Rd. 13W, Mequon, 414/241-8787.

PICARDY SHOE PARLOUR
18900 W. Blue Mound Rd.
Brookfield
414/784-3434   WS
Bringing some of the best accessories from all over the country to Wisconsin, this store carries beautiful leather shoes and purses, costume jewelry, and designer jackets. Wool Boppa jackets feature hand-sewn patterns representative of Frank Lloyd Wright's Prairie Style and abstract florals. Scarves and jewelry pick up these lines to help women create a complete look from earrings to toes. A second, North Side store is located in Mequon.

PROUD PARROT OF PILGRIM SQUARE BROWSING SHOPS
2300 Pilgrim Rd., Brookfield
414/784-0150   WS

Pilgrim Square is a specialty shopping mall that includes a tearoom, a women's clothing shop called the Proud Parrot (traditional casual clothing for women), a young-children's clothing store called Peter Rabbit, and the Stencil Shop, which sells all the necessary materials for home and accessory stenciling.

SALAMANDER
7532 W. State St., Wauwatosa
414/259-0970 WS

The way the story goes, two women became tired of always having to head to the East Side or Third Ward to purchase wearable art, so they opened this little shop in the heart of downtown Wauwatosa. From the day Salamander opened, it has been a huge success, with offbeat fashions, lots of arty wearables, and chunky costume jewelry. The women often host designer trunk shows, with many items designed and produced by local women. They sell such nationally recognized wearable art names as Blue Fish and Christopher Calvin.

STONEWOOD VILLAGE SHOPS
17700 W. Capitol Dr., Brookfield
414/781-9703 WS

Stonewood Village Shops, set in a New England atmosphere of cobbled streets and picket fences, include a flower shop, a Christian bookstore, offices, an antiques shop, and a country crafts shop as well as Brookfield's best deli, the Loaf & Jug.

WILDFLOWER
12326 W. Watertown Plank Rd.
Wauwatosa
414/454-0222 WS

During certain times of the year, butterflies actually flitter around this shop that sells truly creative gardening items. Large and small plants and flowers—some wild, others as tame as peonies—can be purchased here. Outdoor and indoor garden furniture, wonderfully unique planters, and idea after idea to take home and put into play in your own garden spot are found here.

YANKEE TRADING COMPANY
17125 W. Blue Mound Rd.
Brookfield
414/784-6611 WS

A fine collection of gifts and home accessories can be found in this gift shop, which caters to New England– and country-style tastes.

DEPARTMENT STORES

BOSTON STORE
331 W. Wisconsin Ave.
Milwaukee
414/347-4141 or 800/374-3000 DA

With eight stores anchoring major malls in the city, this is the largest chain of department stores in metropolitan Milwaukee. In addition to stores that carry clothing, home accessories, china, and housewares, a Boston Store home furnishings gallery just opened on Blue Mound Road in Brookfield. Other locations include Brookfield Square, Mayfair in Wauwatosa, Bayshore, Northridge, and Southridge.

DRETZKA'S DEPARTMENT STORE
4746 S. Packard Ave., Milwaukee
414/744-8832 SS

Along with Goldmann's (listed below), Dretzka's is one of the last of the locally owned department stores in the city. Only here can you find the truly strange alongside a much-needed piece of hardware. Affordable men's, women's, and children's clothing and a full selection of specialty departments keep this store a viable alternative to Milwaukee's chain department stores.

GOLDMANN'S DEPARTMENT STORE
930 W. Mitchell St., Milwaukee
414/645-9100   SS

Bargain-hunters love to shop the basement sales at this locally owned, 100-year-old landmark department store. It's still the only place to purchase oilcloth by the yard to cover kitchen tables, buttons by the boxful, and other novelties that your mother or grandmother used to keep on hand. Shoppers can finish their day with a treat from the old-fashioned lunch counter.

J.C. PENNEY
Brookfield Square
95 N. Moorland Rd., Brookfield
414/782-2000 or 800/222-6161   WS

While Boston Store and Marshall Field cater to a more upscale clientele, J.C. Penney tends to be a bit more affordable. The company also does a large catalog-order business. Additional stores are at Northridge and Southridge.

KOHL'S DEPARTMENT STORE
2315 N. 124 St., Milwaukee
414/786-8900   WS

A smaller series of department stores originally owned by the Max Kohl family, these stores cater to casual and everyday needs. Some Kohl's stores are attached to small strip malls, but they tend to remain independent of large-scale malls. Additional locations can be found in Menomonee Falls, Grafton, Waukesha, and at other locations on the North and South Sides.

TARGET
3900 N. 124 St., Milwaukee
414/466-8400   WS

The Target stores pride themselves on low prices and good service. Toy and electronics selections tend to

---

Milwaukee Carries Fashion Ties to New York

Milwaukee-bred Donna Ricco of New York women's fashion fame was recently named one of the top ten brand names by Women's Wear Daily for fashion that represents quality and value. Ricco's collections are comprised of a full range of silhouettes, fabrics, patterns, and colors, enabling customers to select styles that suit their needs. "The reason I design dresses is that I wear dresses," said Ricco. "When I'm getting ready in the morning, I don't often have time to create an outfit out of separates and sportswear pieces. Dresses offer women a refreshing option—to choose one garment and be on their way," added this busy mother, whose children range in age from one to five. "I believe there are a lot of women like myself who want fashion as part of their lives—and want it made easier and more accessible."

be strong here. Sales are continuous, and casual clothing can be purchased at reasonable prices. Except for a store at Northridge, most of the Targets are independent of malls. Other locations include Waukesha, Greenfield, the far South Side on Chase Avenue, and West Allis, also on the South Side.

WAL-MART
4500 S. 108 St., Greenfield
414/529-0455   **SS**
Wal-Mart came into Milwaukee during the early 1990s and were seen as direct competition to Target. They also compete with area Kmarts, which have taken a beating, and Walgreen's Pharmacies. Wal-Mart promises low prices, easy exchanges and returns, and well-stocked shelves. The stores also maintain fully staffed pharmacies. Other locations include the Hartland-Delafield area, just off I-94 at Highway 83, and Franklin.

YOUNKERS
7700 W. Brown Deer Rd.
Milwaukee
414/354-2401   **NS**
These complete department stores came into Milwaukee on the heels of the last recession. They offer selections and services similar to the Boston Stores and Marshall Field. Younkers are anchor stores for Northridge and Southridge malls.

SHOPPING MALLS

BAYSHORE MALL
5900 N. Port Washington Rd.
Glendale
414/963-8780   **ES**
Though it's one of the smallest malls, with only 80 specialty stores and ser-

vices, Bayshore contains some of the nicest outlets. Anchored by Boston Store and Sears, the mall contains many jewelry, health and beauty, apparel, gift, sporting goods, and shoe stores. Bayshore was one of the first in the area to carry the teens' favorite clothing source, the Gap, and Gap for Kids.

BROOKFIELD SQUARE
95 N. Moorland Rd., Brookfield
414/797-7245   **WS**
The Gap, Gap for Kids, The Limited, Express, Victoria's Secret, J.C. Penney, and American Eagle Outfitters are just a few of the chain clothing stores found among Brookfield's more than 90 stores. Boston Store anchors one end of this mall, with Sears and a new food court at the other end. The mall provides ample free parking.

GRAND AVENUE MALL
275 W. Wisconsin Ave.
Milwaukee
414/224-0655   **DA**
This downtown mall, covering more than 4 city blocks, can be reached from a covered parking structure and a few offices and area hotels by skywalk, making shopping convenient and practical even in bad weather. The mall contains a Gap, Gap for Kids, Banana Republic, The Limited, a complete food court, Boston Store, Marshall Field, and more. Vendors' carts line the walkways and skywalks, proffering costume jewelry, seasonal items, novelty ties, foods, and puzzles and games. Many area specialty shops began this way.

MAYFAIR MALL
2500 N. Mayfair Rd., Wauwatosa
414/771-1300   **WS**
This was the area's first indoor shop-

ping mall and, with Marshall Field at one end and Boston Store on the other, it remains one of the more upscale in the area. Victoria's Secret, Successories, The Nature of Things, Lang Collectibles, August Max Woman, and a Museum Company store are just some of over 165 specialty stores. Vendor kiosks and a food court make this a pleasant place to spend the day. With lots of open-air parking, it's close enough to the city that it attracts city dwellers as well as suburbanites.

NORTHRIDGE SHOPPING CENTER
7700 W. Brown Deer Rd.
Milwaukee
414/354-2900   **NS**
When Northridge was built, it stood out as an isolated block building. It has since been surrounded by strip malls, restaurants, and apartment buildings. The city of Milwaukee has urbanized this area more quickly than many others. This indoor mall contains over 140 stores, including Younkers and J.C. Penney, and provides plenty of free parking.

Grand Avenue Retail Center

DCD/David LaHaye

SOUTHRIDGE SHOPPING CENTER
5300 S. 76th St., Greendale
414/421-1102   **SS**
Boasting a 450-seat food court and over 145 stores, Southridge bills itself as "Wisconsin's largest." While that may be fact in square footage or food-court seating, the number of stores makes it a fair-sized mall. Anchored by Boston Store and Younkers, Southridge maintains a steady stream of regular customers. Plenty of free parking surrounds the mall.

FACTORY OUTLET CENTERS

DSW SHOES
2265 N. Mayfair Rd., Wauwatosa
414/443-0115   **WS**
Promising 30 to 50 percent off department-store prices, this shoe warehouse is a shoe lovers delight. Dress and casual styles stacked inside open cardboard cartons seem to offer infinite choices for men and women. The store closes on Tuesday for restocking.

T.J. MAXX
12575 W. Capitol Dr., Brookfield
414/783-7223   **WS**
This department store carries a number of outstanding designer bargains, including Jones New York women's clothes, Limited clothes for teens, Limited II for children, Ralph Lauren bedding, knickknacks and housewares, lamps, towels, and shoes. New shipments arrive on Tuesday. Another store in Brookfield and two on the South Side.

NBA Photos/Gary Dineen

10

SPORTS AND RECREATION

If you're a sports fanatic, you can find just about any kind of sports event in this town where "Cheeseheads Rule." You can catch football, baseball, speed skating, hockey, and more. In fact, one little-known Milwaukee fact is that the town is the bowling headquarters of the world. But the city's filled with lots of professional and amateur sports activities besides bowling. Many sports outlets offer classes, workshops, and training sessions for beginners. Leagues and fitness centers sponsor beginning, intermediate, and advanced players and teams of all ages in all manner of amateur sports. You can bowl, hit the courts for tennis and racquetball, and even play a few innings of hardball or slow-pitch softball at any number of city parks. Milwaukee has abundant resources for golfers, swimmers, bikers—whatever your favorite athletic activities may be, you'll probably find them here.

RECREATIONAL SPORTS

Biking

BUGLINE RECREATION TRAIL
Waukesha County Park System
414/548-7790 NS
This 12.2-mile trail, located on the former Chicago, Milwaukee, St. Paul, and Pacific Railroad right-of-way, stretches between Appleton Avenue in Menomonee Falls and Main Street in the village of Merton. The trail is open to bicyclists, joggers, and hikers.

DOCTORS PARK BIKE TRAILS
ES
Located at the east end of Doctors Park Road in Bayside, this trail includes a steep hill. Once you're over the top, the trail winds along Lake Michigan in Bayside and Fox Point.

ESTABROOK AND VETERANS
PARK TRAILS DA
These city trails are groomed on gently sloping paths that follow the Milwaukee River. The trails never merge

DOWNTOWN AREA

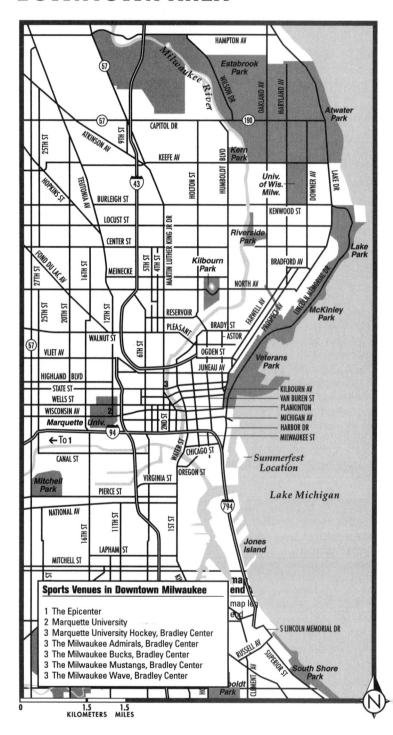

Sports Venues in Downtown Milwaukee

1 The Epicenter
2 Marquette University
3 Marquette University Hockey, Bradley Center
3 The Milwaukee Admirals, Bradley Center
3 The Milwaukee Bucks, Bradley Center
3 The Milwaukee Mustangs, Bradley Center
3 The Milwaukee Wave, Bradley Center

0   1.5   1.5
KILOMETERS   MILES

Milwaukee Mile, page 159

with roads, making this an ideal and relaxing ride for novices and bikers looking for a cruise.

LAKE COUNTRY RECREATION TRAIL
Nagawaukee Park   **NS**
This trail is located on the former Milwaukee-Watertown Interurban Railway. The 8-mile recreation trail now utilizes the Wisconsin Power Company right-of-way, stretching between the Landsberg Center trailhead, just north of I-94 on Golf Road, and Cushing Park in the city of Delafield. Surfaced with crushed limestone, it is open to joggers, bikers, and hikers.

NEW BERLIN RECREATION TRAIL
Waukesha County Parks System
414/548-7801   **SS**
This 6-mile linear recreation trail is located on the Wisconsin Electric Power Company right-of-way in the city of New Berlin. It extends from South 12th Street at the Milwaukee/Waukesha county line to Springdale Road in Waukesha. The trail is

open to bikers, hikers, and joggers. This trail connects to the state Department of Natural Resources run, Glacial Drumlin Trail, a part of the Ice Age Trail.

OAK LEAF TRAIL
Milwaukee County Park System
414/257-6100
An 89.5-mile loop winds throughout Milwaukee County, offering great views of Lake Michigan bluffs and refreshing wooded path respites to bikers on hot days in the Oak Creek and Root River Parkways. Red, white, and blue "76" signs mark the path. Extensive additions and revisions to the path will be completed in late 1997. The path also connects with trails that travel into neighboring counties. Off-the-road paths merge onto bike lanes along municipal streets wherever necessary, making the bike path somewhat treacherous for young or inexperienced bikers. Helmets are not required in Wisconsin, but this is one bike trail where they become a prudent accessory. Bike maps are available through the Milwaukee County Parks Offices.

Bowling

BERT & EDDIE'S FAMILY LANES
1447 S. Muskego Ave.
Milwaukee
414/645-1412   **SS**
Bert & Eddie's was the third certified bowling alley in the United States; its American Bowling Congress certification dates back to 1912. This family-centered bowling alley brings the history of bowling alive.

AMF BOWLERO
11737 W. Burleigh Rd., Milwaukee
414/258-9000   **WS**
This Red Carpet Lanes bowling cen-

Top Ten Reasons to Go Bowling

The following list was compiled by Mark Miller, bowling aficionado and media director of the American Bowling Congress.

1. Because it's what your friends, relatives, and neighbors like to do
2. You're never rained out
3. Size doesn't matter
4. Age doesn't matter
5. Competition
6. Social gathering
7. Moderate exercise
8. One of the few sports in which you can achieve perfection
9. Quality family time
10. You can do it year-round

ter maintains 72 lanes for bumper bowling, "Glow in the Dark Bowling," and championship competitions. Darts, a billiards room, a game room, and volleyball courts offer alternative activities for nonbowlers.

BOWLING HEADQUARTERS
5301 S. 76th St., Greendale
414/421-6400   SS
This is the official national bowling headquarters for the American Bowling Congress, Women's International Bowling Congress, Young America Bowling Alliance, and USA Bowling. The headquarters, which represents over 4.7 million bowlers, is also home to the American Bowling Congress' official magazine.

HOLLER HOUSE
2042 W. Lincoln Ave., Milwaukee
414/647-9284   SS
The Holler House tavern is home to the oldest bowling alley in the country. Established in 1908, the alley still relies on kids to set up the pins. The Holler House was the second ABC-

certified bowling alley, obtaining its certification in 1910 (one year after the Elks Bowling Lanes in Fond du Lac). Open Tue–Sun.

Camping/Day Hiking

MENOMONEE PARK
414/548-7801   NS
Individual and group camping are allowed in this park, which is the only Waukesha County park with scuba-diving access to Quarry Lake. A beach and beach houses provide swimming and shelter. Hiking paths are tied into bridle paths, making horseback riding possible from May 1 though November 1. Cross-country skiing and sledding are the favorite winter sports here.

MUSKEGO PARK
414/548-7801   SS
Part of the Waukesha County Park system, Muskego Park is located in the southeast quarter of Waukesha County on County Highway L, approximately $1/2$ mile west of Racine

Avenue (County Highway Y). This 160-acre site contains 60 acres of hardwoods and is a registered State Scientific Area. The purpose is to preserve plant communities, teach conservation practices, and study the area's natural history. Hiking and cross-country ski trails can be used here.

Curling

WAUWATOSA CURLING CLUB
Hart Park
7300 Chestnut St., Wauwatosa
414/453-CURL **WS**
This club hosted the 1989 World Curling Championship. Membership includes men's, women's, youth, and mixed (men and women) curlers. Although this is an indoor rink, the curling season runs from early November through March. The club is a member of the United States Curling Association. Anyone interested in curling is encouraged to call the club to set up an opportunity to try this original "Scottish" sport.

Fishing

You may already know that whitefish, trout, salmon, and perch are popular catches off the shores of Lake

---

What's Curling?

You might have seen this sport when it made its first appearance in the last Winter Olympics. Then again, maybe not. Curling is a relatively obscure sport that was brought to the United States from Scotland and was originally played on Milwaukee's frozen rivers. The game is similar to shuffleboard, except that only two four-person teams play in each game. A "Skip," or the captain of the team, stands in the middle of a target painted on the ice at one end to call shots, while team members alternate sliding a 40-pound stone down an ice lane. Two members of the team sweep the ice in front of the granite stone to help it stay straight and move quickly toward the target. Each game plays two teams against each other and consists of eight "ends," in which each team member slides two stones down the ice. The team with the most consecutive stones near the center of the target scores one point for each stone. Historically, the game tends to be most played in Canada and the Midwest, where long winters have contributed to its popularity. Nowadays, curling is played on indoor rinks so players don't have to depend on the weather.

SOUTH SIDE

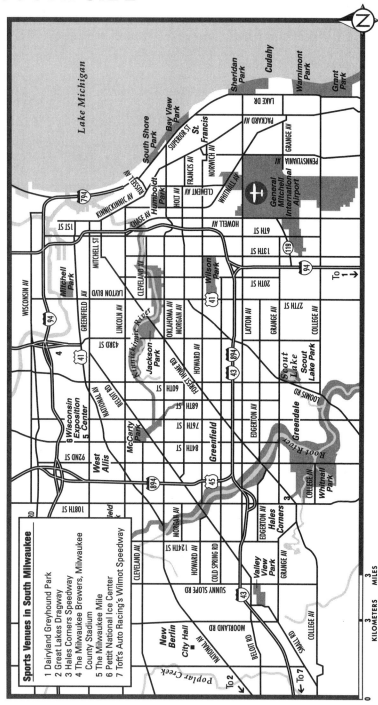

Sports Venues in South Milwaukee

1 Dairyland Greyhound Park
2 Great Lakes Dragway
3 Hales Corners Speedway
4 The Milwaukee Brewers, Milwaukee County Stadium
5 The Milwaukee Mile
6 Pettit National Ice Center
7 Toft's Auto Racing's Wilmot Speedway

Michigan. Smelt fishing, though, might surprise you. It has become a Milwaukee tradition that when the smelt run, usually on an April night, hordes of people line the docks loaded down with equipment that includes nets, flashlights, and plenty of beer. It's also traditional that when you bring your net up and find it filled with smelt, you bite the head off the first one you take out of the net for good luck (your luck, not the fish's). Inland lakes tend to be filled with smaller fish, while bluegill, perch, and bullheads are plentiful in most of the area's lakes and lagoons. In addition, rainbow trout are stocked in Milwaukee County park lagoons each spring.

A A-HOY LUCKY BOY FISHING CHARTER
5600 W. Burnham St., Milwaukee
414/543-9003 or 414/645-2379   DA
Captains Mike and Shirley have 20 years' experience fishing on Lake Michigan. *The Lucky Boy,* a 35-foot Chris Craft, is spacious and clean. The couple will teach novices and operate as guides for more experienced fishing folks. All fishing equipment is furnished. License, stamps, and food are available for all-day excursions.

JACK'S CHARTER SERVICE
2545 S. Delaware Ave.
Milwaukee
414/482-2336 or 800/858-5225   DA
"No Fish—No Charge." Captain Jack Remus has 14 years' experience fish-

ing for trout and salmon. He and his crew will clean and bag all fish caught. His 33-foot boat, the *Leader,* has a head and flying bridge.

JUNEAU PARK LAGOON
Veterans Park, Milwaukee
414/257-6100   DA
Juneau Park Lagoon is situated between Lincoln Memorial Parkway and Lake Michigan, so you can watch sailboats bob on the horizon while you fish for rainbow trout, bluegill, and bullheads. This is probably the most popular fishing spot of 24 Milwaukee County Park lagoons. All anglers need a fishing license and an inland trout stamp.

NAGAWICKA LAKE
Highway 83 and I-94
Waukesha County
414/548-7801   WS
The Nagawicka Lake boat launch and lake access can be reached by exiting I-94 at Highway 83 and heading north for about H mile. The entrance to the park is clearly marked. The boat launch costs $3.75, or $45 for the season.

NEHMABIN LAKE
I-94 and Highway P
Waukesha County
414/548-7801   WS
Nehmabin Lake has an upper and a lower section, with the best fishing in the reedy lower section. Two taverns at the division between upper and lower Nehmabin Lake rent fishing boats and sell licenses and bait.

For licensing information, call the Department of Natural Resources, 414/263-8500. For general fishing information about Milwaukee County Parks lagoons, ponds, and lakes, call 414/257-6100.

WISHIN' & FISHIN'
1244 S. 34th St., Milwaukee
414/835-6570 **DA**
With the logo "Great Fishing on a Great Lake," the 30-foot, twin-screw *Trojan* will take you out; provide rod, reels, and bait; and clean, bag, and ice your catch. The boat has a private head, cabin, and large fishing deck. Multiple boats and licenses are available.

Fitness Clubs

BRICKYARD GYM
2483 S. Kinnickinnic Ave.
Milwaukee
414/481-7113 **SS**
If you're into hard-core bodybuilding, this gym's for you. Individual programs that include diet and vitamin regimens are designed for members. The club is five minutes from downtown and the airport.

GRAND RACQUET & FITNESS CLUB
4801 S. 2nd St., Milwaukee
414/482-3410 **DA**
This fitness center and racquet club offers 24-hour memberships. Eight tennis and six racquetball courts are maintained for all levels of play, lessons, and leagues. Free weight training, aerobics, a running track, steam spa, sauna, whirlpool, and tanning are also available. The club is next to the Grand Hotel, across from the airport.

HIGHLANDER ELITE FITNESS AND RACQUET CLUB
13825 W. Burleigh Rd., Brookfield
414/786-0880 **WS**
Indoor and outdoor tennis courts, a state-of-the-art fitness center, indoor and outdoor swimming pools, basketball, aerobic classes, a running track and challenge course, saunas,

Milwaukee Brewers, page 159

©Joe Picciolo

whirlpools, tanning, a dietitian, and massage therapists provide for a holistic fitness and health experience. A second Elite club is located on the North Side, although daily passes are not generally provided unless you belong to a sister club.

LE CLUB
2001 W. Good Hope Rd., Glendale
414/352-4900 **NS**
Ranked as 1995's best club in which to play tennis by *Milwaukee Magazine,* this site provides a country-club atmosphere. Indoor and outdoor tennis courts are available. State-of-the-art fitness equipment and services are also part of the club's offerings. You must be a member or guest of a member to use the facilities.

YMCA OF METROPOLITAN MILWAUKEE
411 E. Wisconsin Ave., 6th floor
Milwaukee
414/291-9622 **DA**
The Y has something for everyone, from "funk aerobics" to ballroom dancing. Weight and strength train-

The Milwaukee County Parks golf discount card allows residents and nonresidents to golf at a discounted rate the moment the card is purchased. Cardholders immediately become members of the county's automated tee-time reservation system and are allowed to make reservations seven days in advance. Cards can be purchased at Brown Deer, Currie, Grant, and Whitnall clubhouses. For more information, call the Golf Helpline at 414/643-5100.

ing, and fully equipped fitness rooms can be found at more than seven membership branch Ys. Single-day passes can be obtained at most YMCAs in metropolitan Milwaukee, and members may use any location. For the location nearest you, call the association office, 414/224-9622.

Golfing

There are so many excellent golf facilities in metropolitan Milwaukee that it's difficult to narrow them down to a select few. The city claims two golf courses—one private, one public county course—as homes to the nationally acclaimed Greater Milwaukee Open. A few courses were specifically designed to help beginners learn the fundamental skills of the game; others were designed with luxury and environmental beauty in mind. The many courses, rated as some of the finest in the Midwest, are sure to invite and challenge everyone from the novice to the scratch golfer. The ones listed below are just a smattering of the many fine courses in the area.

BROWN DEER GOLF COURSE
7835 N. Green Bay Rd.
Milwaukee
414/352-8080   **NS**

Home of the Greater Milwaukee Open for the past two years, the Brown Deer has a challenging 6,716-yard, par-71 layout. Rated one of the top ten courses in the country, with 60 sand-filled bunkers and water winding throughout the course, it has also played host to three U.S. Public Links Championships.

CURRIE PARK GOLF COURSE
3535 N. Mayfair Rd., Milwaukee
414/453-7030   **WS**

Designed for the middle-handicap golfer, Currie Park is set high on a hill overlooking the west suburban area, with wide fairways, a low rough, and moderately fast greens.

DOYNE GOLF COURSE
5300 W. Wells St., Milwaukee
414/475-9847   **WS**

This nine-hole pitch-and-putt, the perfect place to take up your clubs for the first time, is set high on a hill overlooking downtown Milwaukee. The scenery is a mellow accent on an easy course where you can concentrate on the game's fundamentals.

DRETZKA GOLF COURSE
12020 W. Bradley Rd., Milwaukee
414/354-7300   **NS**

Tailored to the low-handicap golfer, these fast greens and narrow fairways are sculpted and designed for the highest level of challenging play.

OAKWOOD GOLF COURSE
3600 W. Oakwood Rd., Franklin
414/281-6700   DA
Considered a top course, Oakwood provides a challenge to the best golfer and a beautiful setting.

SILVER SPRING GOLF CENTER
N56 W21318 Silver Spring Dr.
Menomonee Falls
414/252-4666   NS
This public 36-hole course also has year-round practice facilities, a multilevel grass and covered driving range, LPGA- and PGA-certified instruction, on-course playing lessons, and even a restaurant. Billing itself as "the public's country club," Silver Spring delivers what it promises.

WANAKI GOLF COURSE
Lisbon and Lannon Roads
Menomonee Falls
414/548-7801   NS
Wanaki is located in the village of Menomonee Falls. The scenic Fox

River meanders through the course, creating water hazards on seven of its 18 holes. Golfers of any age or ability will be challenged by this rolling, 150-acre, irrigated course. Dining and beverage service, a pro shop, and restrooms and locker facilities are featured in the clubhouse.

WHITNALL GOLF COURSE
5879 S. 92nd St., Hales Corners
414/425-7931   SS
Whitnall, along with Dretzka and Oakwood, is one of the three gold-rated courses in the Milwaukee County Park System. Designed for the low-handicap golfer, the course is challenging to play.

Sailboarding/Sailing

MILWAUKEE COMMUNITY SAILING CENTER
1450 N. Lincoln Memorial Dr.
Milwaukee
414/277-9094   DA
Sailboard and sailboat rentals and crew opportunities can be found at this not-for-profit organization.

Volleyball at the Epicenter, page 162

Epicenter

Call for information on prices and weather conditions. The sailing center is open year-round.

SKI JET ZONE
McKinley Beach, Milwaukee
414/630-5387   DA
Offers seasonal rentals of Yamaha Waverunners from Memorial Day to October, depending on weather. Rental includes wet suit and Waverunner instruction.

Skating

BUTLER SKATELAND
12400 W. Custer Ave., Butler
414/783-5012   WS
This indoor roller/in-line skating rink is available for lessons, private parties, and skate hockey. Skate rental available. Butler Skateland is one of three Skate University locations; Waukesha and Cedarburg also have Skate Us. Hours: Fri 5:30–8 p.m.; Sat family skating from 6:30–9 p.m., late skate for teens 8:30–11:30 p.m.; Sun 1–5 p.m.; Mon and Tue, private party rental; Wed, hockey; Thur lessons 5:30–6:30 p.m., open skate 6–9 p.m., open hockey 9 p.m.–midnight.

EBLE PARK ICE ARENA
19400 W. Blue Mound Rd.
Brookfield
414/784-5155   WS
Ice hockey and figure skating popularity seemed to blossom during the late 1980s and early '90s, so Waukesha County developed this indoor ice area for budding ice athletes. Eble is home to the Greater Milwaukee Figure Skating Club, Men's No-Check Hockey League, and Waukesha County Youth Hockey Association. The rink is available for rent 24 hours a day. Skates can be rented or sharpened. Open hockey hours: Sept–April Mon, Wed, and Fri

10:45–11:45 a.m. Public skating: winter, Mon–Fri noon–3 p.m., Sat and Sun 1–3 p.m., Fri night 7:30–9:30 p.m.; summer, daily 1–3 p.m..

MILWAUKEE COUNTY PARKS SYSTEM
414/257-6100
Various county parks offer free outdoor skating on frozen natural lagoons. Signs are posted when the ice is too thin to skate—give them serious attention.

PETTIT NATIONAL ICE CENTER
Wisconsin Exposition Center
500 S. 84th St., Milwaukee
414/266-0100   SS
The Pettit is the only facility in the United States and one of a handful in the world to feature an enclosed ice training and competition center for speed skating, hockey, and figure skating. It is the home training ground of two of the world's most recognizable U.S. Olympic stars, Bonnie Blair and Dan Jansen. The rink features a 400-meter speed-skating oval and two international-sized ice sheets. Open year-round. Daily public skating. Times change depending upon scheduled speed-skating training sessions.

WILSON RECREATION CENTER
4001 S. 20th St., Milwaukee
414/281-4610   SS
This Milwaukee County Parks–owned and –operated indoor ice rink is open year-round for figure skating, hockey, and public skating. The Southeastern Wisconsin Youth Hockey League and the Badger Speed Skating Club hold practices here. A summer adult hockey league, ice dancing, and Learn-to-Skate program are run from this center. Hours vary, depending on club practices. Call for public skating schedule.

Milwaukee Bucks basketball, page 160

©Scott Cunningham

Swimming

Five Lake Michigan beaches, 16 outdoor swimming pools and three indoor pools staffed by the Milwaukee County Parks system refresh Milwaukee during hot summers. The suburbs also rejuvenate the hot and tired, staffing outdoor and indoor community pools, quarries, lagoons, and lakes. Of course, indoor facilities are open year-round.

BRADFORD BEACH
East of Lincoln Memorial Dr.
Milwaukee
414/645-4806 DA
Lifeguards are on duty from June 1 through the end of August. First-class volleyball courts were designed for the annual Miller Lite Million Dollar AVP Tour. Nights in summer get a bit wild at this beach, so teen curfews are enforced by Parks Department staff and the Milwaukee police. Refreshments can be purchased at Bradford Beach Pavilion and the North Point Peninsula

parking lot next to the beach. Street parking.

HOYT PARK POOL
1800 Swan Blvd., Wauwatosa
414/476-0712 WS
One of the first water slides in Milwaukee was constructed at Hoyt because the pool is one of the largest in the area. This Milwaukee County Parks System pool is tucked into a wooded section in the southern reaches of the Menomonee River Parkway. Picnic facilities and a fitness trail are nearby. Adults $1.50; children 50 cents; slides $2.50 per session.

NOYES POOL
8235 W. Good Hope Rd.
Milwaukee
414/353-1252 NS
This pool provides opportunities for recreation and relaxation, lap swimming, fitness workouts, special events, and education. Adults $2; children 75 cents. Lap swimming Mon–Fri 9–10 a.m., 10–11 a.m., 7–8 p.m., and 8–9 p.m.; weekends noon–1 p.m.. Open swim Mon–Fri 12:45–3:45 p.m. and 5–6:45 p.m. Weekends 1–5 p.m.

SOUTH SHORE
2900 South Shore Rd., Milwaukee
414/747-0514 DA
This great people-watching beach is located next door to the South Shore Yacht Club, so bathers' thoughts often drift to the sails bobbing out beyond the breakwater. A large sand beach makes this an ideal setting for building sand castles. A concession stand located in the South Shore Pavilion provides refreshments. This beach has been closed periodically because of high bacteria and pollution warnings, especially after severe thunderstorms.

WASHINGTON PARK POOL
1859 N. 40 St., Milwaukee
414/342-0215 **WS**
During summer hot spells, this and many other outdoor Milwaukee County pools extend their hours until 9 p.m. weekdays and 7 p.m. weekends. This particular pool is located less than five minutes from downtown in Washington Park, which also includes a picnic area; walking, jogging, and bike paths; and a band shell for summer concerts.

PROFESSIONAL SPORTS

Auto Racing

GREAT LAKES DRAGWAY
Union Grove
414/878-3783 **SS**
Fast cars and funny cars for auto race enthusiasts. Drag-racing Tue, Wed, Fri–Sun, and holidays April–Nov. Many special events feature funny cars, jets, wheelstanders, pro stocks, and more. The dragway is billed as a quality family entertainment center.

HALES CORNERS SPEEDWAY
6531 S. 108th St., Franklin
414/778-4700 **SS**
Hosting sprint and drag races on a N-mile clay oval, the speedway is open from April through September.

THE MILWAUKEE MILE
7722 W. Greenfield Ave.,
West Allis
414/453-8277 **DA**
Record crowds have enjoyed races at America's "Legendary Oval," located at State Fair Park (or the Wisconsin Exposition Center). This track hosts major-league auto racing each summer. Indy Car Weekend is usually the last weekend in

May. The Miller 200 Indy Car Race is traditionally held over Memorial Day weekend.

NASCAR races are traditionally held the weekend closest to Independence Day.

The ASA AC Delco Challenge Series Badgerland 200 stock car races run the last weekend of August. The Hooders Cup series and Hooders Pro Cup Series, called the AK Memorial 207, commemorates race car driver Allen Kulwicki, who died in a plane accident.

TOFT AUTO RACING'S WILMOT SPEEDWAY
Kenosha County Fairgrounds,
Kenosha
414/862-2446 **SS**
This speedway is a N-mile clay track that hosts Saturday night racing from April to September, featuring sprints, modifieds, sportsman, mini-sprints, mini-modifieds, and street stocks.

Baseball

MILWAUKEE BREWERS BASEBALL
Milwaukee County Stadium
201 S. 46th St., Milwaukee
414/933-9000 **SS**
Providing exciting major-league action and reasons to continue the tradition of Wisconsin tailgate picnics,

the Brewers play about 80 home games each year from April through September. County Stadium, one of the oldest major league stadiums, will be replaced with a new stadium called Miller Park, complete with retractable roof, by opening day 2000. Notable players include Robin Yount and Paul Moliter.

Basketball

MARQUETTE UNIVERSITY GOLDEN EAGLES
1212 Building
Marquette University, Milwaukee
414/288-7447   DA
This college team has stacked up more than 30 tournament appearances over the last 40 years, under such coaches as Al McGuire, Hank Raymonds, and now, Mike Dean. Members of the newest intercollegiate athletic conference, Conference USA, the Golden Eagles have proven they can beat the best—playing against such powerhouses as DePaul, Louisville, UNC-Charlotte, and St. Louis, the team made it to the second round of the NCAA tournament in 1996.

MARQUETTE UNIVERSITY GOLDEN EAGLES WOMEN'S BASKETBALL TEAM   DA
This women's championship team has earned a place in four postseason tournaments, including the NCAA, and was the 1995 Great Midwest Conference Tournament Champion. The team made it to the second round of the 1997 NCAA tournament. Like the men's team, the women are members of the nation's newest conference, Conference USA. Competitive challenges include Memphis, Louisville, and DePaul. The women's team plays at the Wis-

consin Center under coach Terri Mitchell, who began training this award-winning team in 1996, replacing previous head coach Jim Jabir.

MILWAUKEE BUCKS BASKETBALL
Bradley Center
1001 N. 4th St., Milwaukee
414/227-0500   DA
Exciting National Basketball Association games are played at the state-of-the-art sports and entertainment center, the Bradley Center. The Bucks play October through April. Wheelchair accessible.

Football

MILWAUKEE MUSTANGS ARENA FOOTBALL INC.
740 Plankinton Ave., Milwaukee
414/272-1555   DA
Beginning its fourth year in 1997, the Mustangs are Milwaukee's indoor football team. The football, pads, helmets, and tackles are the

Despite great protest from Marquette alumni, the name of the university's basketball team was changed, in 1995, from the Warriors to the Golden Eagles by the college's president, Father Albert De Ulio, who believed the original name was insensitive to the community's Native American population.

same as in the National Football League, but the field is 50 yards instead of 100, and teams have eight (instead of 11) players on a side. Members of the 15-team Arena Football League, the Mustangs play home games at Bradley Center. Catch all the hard-hitting action of arena football at a Mustangs game April through August.

Greyhound Racing

DAIRYLAND GREYHOUND PARK
5522 104th Ave., Kenosha
800/233-3357 SS
This greyhound dog-racing park provides premier live greyhound racing and horse-race simulcasting year-round. Clubhouse, restaurant, and sports bar.

Where Did Bernie Brewer Come From?

The Brewers organization was into its third month as Milwaukee's baseball club in 1970 when spotty attendance prompted retired aviation engineer Milt Mason to take matters into his own hands. The 69-year-old retiree climbed to the top of the right-field scoreboard on July 6, 1970, and swore he would live in a specially constructed trailer there until the Brewers drew a sellout crowd.

In August Mason lowered his expectations to a crowd of 40,000. Meanwhile, his publicity stunt was played out before the media, and admiring fans made every effort to fill the stadium. Finally, on August 16, the Brewers played the Cleveland Indians before a crowd of 44,387. Mason descended from his scoreboard home by sliding down a rope, amid such cheers you'd think the Brewers had hit one out of the stadium! The Brewers organization took the opportunity to create Bernie Brewer, who sits on the porch of his chalet in the center-field bleachers, waiting for a Brewers home run so he can slide from his perch into a foaming beer mug.

Hockey

MARQUETTE UNIVERSITY HOCKEY
714/288-6976   **SS/DA**

Home games for Marquette Hockey are played at Wilson Park Arena and Bradley Center. This fast-paced, hard-hitting season runs from October through February.

MILWAUKEE ADMIRALS
Bradley Center
1001 N. 4th St., Milwaukee
414/227-0550   **DA**

Milwaukee's hockey team is owned by Jane and Lloyd Pettit, who built the state-of-the-art Bradley sports and entertainment center in order to bring Milwaukee hockey into the national limelight on a regular basis. The 26-year-old Admirals have consistently been contenders for the International Hockey League's top prize, the Turner Cup.

Soccer

MILWAUKEE WAVE
10201 N. Port Washington Rd., Mequon
414/240-2000   **DA**

Milwaukee's exciting indoor soccer team is one of the only remaining charter members of the National Professional Soccer League. The season runs from October through March, with playoffs in April and May. The team, founded in 1984, has proven to be a contender, tying for a division title at least once.

SPORTS FACILITIES

THE BRADLEY CENTER
1001 N. 4th St., Milwaukee
414/227-0400   **DA**

TRIVIA

On January 14, 1990, the Milwaukee Wave and Hershey Impact soccer teams played the longest game in Wave franchise history. Lee Rogers, nicknamed Robocop, finally scored a goal, ending the game with a 14–12 victory.

Built with a substantial donation from Admiral hockey club owners Lloyd and Jane Pettit, the Bradley Center is a multipurpose sports and entertainment facility. The glass and steel-girded building is home to National Basketball Association (NBA) Milwaukee Bucks, International Hockey League (IHL) Milwaukee Admirals, Arena Football League (AFL) Milwaukee Mustangs, National Professional Soccer League (NPSL) Milwaukee Waves, and the Marquette University Golden Eagles men's basketball team. Concerts, figure-skating, and family shows are also featured here. Concessions are staffed by volunteer organizations. A percentage of the evening's profits go to these groups.

THE EPICENTER
815 Northview Rd.
Waukesha
414/548-3838   **WS**

This premier indoor volleyball facility and banquet complex hosts U.S. Volleyball Association tournaments and attracts top tour players. The banquet/meeting facility can accommodate up to 350 guests. The center is designed for weddings and social events as well as for educational seminars and trade shows.

Super Bowl '97: A Packer Treat

The 1997 Super Bowl–winning Packers failed to surprise the country when they walked away with this win, yet Milwaukee and Wisconsin haven't seen as much green-and-gold excitement since the late 1960s, when Vince Lombardi's Packers brought two consecutive championships to Wisconsin. It's likely that the excitement goes well beyond state team support. Local fans can't get enough of the personalities who took the team to Super Bowl XXXI. Coach Mike Holmgren is loved and respected for his teddy-bear appearance and gentle manner. Reggie White, Green Bay's "Minister of Defense," captured America's attention when this honest-to-goodness preacher augmented his uniform by wearing a green turtleneck shirt with the word "Jesus" emblazoned in gold on the neckband. Quarterback Brett Favre received acclaim when he courageously fought a public battle against an addiction to painkillers, then came back to the Pack to play consistently better than ever before. Desmond Howard (named Most Valuable Player of Super Bowl XXXI, a first for a special-teams player) and Anthony Freeman received national attention for creating amazing end-zone dances after touchdowns, and all the scoring Packers will be remembered for their "Leaps of Faith" into Lambeau Field stands after scoring. They're a team that's so talented, personable, and clean-cut, they've stolen Wisconsin's heart. The Monday after the team's Super Bowl win, fans proved their love of the green and gold when hundreds of thousands from Milwaukee and other Wisconsin towns turned out at Lambeau Field in Green Bay to cheer the Packers' return home.

GRAND SLAM USA
4905 S. Howell Ave., Milwaukee
414/483-8400 SS
Batting cages, basketball and volleyball courts, and an indoor driving range make this a must-see for sports enthusiasts.

MILWAUKEE COUNTY SPORTS COMPLEX
6000 W. Ryan Rd., Franklin
414/421-9733 SS
This 55,000-square-foot facility is available for sports activities, conventions, and shows. Take a moment

Looking for Din-O-Mite!

When watching a Wave game at the Bradley Center, it's a sure bet that you'll see Din-O-Mite—the team's dinosaur mascot—jumping around the field or popping up in unexpected places. Din-O-Mite has earned a reputation for mischievously hiding the ball from referees, warming up with the players, sassing the visiting team, and extending birthday wishes to fans in their seats. Wave fans love Din-O-Mite, who demonstrates his love in return by snatching their hats, dancing the Macarena, and throwing kisses to his fans.

to play a pickup game or to schedule a tournament of your own.

WILSON PARK
1601 W. Howard Ave., Milwaukee
414/384-4748   SS
These facilities give amateur sporting events a special home in Milwaukee. An indoor ice rink allows year-round skating whatever the weather. A softball stadium complete with lighting system, press box, and a 300-foot outfield fence, seats 3,600. The adjacent seniors' center, which opened in 1982, has three separate rental areas, including an auditorium with a stage and an attached kitchen. The park itself covers 79 acres. Picnic areas, paddle boat rentals on the park lagoon, softball diamonds, and a tot lot are enjoyed by all.

DCD/David LaHaye

11

PERFORMING ARTS

Milwaukeeans don't need to head off to Chicago or New York to get a solid dose of performing arts—there's plenty available right here. From dance to symphony, Milwaukee employs world-class performers through the Milwaukee Ballet, Milwaukee Repertory Theater, Skylight Opera, and Milwaukee Symphony Orchestra. Community dance corps and theaters are also plentiful and offer a variety of entertainment, including classical performances, Broadway musicals, contemporary and groundbreaking plays, even ethnic acting and dance troupes. Concerts have become a Milwaukee staple. Marcus Amphitheater, built to support big-name musicians for summer festivals, has drawn a steady stream of headline acts, such as Jimmy Buffet, James Taylor, Bonnie Raitt, Paul Simon, Metallica, and the BoDeans. Other large venues, such as County Stadium, Bradley Center, Alpine Valley Music Theater, and Riverside Theater, have hosted Crosby, Stills, and Nash, John Denver, Tony Bennett, and many others.

THEATER

ACACIA THEATRE COMPANY
3300 N. Sherman Blvd.
Milwaukee
414/769-3200   **DA**
Performing in an intimate, 132-seat theater, the Acacia Theater Company is open to experienced and aspiring actors. Among its varied productions, last fall the company performed an off-Broadway musical

and, in December, their Christmas production added to the city's holiday spirit. The company's diverse offerings to the community include biographies, comedies, musicals, and dramas.

BOULEVARD THEATER
2250 S. Kinnickinnic, Milwaukee
414/672-6019   **SS**
This storefront theater, home to the Boulevard Ensemble, seats 35 to 40

DOWNTOWN AREA

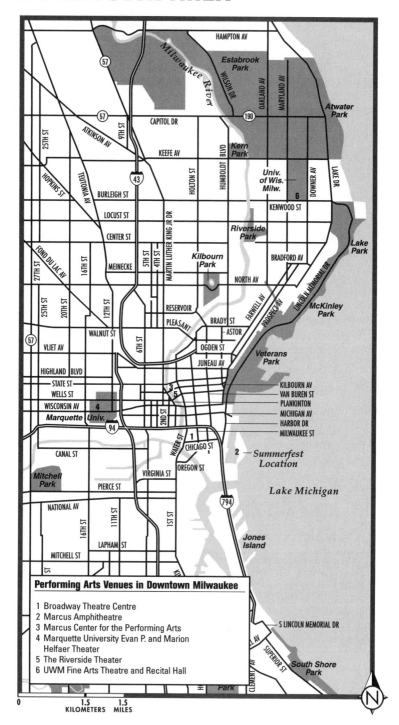

Performing Arts Venues in Downtown Milwaukee

1 Broadway Theatre Centre
2 Marcus Amphitheatre
3 Marcus Center for the Performing Arts
4 Marquette University Evan P. and Marion Helfaer Theater
5 The Riverside Theater
6 UWM Fine Arts Theatre and Recital Hall

2 — *Summerfest Location*

Lake Michigan

0   1.5   1.5
  KILOMETERS MILES

per show and presents romantic comedies. Snacks and soft drinks are provided before and after shows, which are held Thur–Sun.

BROADWAY THEATRE CENTRE
Box Office
158 N. Broadway, Milwaukee
414/291-7800 **DA**
The Broadway Theatre Centre houses the Studio Theater, which seats about 100; and the Cabot Theatre, which seats 358. It is located in the heart of the Historic Third Ward. Regular performers include the Skylight Opera Theatre, Theatre X, and the Milwaukee Chamber Theater. Light meals and beverages are served in the theater bar, which usually opens about an hour before each performance.

FIRST STAGE MILWAUKEE
929 N. Water St., Milwaukee
414/273-7121 **DA**
The fact that First Stage has gained a reputation as a children's training center belies the high-quality performances that appear here. Adult and child actors appear in the productions. Although they lean decidedly toward children's interests, they also appeal to the entire family.

HANSBERRY-SANDS THEATRE COMPANY
P.O. Box 93456, Milwaukee
414/444-7529 **ES**
This roving company performs dinner theater at the Wisconsin Club and

local theaters. Minimalist costuming and stage design don't detract from strong performances of contemporary works.

MARCUS CENTER FOR THE PERFORMING ARTS
929 N. Water St., Milwaukee
414/273-7121 **DA**
Marcus Center, which underwent a major exterior facelift in 1996, houses three performing spaces: Uihlein Hall, which seats 2,305; Todd Wher Theater, seating 500; and Vogel Hall, seating 484. The center is home to the Milwaukee Ballet Company, Florentine Opera Company, Milwaukee Symphony Orchestra, and First Stage Milwaukee.

MARQUETTE UNIVERSITY-EVAN P. AND MARION HELFAER THEATER
513 N. Clybourn St., Milwaukee
414/288-7504 **DA**
The Marquette Players, comprised of theater arts majors and graduate students, put on four performances each year. Offerings include musicals, Broadway productions, contemporary and classic dramas, and Shakespearean and Greek tragedy.

MILWAUKEE CHAMBER THEATRE
158 N. Broadway, Milwaukee
414/276-8842 **DA**
The Milwaukee Chamber Theatre performs classical and contemporary theater. It is the only company in the Broadway Theater Centre that per-

If you want to attend one of Milwaukee's theater productions, pick up a copy of *Milwaukee Footlights*. This official publication of the Marcus Center for the Performing Arts provides provocative and insightful features about the community's theater events.

Milwaukee's "Little" Theater Produces Artistic Visions

Since its inception in 1975, Milwaukee Chamber Theatre (MCT) has been dedicated to producing classic and contemporary plays with a literate or philosophical base while developing a pool of the finest local actors and artisans. Under the direction of founder and Artistic Director Montgomery Davis, the company has remained true to that mission. In the past several years, MCT has moved from a small touring company to an internationally recognized theater with a permanent home in Milwaukee's newest performing-arts facility, the Broadway Theatre Center (BTC). The facility provides Milwaukee Chamber Theatre with an administrative office, rehearsal rooms, a beautiful 360-seat baroque opera house (Cabot Theatre), and the Studio Theater box office. MCT performs four plays each season in the large theater and two in the intimate Studio Theatre. In recent years, MCT has received national and international recognition in the New York Times, Harper's Magazine, *and the* London Times.

forms in both the smaller Studio Theatre and in the mainstage opera house, the Cabot Theatre. Each season the Chamber Theatre features plays that emphasize the importance of language, through productions that range from Restoration comedies to plays drawn from letters to dramas addressing contemporary social, gender, and age issues. The cornerstone of the group is its Shaw Festival, held every March.

MILWAUKEE REPERTORY THEATER
108 E. Wells St., Milwaukee
414/224-9490   DA
The Rep, Milwaukee's largest professional theater company, performs a variety of contemporary and

classic dramas. Its annual production of *A Christmas Carol* is one of the best around.

THE RIVERSIDE THEATER
116 W. Wisconsin Ave.
Milwaukee
414/224-3000   DA
This 2,550-seat theater hosts a variety of productions with nationally recognized casts. One of the most recent was *A Chorus Line* with many of the original cast members.

STACKNER CABARET
108 E. Wells St., Milwaukee
414/224-9490   DA
This intimate dinner theater, located in the Milwaukee Center, has developed a following by producing musical re-

vues that fill the house each night simply through word-of-mouth. One particular production, the 1950s review *Hula Hoop Sha Boop*, proved so popular that performances were extended for an additional two-week period two years in a row. If it should return to the Stackner, make a point to see this funny, sweet musical memoir.

SUNSET PLAYHOUSE
800 Elm Grove Rd., Elm Grove
414/-782-4430   **WS**
This community theater, using community actors, produces about four plays each year. They rely heavily on plays with popular appeal, such as *Nunsense* and *The Lion in Winter.*

THEATRE X
158 N. Broadway, Milwaukee
414/278-0555   **DA**
This avant-garde theater proves that Milwaukee audiences have a taste for the absurd and unusual. The company is located in the Broadway Theatre Center.

UWM FINE ARTS THEATRE AND RECITAL HALL
Fine Arts Complex
University of Wisconsin Campus, Milwaukee
414/229-4308   **DA**
This training ground for the UWM professional theater training program, the UWM Fine Arts Quartet, and the Northern Stage Company includes the 576-seat Fine Arts Theater, 301-seat Arts Recital Hall, and 100-seat Studio Theater. A variety of dramas and concerts are held here.

DANCE

AMADEUS DANCE COMPANY
1375 S. 72nd St., West Allis

414/774-9233   **SS**
Ballroom dance, jazz, hip-hop, and more. Private classes available.

DANCECIRCUS
3195 S. Superior St., Milwaukee
414/481-4324   **SS**
Workshops for this contemporary dance troupe are held at Danceworks studios. The company, under the direction of Betty Salamun, creates collaborative pieces with many artists in many media, and works with different community groups to develop performances. The company collaborated with the Milwaukee Women's Center and Elders in the Golda Meir House on an original production of *Stones and Bones: Journeys of Barefoot Sole*, which was presented at Wisconsin Lutheran College in April 1997. Plans are also underway for a touring production, *A Sand County Almanac,* for the Wisconsin sesquicentennial in 1998. The

TRIVIA

Ten Famous Actors Who Received Their Training at the Milwaukee Repertory Theater

Glenn Close
Tom Berenger
Jeffrey Tambor
Charles Kimbrough
Michael Tucker
Tom Hulce
Erika Sleazak
Judith Light
Sada Thompson
John Hancock

dance and music are based upon the work of Aldo Leopold, the man who coined the word "ecology," and his ecological almanac.

IBERIAN SPANISH DANCERS
2937 N. Hackett Ave., Milwaukee
414/963-8850 DA
Seen at different Milwaukee area locations and ethnic festivals, the Spanish Dancers are an ethnic troupe with a strong following.

KO-THI DANCE COMPANY
342 N. Water St., Milwaukee
414/273-0676 DA
This African American dance troupe has received endowments from the Wisconsin Arts Board and the National Endowment for the Arts and has gained a worldwide reputation for its work of renewing understanding and appreciation of the United States' African heritage. The troupe has evolved into a creative force that interprets contemporary culture in the community. African drums beat out the rhythms of dance as this troupe takes the stage, but they've been accompanied by the full Milwaukee Symphony Orchestra. Their performances are thoroughly mesmerizing.

MILWAUKEE BALLET
504 W. National Ave., Milwaukee
414/643-7677 DA
The Milwaukee Ballet, a world-class company under the art direction of Basil Thompson, produces dazzling seasons offering everything from classic to contemporary story ballet and groundbreaking dance. Their annually scheduled holiday fare is *The Nutcracker.* Recent seasons have included *Swan Lake, Billy the Kid, A Midsummer Night's Dream,* and *Unknown Territory.*

First Stage Productions

First Stage Productions, page 167

TRINITY IRISH DANCERS
W30 11200 N. Bobolink Dr.,
Mequon
414/242-0203 NS
Members of this award-winning dance group have appeared on *The Tonight Show* and in New York City's Thanksgiving Day Parade. The Trinity dancers are an ethnic performance group of children and adults of all ages, who perform the original dances of their Gaelic ancestors.

CLASSICAL MUSIC AND OPERA

FLORENTINE OPERA COMPANY
735 N. Water St., Suite 1315
Milwaukee
414/291-5700 or 800/32-OPERA
outside Milwaukee DA
Performing at Marcus Center, in Uihlein Hall, the Florentine is the only grand-opera company in Wisconsin. In fact, it is the fifth-oldest in the United States and Wisconsin's oldest arts organization. The company,

Milwaukee's Grand Opera: A History of Classic Art

From its meager beginnings in 1933 as the Italian Opera Chorus, founded by John Anello, the Florentine assumed its own identity as it extended its efforts to the production of complete operas in 1950. The Florentine now presents three complete operatic productions each season under General Director Dennis Hanthorn. During the record-breaking 1993–94 season, more than 24,700 people attended.

Combining the best from the art forms of music, dance, drama, and visual spectacle, the Florentine is Wisconsin's oldest, as well as one of its most respected, arts organizations in the state. The 1997–98 season heralds the company's 65th year of continuous operation, making it the fifth-oldest opera company in the United States.

The company constantly strives to promote artistic excellence as it casts professional performers in principal roles. Internationally known artists featured over the years include Placido Domingo in Samson et Dalila *(1965); Richard Tucker in* Aida *(1969); Sherrill Milnes in* The Barber of Seville *(1970),* Il Trovatore *(1973),* Tosca *(1995), and* La Traviata *(1997); Carol Neblett in* La Traviata *(1971); James McCracken in* Otello *(1974); Beverly Sills in* Lucia di Lammermoor *(1975) and* Daughter of the Regiment *(1978); John Meier in* Tosca *(1980),* Turandot *(1988), and* Elektra *(1994); Maria Spacagna in* Rigoletto *(1986),* La Traviata *(1991 and 1997),* The Marriage of Figaro *(1991), and* Otello *(1994); Erie Mills in* Ballad of Baby Doe *(1988),* Ariande Auf Auxos *(1990),* The Barber of Seville *(1991),* Lucia di Lammermoor *(1994), and* Don Giovanni *(1996). In February 1992, the Florentine presented Luciano Pavarotti at the MECCA (Midwest Express and Wisconsin Center) for a sold-out concert, and in June 1995, the company hosted Jose Carreras in a critically acclaimed recital at Uihlein Hall.*

Ko-Thi Dance Company, page 170

which celebrated its 60th year in 1992–93, casts such nationally recognized stars as Beverly Sills and Placido Domingo, utilizes gifted young regional artists to fill its cast roster, and has presented such classic operas as *Otello* and *La Traviata*. The company's planned schedule for 1997–98 includes *La Boheme*, Nov 21–23, 1997; *Abduction from the Seraglio (Die Enthuhrung aus dem Serail)*, Feb 20–22, 1998; and *The Flying Dutchman (Der Fliegender Hollander)*, May 1–3, 1998.

MILWAUKEE MANDOLIN ORCHESTRA
6275 N. Lydell Ave., Milwaukee
414/964-5161   DA
This group, which has been together for decades and recently celebrated the 100th anniversary of mandolin groups in Milwaukee, plays traditional mandolin music found in Europe, but they've also embraced a philosophy of experimentation, adding newly created music to their repertoire. The mandolin orchestra has played at Festa

Italiana, with the Milwaukee Symphony Orchestra, and at Marcus Center for the Performing Arts.

MILWAUKEE SYMPHONY ORCHESTRA
330 E. Kilbourn Ave., Suite 900
Milwaukee
414/291-7605 or 800/291-2605   DA
The MSO usually performs at the Milwaukee Center, with some concerts also held in the Elmbrook area. The MSO presents nearly 90 classical and pop-music concerts each year, offering a variety of music, a first-rate chorus, student performances, Classical Conversations, holiday concerts, and the ever-popular Pops Series that features such guest artists as Doc Severinsen, Lou Rawls, Bobby McFerrin, and Maureen McGovern.

SKYLIGHT OPERA THEATRE
Broadway Theatre Center
158 N. Broadway, Milwaukee
414/291-7811   DA
This diverse and talented company has made its mark on Milwaukee, presenting music from Lerner and

The Milwaukee Symphony Orchestra

The Milwaukee Symphony Orchestra, founded in 1959, has reached such a level of artistic maturity as to be classified by the New Yorker as "one of America's great virtuoso orchestras." Annual attendance has surpassed 25,000 people statewide. The orchestra reaches more than 300,000 people every year through national radio broadcasts, free summer concerts, and arts education programs.

Under the direction of MSO Artistic Advisor Stanislaw Skrowaczewski, the symphony has created season after season of presentations that stun the imagination. Each year the conductor programs a variety of works, spanning at least two centuries and demonstrating such themes as "The Classical Tradition," or "The Romantic Imagination."

The MSO also takes its leadership role in arts education seriously. The Arts in Community Education program is the most comprehensive and progressive arts education program of any American orchestra. A youth orchestra and choir have become an integral part of the MSO.

Says Skrowaczewski, "There is a deep hunger and thirst today for the kind of experience the symphony can provide. Think of it as a spiritual harbor in the storm of modern life."

Loewe's *My Fair Lady* to Donizetti's *The Elixir of Love.*

CONCERT VENUES

MARCUS AMPHITHEATER
Henry W. Maier Festival Park
200 N. Harbor Dr., Milwaukee
414/273-FEST   **DA**
This site is the largest concert stage at the Summerfest grounds. Top name acts perform here throughout that festival and play the outdoor amphitheater spring through fall. The amphitheater holds 24,000. Acoustics tend to make audience noise a problem that can hinder enjoyment, but this is still the best place in town to hear and see nationally recognized rock and pop artists.

THE MARCUS CENTER FOR THE PERFORMING ARTS
929 N. Water St., Milwaukee
414/273-7206   **DA**
Originally the Performing Arts Center, or PAC, the Milwaukee Center for the Performing Arts is the home of the Milwaukee Repertory Theater, the Milwaukee Ballet, the Milwaukee Symphony, and the Milwaukee Pops.

Performance of Abraham and Isaac *by the Acacia Theatre Company, page 165*

ever, has had some problems with last-minute performer cancellations—leaving fans with reserved seats standing outside the doors moments before a performance should have begun, only to find the show cancelled.

TICKET SALES

MILWAUKEE WORLD FESTIVAL, INC., BOX OFFICE
200 N. Harbor Dr., Milwaukee
414/273-2600   DA
Tickets for select summer festivals and Marcus Amphitheater concerts can be purchased at the box office.

TICKETMASTER
414/276-4545
Reservation ticket outlet 414/272-6446
Tickets can be purchased either by calling the Ticketmaster number or from outlets at most Boston Stores, Piggly Wiggly grocery stores, Mainstream record stores, the Midwest Express and Wisconsin Center Box Office, and Vibes on 16th and Wells.

THE RIVERSIDE THEATER
116 W. Wisconsin Ave.
Milwaukee
414/224-3000   DA
This 2,550-seat theater has hosted many well-known contemporary artists. The booking company, how-

12

NIGHTLIFE

It's a safe bet that only in Milwaukee will you find a cabaret that features a tap-dancing crooner one night and a Spanish dance troupe the next, where the jazz renditions of Paul Cebar and the Milwaukeeans can draw a crowd as large as the rock 'n' roll crowd that traditionally turns out for the Milwaukee-bred but nationally recognized BoDeans. Late night on top of the Pfister often means slow dance or jazz. Or you can rock the night away at The Rave or Shank Hall, laugh until your sides hurt at ComedySportz, or spend an intimate evening listening to blues and progressive rock at one of the Riverwest taverns. If all else fails, there's always a cozy spot for two on the rock ledges along the shores of Lake Michigan, where you can catch an early morning sunrise and listen to the music of the crashing waves.

LIVE MUSIC

Blues, Country, and Rock

BBC'S
2022 E. North Ave., Milwaukee
414/272-7263 **DA**
This popular club brings a little bit of everything—rock, blues, reggae, funk—to late-night crowds. There is a basic and affordable bar menu. Open for lunch daily. Live music Thur and Fri. Cover charge.

BINGO'S
4928 W. Vliet St., Milwaukee
414/453-6200 **WS**
This used to be one of Milwaukee's German restaurants and still bears the Tudor decor and styling of by-gone days. Walk inside and you know you're in a tavern and music hall. Tall stools line the bar, spilled beer flavors the air, and peanuts litter the floor. But when Bingo's brings on blues, it's some of the best around. Only here can you see blues performers who

DOWNTOWN AREA

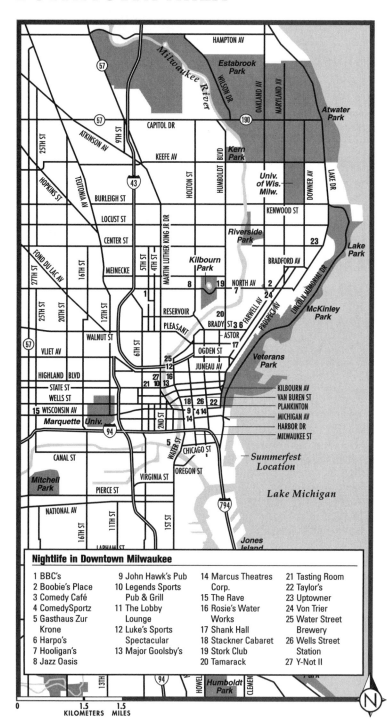

Nightlife in Downtown Milwaukee

1 BBC's
2 Boobie's Place
3 Comedy Café
4 ComedySportz
5 Gasthaus Zur Krone
6 Harpo's
7 Hooligan's
8 Jazz Oasis
9 John Hawk's Pub
10 Legends Sports Pub & Grill
11 The Lobby Lounge
12 Luke's Sports Spectacular
13 Major Goolsby's
14 Marcus Theatres Corp.
15 The Rave
16 Rosie's Water Works
17 Shank Hall
18 Stackner Cabaret
19 Stork Club
20 Tamarack
21 Tasting Room
22 Taylor's
23 Uptowner
24 Von Trier
25 Water Street Brewery
26 Wells Street Station
27 Y-Not II

Top *Twelve* Places to Hear Live Music

Mayor John Norquist gained a reputation for being a music aficionado soon after being elected to office. And why not? The mayor has some musical training and his sister is a professional musician. From the Summerfest stage to Café Mélange, he has been known to exercise his vocal cords along with members of local bands. When asked to provide a list of his top ten places to hear live music, the mayor couldn't stop there, so his list numbers 12.

1. Café Mélange
2. Boobie's Place
3. Blue Canary (now Cedarwoods)
4. Shank Hall
5. Harpo's
6. Christopher's Jazz Club
7. Riverside Theater
8. The Milwaukee Symphony at the Milwaukee Center for the Performing Arts
9. The Rave
10. Club Garibaldi
11. Summerfest
12. The Milwaukee Center lobby at lunchtime

really understand how to slide on a Dobro, listen as a blues riff is strung out, or close your eyes and hear the wail of a classically bluesy voice.

BRASS'
16755 W. Lisbon Rd., Brookfield
414/781-3680   **WS**
Bringing in the best and some fair-to-middling rock 'n' roll, blues, and more, Brass' gained its reputation as a West Side steak and rib joint. Family dining turns into a nightclub atmosphere most weekends after 9 p.m.

HARPO'S
1339 E. Brady St., Milwaukee
414/278-0188   **DA**
Rock, blues, and funk are featured in this hippie-era nightclub, located in the heart of the original psychedelic district.

HOOLIGAN'S
2017 E. North Ave., Milwaukee
414/273-5230   **DA**
This bar seems to have been into the contemporary band scene since the beginning of rock 'n' roll, and it still reigns supreme. Hooligan's stereo system provides a steady stream of rock at earth-shattering (or ear-shattering) decibels. Deli sandwiches available. A $3 cover is charged for live music on Monday.

Milwaukee's BoDeans Become the Sound of the Times Thanks to TV's *Party of Five*

Emerging on the national music scene during the late 1980s, the BoDeans have shrugged off efforts to pigeonhole their style by keeping their sound diverse. Their debut album, Love & Hope & Sex & Dreams, *had a fresh style that soon earned the nickname "The Heartland Sound." The album was noted for the resonating voice of lead singer Sam Llanas, coupled with the harmonies of his partner Kurt Neumann.* Time *magazine declared it one of the best of the year.*

After their initial success, the BoDeans went on to produce several more albums, each of which departed from their original style; these albums were received with less enthusiasm than their first, and fame eluded the Bodeans. However, eventually somebody who counted heard their music and brought it to the hit TV show, Party of Five. *The show's characters play BoDeans tunes to trace the emotions of their love- and angst-ridden lives. With a little luck and the constant exposure from a major television show, the BoDeans could capture the nation's rock 'n' roll heart once again.*

IRISH SPRINGHOUSE
1849 S. Calhoun Rd., New Berlin
414/782-6110   SS
The hamburgers here are outstanding. The blues ain't bad, either. From the outside this saloon looks like an old cowboy ranch; the contemporary inside is nightclub all the way.

NASH'S IRISH CASTLE
1328 W. Lincoln Ave., Milwaukee
414/643-9654   SS
Owner Nash (who likes to be called by his last name) insists on Celtic music in this honest-to-goodness Irish tavern; that is, when he isn't opening his stage to one of the area's bluegrass bands. The Castle, which is more reminiscent of a stone cottage, is good choice if you're looking for the neighborhood spirit that has made Irish pubs famous throughout the world.

THE RAVE
2401 W. Wisconsin Ave.
Milwaukee
414/342-RAVE   DA
Featuring alternative rock and national acts, the setting for the Rave is the Eagles Club, where local boxing matches rule.

SHANK HALL
1434 N. Farwell Ave., Milwaukee
414/276-7288   DA
This is Milwaukee's hot spot for national acts ranging from one-

person folk singers to larger rock bands, it's also the ideal hangout for some of Milwaukee's own who have made a name in the music industry. Located in East Town, a downtown area of elite hotels, eateries, shops, homes, and nightclubs, Shank Hall's interior fails to seduce, but the entertainment scene can be set with a pitcher of beer. While you check out the national sounds, you might find a member of the BoDeans or the Spanic Boys at the bar. The acts—including Jonathon Richmond, Paul Cebar and the Milwaukeeans, and alternative musicians from the community—are refreshing, usually talented, and eclectic. No food served.

TAMARACK
322 W. State St., Milwaukee
414/225-2552   DA
This intimate gathering spot, close to Bradley Center and the Milwaukee Center for the Performing Arts, provides blues, pop, rock, and folk music to late-evening crowds.

UPTOWNER
1032 E. Center St., Milwaukee
414/372-3882   DA
This low-key Riverwest neighborhood tavern features gospel, rock, blues, and bluegrass. Cover charges vary according to the entertainment.

Y-NOT II
706 E. Lyon St., Milwaukee
414/347-9972   DA
From poetry to progressive rock, this tiny club provides creative entertainment that is sure to generate an imaginative spark in the audience.

Jazz

CEDARWOODS
546 W. College Ave.

Milwaukee
414/764-5440   SS
This intimate club offers some of the best in local jazz and blues sounds in the city.

CIBANI'S
4704 W. North Ave., Milwaukee
414/444-2001   WS
Cibani's claims to be Milwaukee's newest jazz hotspot, featuring live jazz and dancing Wednesday through Sunday nights from 5 p.m. until closing. A dress code is enforced, and the club tries to be strict about a 25-and-over age minimum. Closed Mon and Tue.

JAZZ OASIS
2379 N. Holton Ave., Milwaukee
414/562-2040   DA
Regular jazz favorites include the Dean Lea Trio on Sunday, Abduali Quartet on Tuesday, and Lee Forster Quartet on weekends. Wednesday is Oasis guest-band night. This club should be first on the list of nightspots for serious jazz fans.

Jimmy D's Restaurant, page 180

©Filmsmith

JIMMY D'S RESTAURANT
5108 W. Blue Mound Rd.
Milwaukee
414/774-9100 **WS**
Across from Milwaukee County Stadium, this restaurant tends to draw oversized crowds before and after Brewers games. The restaurant recently changed owners, and the new management's first act was to hire a cook from Coerper's Steakhouse, considered by many to be the best steakhouse in Milwaukee. Prices were raised to reflect the fact that it is now possible to get a side of beef as your meal. The restaurant features live jazz and dinner music in the dining room. Go there for the music—it's too smoky to taste the food, and the crowd tends to be a post-game group.

THE RED MILL EAST
4034 E. Good Hope Rd.
Milwaukee
414/228-6800 **NS**
In addition to specializing in steaks and beer-batter fish and chicken fries, this dinner club has developed a statewide reputation as Milwau-

Paul Cebar and the Milwaukeeans: A Hard Act to Follow

This twenty-something local music legend and his band, the Mil-waukeeans, provide a sound that mixes jazz, rock, Dixieland, and blues they label "eccentric sonic accouterments." Paul Cebar and the Milwaukeeans' recent release, Upstroke for the Downfolk, *is passionate and dapper, what Cebar calls "a maximalist racket replete with the percussive legerdemain; saxophonic derring-do; buzzing, whirring, and keening guitarists; and the sighs, shouts, and murmurs of an elite cadre of additional sound organizers."*

Whatever that means, the band is good listening if you like your music fresh, experimental, and jazzy, with a little ethnic beat thrown in. Cebar writes the songs, sings, and plays guitar and some percussion instruments, while his crew fills in with a tremendous sweep of rhythmic sound. The Milwaukeeans include McKinley Perkins on percussion and vocals; Reggie Bordeaux on drums; Bob Jennings on saxophones, organ, accordion, and vocals; and Terry Vittone on guitar, lap steel, slide, and vocals. The group plays college and university gigs, as well as in small theaters and auditoriums throughout the Midwest, and has shown up as far away as the Warfield Theater in San Francisco.

kee's premier jazz club. In fact, some of the best jazz musicians in the country have been guests here. Up to two dinner shows per night, featuring nationally acclaimed artists such as Lou Rawls and Nancy Wilson. Reservations required.

STORK CLUB
2778 N. Weil St., Milwaukee
414/265-2300 **DA**
This upscale club, located near the Performing Arts and Bradley Centers, offers a mellow alternative to the sports bars. Local musicians hang out here to listen to solo jazz and other music.

Other Notable Music Spots

BOOBIE'S PLACE
502 W. Garfield Ave., Milwaukee
414/263-3399 **DA**
You might be able to catch Mayor Norquist and other City Hall types here. This more than 40-year-old establishment offers late-night burgers, soul food, ribs, chicken, and shrimp to go with a variety music in a neighborhood tavern setting. Open weekends until 2:30 a.m.

CLUB GARIBALDI
2501 S. Superior St., Milwaukee

TRIVIA

Milwaukee's own Luis Diaz Quintet won second place in *Musician* magazine's 1996 "Best Unsigned Band" competition. The quintet, with a decidedly Afro-Caribbean sound, are veterans of the local jazz scene.

414/747-1007 **SS**
Another Mayor Norquist–spotting station, this mellow club hosts a range of musicians and musical styles.

GASTHAUS ZUR KRONE
839 S. Second St., Milwaukee
414/647-1910 **DA**
Weekly acoustic and low-decibel music provides the over-40 crowd with a mellow place to stop and sip a brew. The Box Turtles, Milwaukee's own bluegrass band, are regulars here.

THE LOBBY LOUNGE
The Pfister Hotel
424 E. Wisconsin Ave.
Milwaukee
414/273-8222 **DA**
Piano music that soothes the souls of weary travelers can be heard in the Pfister's Lobby Lounge most evenings. This sedate area is an ideal location for a before-dinner rendezvous, an after-theater drink, or any in-between moment for an intimate conversation with a friend.

STACKNER CABARET
108 E. Wells St., Milwaukee
414/272-1994 **DA**
Sometimes the cabaret is booked with a musical revue, at other times it's a one-person show. Some dinner shows are scheduled here, too. But most Milwaukeeans agree that this is the perfect spot for after-theater dessert and coffee or a brandy.

TASTING ROOM
1100 E. Kane Pl., Milwaukee
414/277-9118 **DA**
This neighborhood tavern caters to a variety of musical tastes, offering jazz, blues, and acoustic sounds. Call for scheduled performers.

NORTH SIDE

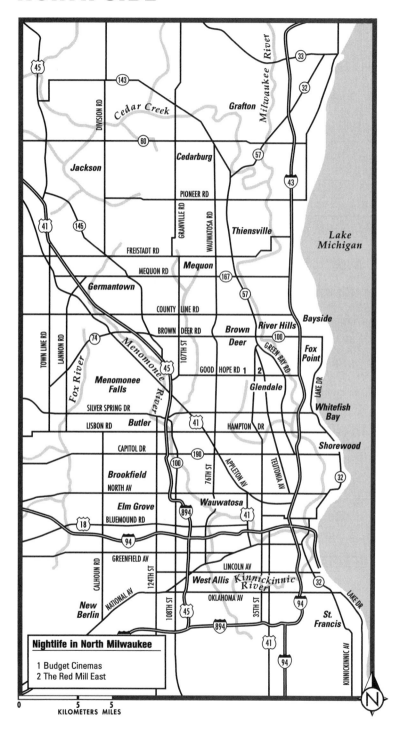

45

143

Cedar Creek

Grafton

Milwaukee River

33

32

DIVISION RD

60

Jackson

Cedarburg

57

43

PIONEER RD

GRANVILLE RD

WAUWATOSA RD

Thiensville

Lake Michigan

41

145

FREISTADT RD

MEQUON RD

Mequon

167

57

Germantown

COUNTY LINE RD

TOWN LINE RD

LANNON RD

BROWN DEER RD

Brown Deer

River Hills

Bayside

100

74

Menomonee River

Fox River

45

107TH ST

GREEN BAY RD

Fox Point

LAKE DR

GOOD HOPE RD 1 2

Menomonee Falls

Glendale

SILVER SPRING DR

Whitefish Bay

LISBON RD

Butler

41

HAMPTON DR

CAPITOL DR

Shorewood

190

Brookfield

100

76TH ST

APPLETON AV

TEUTONIA AV

32

NORTH AV

Elm Grove

BLUEMOUND RD

894

Wauwatosa

41

18

94

GREENFIELD AV

CALHOUN RD

124TH ST

LINCOLN AV

West Allis

Kinnickinnic River

32

New Berlin

NATIONAL AV

108TH ST

45

OKLAHOMA AV

35TH ST

94

LAKE DR

894

St. Francis

41

94

KINNICKINNIC AV

Nightlife in North Milwaukee

1 Budget Cinemas
2 The Red Mill East

0   5   5
KILOMETERS MILES

N

COMEDY CLUBS

COMEDY CAFÉ
615 E. Brady St., Milwaukee
414/271-5532   **DA**
Hosting nationally recognized comedians as well as local talent, the Comedy Club brings night after night of humor to Milwaukee. Some of the comedians can be a bit raunchy, so check the bill before bringing young or tender souls.

COMEDYSPORTZ
126 N. Jefferson St., Milwaukee
414/272-8888 or 800/277-8887   **DA**
This troupe can play with the most demanding of audiences and still win laughs. ComedySportz teams use audience suggestions to ad-lib some of the best routines imaginable. The longest-running comedy show in Milwaukee has 21 locations throughout the country. Reservations required. ComedyCuizine bar and restaurant.

PUBS AND SPORTS BARS

BOB EO'S
6317 W. Blue Mound Rd.

Milwaukee
414/453-3580   **WS**
Local legend has it that the new owner of this restaurant is a former regular customer of the place (when it was called Cassidy's) who won the lottery. He wanted to maintain a neighborhood establishment that sold affordable tap beer. When he took over, he actually lowered the price of a hamburger to $1.50 and a tap beer to a half-dollar. Whether or not the legend is true, enough curiosity-seekers are showing up for the Friday fish fry to assure that business is booming.

DERRY HEGARTY'S
5328 W. Blue Mound Rd.
Milwaukee
414/453-6088   **WS**
This corner tap maintains a steady stream of thirty-something regulars and, because of its location near the stadium, picks up a hefty post-game crowd. When it's crowded the bar can be three- or even four-deep, and the din is astounding. Still, it's one of Milwaukee's favorite meeting-and-greeting places.

JOHN HAWK'S PUB
100 E. Wisconsin Ave.
Milwaukee
414/272-3199   **DA**
This intimate pub is a solid choice when looking for a light supper or a nightcap and mellow music, especially jazz and blues. Located just east of the Milwaukee River, umbrella tables set up on the pub's river-facing patio create a vacation atmosphere. Indoor seating is charming, reminiscent of an old English cottage. Weather permitting, musicians set up outside.

KELLEY'S BLEACHERS
5218 W. Blue Mound Rd.

Milwaukee
414/258-9837   **WS**

Kelley's is located directly across
from Milwaukee County Stadium
and tends to be packed before and
after Brewers games. They also do
a huge business after Bradley Center sporting events. Two bars cater
to beer drinkers. Kelley's is home to
the four-pound burger, but late-
night cuisine goes well beyond
burgers. The kitchen staff makes
shrimp stir frys and a prime rib
sandwich that satisfies the grizzliest
post-game hunger. Live music, usually rock 'n' roll, Saturday nights.
The bar tends to become over-
crowded and loud, but it's as good a
place as any to see what's happening and to meet people. Kelley's is
scheduled for a major remodeling to
coincide with the opening of the
new stadium.

LEGENDS SPORTS PUB & GRILL
1118 N. 4th St., Milwaukee
414/283-5300   **DA**

Located in the parking structure
across from Bradley Center, Legends
is decorated with signed sports jerseys and photos of sports teams.
Service, even on slow nights, tends
to crawl, and the food is mediocre,
but Legends' proximity to Bradley
Center seems to generate decent be-
fore- and after-event crowds.

LUKE'S SPORTS SPECTACULAR
1225 N. Water St., Milwaukee
414/223-3210   **DA**

When the local broadcast media
want to catch a crowd's reaction to a
sports happening, a major catastro-
phe, or even elections, this is where
camera and crew are sent. The bar
crowd provides a steady stream of
commentary, while eyes are glued to
one of over 50 televisions or five big-

John Hawk's Pub

John Hawk's Pub, page 183

screen sets. This is Milwaukee's
most popular sports bar, able to
broadcast eight events at once.

MAJOR GOOLSBY'S
340 W. Kilbourn Ave., Milwaukee
414/271-3414   **DA**

Goolsby's is more than just a sports
bar, it's one of Milwaukee's top post-
game hangouts. The bar that began
as a corner tap and now seems to
encompass half a city block is located directly across from the Hyatt
and 1 block south of Bradley Center.
It is one of the busiest after-event
meeting places in town. Over 30 tasty
appetizers and sandwiches make
this one of the most palatable late-
night menus in town.

ROSIE'S WATER WORKS
1111 N. Water St., Milwaukee
414/274-7215   **DA**

Considered by thirty-somethings to
be the best bar in town. Rosie's features a full selection of stacked deli
sandwiches, salads, and burgers.
The long, narrow tavern, decorated
with barstool-height tables, is located

WEST SIDE

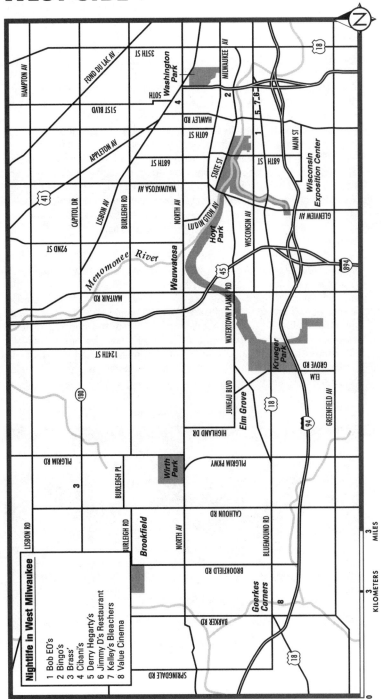

Nightlife in West Milwaukee

1 Bob EO's
2 Bingo's
3 Brass'
4 Cibani's
5 Derry Hegarty's
6 Jimmy D's Restaurant
7 Kelley's Bleachers
8 Value Cinema

near Bradley Center and the Milwaukee Center for the Performing Arts. Serves lunch and dinner and is open nightly.

TAYLOR'S
795 N. Jefferson St., Milwaukee
414/271-2855   DA
This Euro-style cocktail lounge, which sometimes hosts reggae musicians, is located in Milwaukee's East Town. Happy Hour each day from 3 to 7 p.m. French doors frame Cathedral Square, making this one of Milwaukee's most scenic late-night spots. The doors open out to sidewalk seating in summer.

VON TRIER
2235 N. Farwell Ave., Milwaukee
414/272-1775   DA
One of the best selections of domestic and imported beers in the city and a wide variety of hot drinks are available at this Old German establishment. The bartender boasts over 60 imported bottle beers and over 20 imported draft beers on tap at any given time. An enclosed beer garden provides ambiance. No food served.

WATER STREET BREWERY
1101 N. Water St., Milwaukee
414/272-1195   DA
Located near Bradley Center and the Milwaukee Center for the Performing Arts, this microbrewery is a favorite stopover for both crowds. House brews are created in copper vats within viewing. A wide variety of menu items keeps hunger at bay. Herb-garlic-stuffed mushrooms and the New England crab melt are delectable appetizer choices, but if you're really hungry, try the jerk chicken dinners.

WELLS STREET STATION
117 E. Wells St., Milwaukee
414/276-7575   DA
Located directly across from the Pabst Theater, Wells Street Station is a turn-of-the-century building that received its name from the trolley memorabilia theme that surrounds its casual diners. The open galley kitchen allows diners to see

Water Street Brewery

Family Entertainment Center/Water St. Brewery

Top Ten Sporting Events to Watch at Milwaukee Sports Bars

"Preferably at Luke's," says John Lukas, president of Luke's Sports Spectacular and the source for this list, but this list serves all Milwaukee-area sports bars

1. NCAA Tournament—constant college hoops for three weeks—could life get any better?

2. Super Bowl

3. NBA Finals—if Dennis Rodman wears a dress

4. World Series—when the players are not on strike

5. Packers Football—"Cheeseheads Rule!"

6. Electronic pole vaulting

7. The annual *Sports Illustrated* swimsuit edition on video

8. Same as number 7

9. College Bowl games while your spouse returns Christmas gifts at the mall

10. Synchronized swimming in stereo

their meals being prepared, but you'll find people-watching even more interesting at this popular establishment. The menu offers pizza, deli-style sandwiches, and hamburgers. Live entertainment is frequently offered. Open nightly.

MOVIE HOUSES

BUDGET CINEMAS
7222 W. Good Hope Rd.
Milwaukee
414/358-1999　　　　　　　**NS**
4475 S. 108 St., Milwaukee
414/529-4050　　　　　　　**SS**

These cinemas offer second-run movies to those theater buffs who don't want to pay full price for a new release movie but also don't want the small-screen effect that home video rentals afford. Movies

shown here have usually played local full-price houses but won't be offered on video for a few more months. Ticket prices are $1.25 before 5:30 p.m. and $2 after 5:30 p.m. Special discounted holiday gift certificates are available. Buy a book of ten certificates for $10, and you receive one free movie pass.

MARCUS THEATRES CORP.
250 E. Wisconsin Ave.
Milwaukee
414/291-3456　　　　　　　**DA**

Its 13-plus locations and two value-cinema locations, with more than 100 screens showing as many first-run films throughout metropolitan Milwaukee, make Marcus Theatres the area's top provider of film entertainment. All theaters feature stadium seating for optimum viewing ability; some have digital sound.

SOUTH SIDE

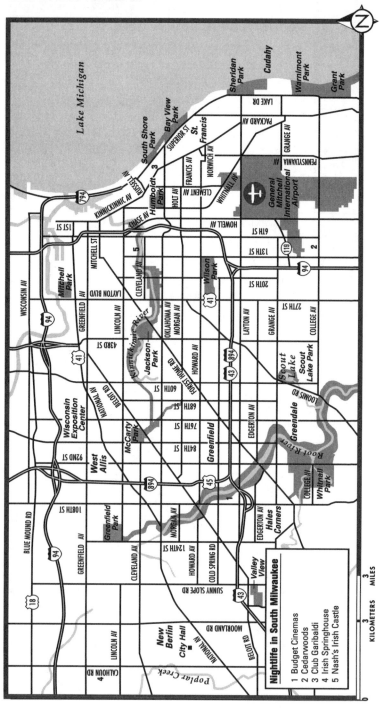

Nightlife in South Milwaukee

1 Budget Cinemas
2 Cedarwoods
3 Club Garibaldi
4 Irish Springhouse
5 Nash's Irish Castle

3 KILOMETERS
3 MILES

Adult ticket prices range from $4.50 to $6, depending on the movie and time of day.

VALUE CINEMA
20075 Watertower Blvd.
Brookfield
414/798-9300   **WS**
This newest budget theater, owned and operated by the Marcus Theatre group, shows second-run films similar to those at Budget Cinemas and for the same low prices: $1.50 before 5:30 p.m.; $2 after 5:30 p.m.

ComedySportz, page 183

Door County Chamber of Commerce

13

DAY TRIPS FROM MILWAUKEE

Day Trip: Baraboo

Trip time: About 1 hour and 45 minutes

A little more than 120 miles northwest of Milwaukee, Baraboo is best known as home of the **Circus World Museum** (426 Water St., 608/356-0800), Barnum and Bailey's winter home and probably the only place that clowns are revered. While here, you'll be transported to the golden days of the American circus with exciting shows, exhibits, and attractions. The museums' two resident clowns, Mr. Bill and Happy, often bumble around the museum, evidence that the Circus Clown School is also a Baraboo attraction. Daily shows provide "real-life" enactments and job demonstrations.

Genuine draft-horse-powered and antique vehicles still load circus wagons onto train cars for the annual Great Circus Train Ride to Milwaukee for the Great Circus Parade. Those who can't make the parade can witness similar demonstrations throughout the summer. The circus museum's Big Top performances are held May through October each year; the museum is open daily, year-round.

The city itself is a charming shopper's paradise, filled with craft shops, art galleries, antique shops, gourmet restaurants, and cozy bed and breakfasts.

Devil's Lake, Wisconsin's Premiere State Park

Just minutes from downtown Baraboo and 90 minutes from Milwaukee, Devil's Lake State Park offers visitors fishing, swimming, hiking, camping, and bluff-climbing. Amateur and professional geologists from all over the

MILWAUKEE REGION

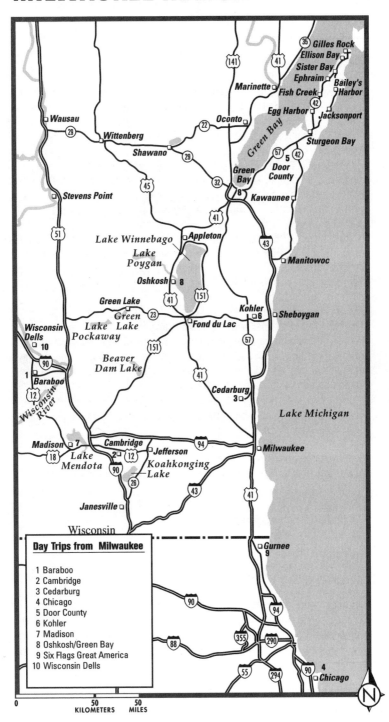

Day Trips from Milwaukee

1 Baraboo
2 Cambridge
3 Cedarburg
4 Chicago
5 Door County
6 Kohler
7 Madison
8 Oshkosh/Green Bay
9 Six Flags Great America
10 Wisconsin Dells

0   50   50
KILOMETERS   MILES

world appreciate the park's unique topography, a result of glacial melting hundreds of thousands of years ago. Devil's Head ski resort and golf course are near the park, and Christmas Mountain and Cascade Mountain ski areas provide a versatile selection for downhill enthusiasts.

The International Crane Foundation

The International Crane Foundation (ICF), 5 miles north of Baraboo off Highway 12, works to conserve cranes and the wetland and grassland communities on which they depend. ICF imparts firsthand experience, knowledge, and inspiration to the thousands of visitors who come each year to learn about captive breeding and reintroduction into the wild. The foundation's work also demonstrates endangered-species management for the public. ICF differs from most nature preserves in that its activities single out a specific subject rather than treating the natural history and general ecology of a region. But the focus on cranes is far from limiting; rather, it allows the foundation to address a series of issues not tied to a particular place, such as species management, wetland ecology, habitat restoration, and the critical need for international cooperation. ICF visitors see the world's most complete collection of cranes—adults and chicks—through guided tours. Self-guided tours are also available. The foundation is open daily May 1–Oct 31. A gift shop is on-site.

The Railway Museum

The Mid-Continental Railway Museum is also located in this area, in North Freedom. This outdoor living museum shows the small-town/short-line railroad way of life, with operating trains, educational exhibits, and displays of restored, pre-1900 wooden passenger and freight cars. For more information about the museum, call 800/930-1385.

For more information about the Baraboo area, contact the Baraboo Area Chamber of Commerce, P.O. Box 442, Baraboo, WI 53913-0442, or call 800/BARABOO.

Getting there from Milwaukee: *Take I-94 west to Madison. Follow I-90-94 to Portage. Exit at Highway 33 and go west until you reach Baraboo.*

DAY TRIP: Cambridge

Trip time: About 1 hour

This tiny village, known as the Salt Glaze Capital of the World, has just over 1,000 residents and is the halfway point between Milwaukee and Madison. Founded in the early 1800s, the Cambridge community is a pleasant mix of farmers, artists, and entrepreneurs. Known for over half a century as the "Umbrella City," the village centered on scenic Lake Ripley has been a popular Chicagoland vacation spot. Cambridge's location makes it an ideal day trip for Milwaukee and Chicago visitors seeking pottery, antiques, and gift items.

Small as it is, Cambridge, with an increasingly diverse artists' community, is well worth a day trip all by itself.

Salt Glaze Pottery

James Rowe, of **Rowe Pottery Works**, is responsible for putting Cambridge on the map as the "Salt Glaze Capital of the World." His original dishes bore a blue fingerpainted leaf print on the gray pebbled surface that has become his trademark. The potter then branched out to prints and patterns that include checks, birds, and floral motifs. Before long, Rowe started making wrought-iron lamps, stove racks, and accessories. Today Rowe pottery lamps, plates, and candlesticks are seen around the world in impressive pottery collections. But Rowe isn't the only potter in town. A number of other salt-glaze experts, including **Rockdale Union Stoneware**, have opened studios, factories, and storefronts along Highway 18. Potters and artisans from all over the Midwest come to display their crafts at Cambridge's **Annual Pottery Festival**, held each fall.

Antiquing and a Place to Rest Your Weary Head

The **Cambridge Antique Mall**, located in a 100-year-old church, displays the collections of over 25 dealers. One of the best antiquing spots in all of Wisconsin is located just east of Cambridge in **Gays Mills**. This tiny farm community boasts a streetful of shops that contain rare country finds.

The **Night Heron Bed, Books & Breakfast**, a three-bedroom inn on Highway 18, is a romantic getaway among flowering crab apple trees across from a river. Hearty country meals are served nearby at the **Cambridge Country Inn & Pub**, while the **Clay Market Café** sets original standards with Italian entrees and vegetarian specials.

Getting there from Milwaukee: *Take I-94 west from Milwaukee to Highway 26. Head south to Jefferson. Turn right on Highway 18 and follow it north to Cambridge.*

DAY TRIP: Cedarburg

Trip time: 30 minutes

Cedarburg residents and visitors may have coined the term "quaint." This picturesque village only 30 minutes north of Milwaukee has a Currier & Ives beauty that is unsurpassed. Old stone houses, spire-topped churches, a settlement near the creek with waterwheel-driven power, and one of Wisconsin's only standing covered bridges prepare visitors for scenes of horse-driven sleighs and long-skirted ice skaters. Indeed, winters seem to stir up the sleighs and skaters—only the clothing styles have changed.

Cedar Creek Settlement and Other Attractions

The settlement is worth a day trip all by itself. The stone mill was built in 1864 by three pioneers to process wool needed during the Civil War. The waterwheel originally generated enough power for 21 looms and knitting machines. The Wisconsin wool was processed into worsted flannels for Union troops. In 1971 Jim and Sandra Pape preserved the mill, opening a group of artist studios, antique shops, and the **Cedarburg Winery**. Today visitors can wile away the day browsing, munching on fudge and popcorn, eating at one of the many local pubs or restaurants, or joining a wine tour.

Take Washington Avenue (which becomes Highway 143) about 3 miles north of Cedarburg, and you'll reach **Covered Bridge Park**, listed on the *National Register of Historic Places.* The park is a charming place in which to picnic along Cedar Creek.

Head further north to the **Riveredge Nature Center**, where you can traverse 350-plus acres of forests, meadows, and prairies on cross-country skis or hiking trails. **Pioneer Village**, a historic living museum with 17 buildings representing Wisconsin from about 1840 to 1907, is just north of the nature center.

Bed and Breakfasts

Although Cedarburg is close enough to Milwaukee to make this an easy day trip, many history buffs, who admit to a passion for antique hunts and gift buying, like to stay longer so they have time to comb the village's nooks and crannies for that one-of-a-kind find. The village's bed and breakfasts make an overnight stay a romantic interlude before returning to Milwaukee's fast pace.

The **Washington House Inn**, on Washington Avenue, the main street, dates back to 1846. The inn's 34 rooms are refurbished with antiques and historic memorabilia. Originally serving the community as a hotel, the inn had fallen into disrepair and appeared destined for the wrecking ball when Cedar Creek Settlement owner Donald Pape restored it to its current charm. Make sure to join other guests in the gathering room in the morning, when the inn serves a continental breakfast, or for evening refreshments. You can't help noticing the tin ceiling, wainscotting, and wood floors, parts of the original decor. The inn is listed on the National Register of Historic Places. For more information about the inn, call 800/554-4717.

The **Stagecoach Inn**, also on

Two Red Crowned Cranes, page 192

International Crane Foundation

Washington Avenue, was restored by historians and owners Brook and Liz Brown. The 12-room inn was originally established in the 1850s. The Stagecoach Pub, on the ground floor of the inn, serves as the breakfast dining area. A chocolate shop is also located in the inn. All 12 rooms have private baths.

Shopping

A few noteworthy shops exist along Washington Avenue. **Cedarburg Woolen Mill**, a wool-carding business, manufactures, restores, and sells wool products and quilts. The **Timber Haus** is a moderately priced furniture and gift store that combines primitive craft with antique and painted pieces. Jewelers Michael and Beth Eubobanks work on their traditional-style custom-designed jewelry at the **Jewelry Works**. The Jewelry Works also does a fine job of restoring antique jewelry. Nearby on Columbia Road, metalsmith **Catherine Laing** makes unique jewelry of silver, 14-karat gold, gemstones, and pearls. Many of her geometric designs hint at Scandinavian and Native American influences.

For more information on this area, contact the Cedarburg Chamber of Commerce & Visitors' Center, W63 N645 Washington Ave., P.O. Box 104, Cedarburg, WI 53012-0104, or call 800/237-2874.

Getting there from Milwaukee: *The easiest route to Cedarburg is to take Highway 43 north and follow the signs to Washington Avenue.*

DAY TRIP: Chicago

Trip time: 2 hours

Chicago's vast museums, cultural centers, shopping, restaurants, and theaters are just a little more than two hours south of Milwaukee off I-894. The most difficult thing about visiting this cultural and financial center to the rest of the Midwest is narrowing down sights to fit into one day.

Fine-arts enthusiasts will want to see the **Art Institute of Chicago**, which houses famous paintings from the thirteenth century to the present. The nineteenth- and twentieth-century French collection is among the finest in the world. Other outstanding holdings include the Thomas F. Harding Collection of arms and armor and the Mrs. James Ward Thorne Collection of miniature famous rooms. The **Junior Museum** is designed especially for children, with an auditorium, library, work rooms, and gallery.

The city's music scene is almost unlimited in scope. Check out the **Chicago Symphony Orchestra**, the **Lyric Opera of Chicago**, and the **Chicago Opera Ballet Company**. The historic **Ariae Crown Theater** in McCormick Place presents ballets and national theater productions with big-name entertainers all year.

Exhibits of applied sciences, engineering, and industry offer hands-on opportunities to cover the inventive genius of the last three centuries at the **Museum of Science and Technology**. Tour the full-size operating coal mine, or a German submarine captured during World War II. The Space Age is represented by the *Apollo 8* command module that first orbited the moon. The history of the newspaper industry is traced in a walking tour that includes oversize pages from the most important headlines of the century.

Shedd Aquarium, in Grant Park along the Lakeshore, exhibits more than 7,000 fish and sea creatures, including whales, octopi, and sharks. Coral reefs help visitors understand the complexities of our underwater world.

Shopping and Dining

Many Milwaukeeans still insist that Chicago is the only place to go for special-occasion formalwear or fine gifts. More than 7 blocks along State Street and Michigan Avenue's **Magnificent Mile** are dedicated to shopping at its finest. Carson Pirie Scott, Marshall Field, Gucci, Bonwit Teller, Saks Fifth Avenue, and others easily prove to be worth more than a day's shopping entertainment.

More offbeat shops can be found in the bazaars of Chicago's **Old Town**, where handcrafted items and imports can be purchased. This is also the first area to head for when you're craving a good selection of international food. You can also find great food in the old ethnic neighborhoods; simple, family-owned eateries and elegant gourmet restaurants are widely available all over Chicago.

For an updated listing of restaurants, accommodations, shops, or rotating exhibits, contact the Chicago Visitor's Bureau at 312/744-3400.

Eagle Bluff Lighthouse in Peninsula State Park, Door County, page 197

Door County Chamber of Commerce

Getting there from Milwaukee: *Take I-94 south to I-894 into Chicago. You can't miss it.*

DAY TRIP: Door County

Trip time: About 3 hours

Whether you're interested in biking through Peninsula State Park, fishing for sturgeon in the bay, trout-fishing in Lake Michigan, or sailing along the peninsula, Door County can provide pleasant overnight accommodations, breathtaking scenery, and mile after mile of trails and paths. Over 250 miles of shoreline along **Sturgeon Bay** on the west and Lake Michigan on the east ensure that you'll be within moments of scenic waves and beaches. More than 40 islands—some private, some public—dot the peninsula's coastlines.

    Jacksonport, on Lake Michigan, is the first village you reach if you remain on Highway 57 when you drive through Sturgeon Bay. Here you will find **Whitefish Dunes State Park**, the shoreline with the highest sand dunes in Wisconsin. Only one other village, **Bailey's Harbor**, provides respite for tourists. This is considered the quiet side of the peninsula.

    If you veer off Highway 57 and take Highway 42, you head into the tourist towns that have expanded to almost bursting with hotels, condominiums, restaurants, and shops in order to meet tourism's demands. **Egg Harbor**, on the shores of Green Bay, is a protected harbor with a vibrant business district. The annual **Birch Creek Music Festival** is held here. **Fish Creek** is the village in which most tourists experience their first fish-boil, at the historic **White Gull Inn**. This community bustles with outdoor activity year-round because **Peninsula State Park**, which follows the bay all the way to Ephraim, begins here. **The Peninsula Players** and the **American Folklore Theater** make their home here, as does the **Community Auditorium**. Ephraim, the next town north, boasts a Moravian enclave of white-clad historic buildings along the bluffs of **Eagle Harbor**. **Sister Bay** is the largest community, with 700 year-round residents, extensive shopping, and the Great Marina; it's the site of the annual **Door County Fall Festival. Ellison Bay** has managed to remain unchanged despite the commercial hubbub that surrounds it, while **Gills Rock** on the northern tip of the peninsula remains an active commercial-fishing hub. **Washington Island** ferries depart and arrive here almost hourly during the summer.

    Cherry and apple orchards, grazing cows and sheep, and many miles of rugged stone walls testify to the area's continued reliance on agricultural businesses. Much of the Door area's farmland has been retired, allowing nature to sow a colorful, constantly shifting crop of perennials and wild grasses to contrast with the ever-changing leaves on the many varieties of trees.

Door County Lighthouses
Over 250 miles of shoreline and rocky shores make the lighthouse an important part of Door County's heritage. Early on, sailors searched the shoreline for its guiding beams so they could safely navigate the lake and bay waters around the peninsula. Besides other navigational aids, there were ten lighthouses in the county, more than in any other county in the United States.

Today only **Eagle Bluff Lighthouse**, in Peninsula State Park, is open to the public. The lighthouse has been restored and furnished just as it was when the lighthouse keeper and his family lived there. Other lighthouses may be viewed from a distance in lighthouse grounds areas: Sturgeon Bay Ship Canal, Bailey's Harbor Rangelight and Lighthouse, Cana Island, and Sherwood Point. Lighthouses on Chambers Island, Rock Island, Plum Island, and Pilot Island are accessible only by water.

There are many, many bed and breakfast, hotel, and condominium choices for vacationers interested in staying in Door County overnight, over the weekend, or longer. For more information, contact the Door County Chamber of Commerce at 800/52-RELAX.

Getting there from Milwaukee: *Take I-43 North to Highway 57 North.*

DAY TRIP: Kohler

Trip time: 1 hour

An exceptional array of recreational, cultural, and social activities in this residential community draws Milwaukeeans and others to this heartland spot. In 1917 Walter Kohler decided to use this setting for one of the first planned communities in the United States. The village of Kohler was designed by several notable land planners of the time, under guidelines established by the Frank Lloyd Wright Foundation, to blend architectural treasures with pragmatic utilization.

The Kohler Design Center and the Kohler Company Factory, both dedicated to the world of plumbing fixtures, are two of the most unusual attractions anywhere in Wisconsin. The Design Center showcases the most innovative plumbing-fixture and power-system designs in the world. More than 25 designer baths and kitchens offer decorating ideas. A video presentation, art gallery, and museum provide a glimpse of plumbing history. Factory tours, for visitors age 14 and over, give an overview of the production of vitreous china and enameled cast-iron plumbing products.

Lest you think that Kohler villagers believe only plumbing can be art, visit **Artspace**, a gallery of the **John Michael Kohler Arts Center**, which hosts contemporary exhibitions of American art forms. Meanwhile, daily tours of **Walerhaus**, the Kohler family's ancestral home, provide a look at architecture found in the Bergenzerwald region of Austria. Austrian life of the 1800s is presented during the free tour.

What would a planned community be without a PGA championship golf course? **Blackwolf Run** golf course is two 18-hole championship courses designed by Pete Dye. The **River** course has been named one of the top seven public courses in the country by *Golf Digest*. The log clubhouse offers dining and a pro shop.

The **Sports Core Salon and Day Spa** provides complete hair and nail care, plus a variety of full- and half-day pampering spa services, such as herbal wraps, massages, and skin-care treatments.

The **Shops at Woodlake** offer quality merchandise and personalized service in a picturesque lakeside setting. Shops feature men's, women's, and children's clothing, leather goods, gifts and collectibles, sporting goods, artwork, books, home furnishings—even a cooking school.

There are only two places to stay in Kohler, should you decide to turn your day trip into an overnight or weekend retreat. The **American Club** is the only AAA Five Diamond resort hotel in the Midwest, and is in the *National Register of Historic Places*. The **Inn at Woodlake** is a 60-room, moderately priced hotel on the shores of Wood Lake.

For more information about Kohler, contact the Visitor Information Center at 414/458-3450.

Getting there from Milwaukee: *Take I-43 north to Highway 23 (Exit 126). Head west two-thirds of a mile to the Kohler exit at County Trunk Y.*

DAY TRIP: Madison

Trip time: About 90 minutes

Wisconsin's capital city, a genial mix of small-town politeness and big-city convenience, is known for its beauty, diversity, and culture. The city rests on an isthmus stretching between two inland lakes, **Lake Mendota and Lake Monona**. The capitol building stands proudly, a bronze statue of Wisconsin reaching over 285 feet into the sky. She oversees the making of state law, the **University of Wisconsin-Madison** campus, a symphony and repertory theater, nature preserves, and more.

On summer weekends a farmer's market around the capitol rotunda allows visitors to purchase any number of organically grown fruits and vegetables, baked goods, and fresh flowers from all over the state.

This capital city is also home to the 1994 Rose Bowl winners, the **Wisconsin Badgers** football team, whose home field, Camp Randall Stadium, along with the UW Fieldhouse, also hosts state collegiate and high-school sporting events.

The University of Wisconsin-Madison is acclaimed for academic excellence and state-of-the-art technology, making Madison a unique blend of politicians and academics. If you can't capture enough of this strange blend on the streets, make sure to spend some time at the **Wisconsin Union**, Madison's most obvious student scene.

Bike trails wind around both Lakes Mendota and Monona and through the **UW Arboretum** and **Law and Olin Parks. Vilas Park Zoo** is a pleasant place to spend an afternoon, while Olbrich Botanical Gardens provide attractive ideas for planting. Or take a countryside ride out to **Spring Green**, where you can view a Shakespearean play or Greek tragedy under the stars at the **Spring Green Theater. Taliesin,**

Wisconsin State Capitol in Madison

Frank Lloyd Wright's Prairie-Style home, is nearby, as is one of the biggest tourist attractions in the state, the **House on the Rock**, which tends to become overly crowded in summer.

Don't leave Madison without stopping at the **Canterbury Bookseller Coffeehouse**, where you can eat, drink, and be merry in a Chaucerian sort of way. The bookseller hosts many national and local authors for readings and signings of their newest works. The **Canterbury Inn**, located above the store, provides six elegant sleeping rooms, each featuring a different character from *The Canterbury Tales*. Each room contains a private bath and includes such amenities as wine, cheese, and homemade cookies.

For more information, contact the Greater Madison Convention and Visitors' Bureau at 800/373-6376.

Getting there from Milwaukee: *Take I-94 west to Madison. Exit on Washington Street, which leads directly to the state capitol.*

DAY TRIP: Oshkosh/Green Bay

Trip time: About 2 hours

The best reason to head to this part of the state is to visit Green Bay's huge green Packer stadium, **Lambeau Field**. Here, in the heart of Wisconsin, the Cheesehead comes to life. The **Packer Hall of Fame** provides a historical look at this publicly held franchise's winning history, from the days of Vince Lombardi to the club's resurgence in the late 1990s as a powerhouse team (and winners of the 1997 Super Bowl). Head home via Highway 41/45 and you'll drive through the **Fox Valley**, where you can shop at countless factory outlets, including Oshkosh B'Gosh, Lenox, Eddie Bauer, J. Crew, and more. Check out the **Experimental Aircraft Association (EAA) Air Adventure Museum** and annual Fly-In in Oshkosh. If you decide to remain overnight, make reservations at the **Paper Valley Hotel** in Appleton or at the **Pioneer Inn** on Lake Winnebago.

Getting there from Milwaukee: *Take I-43 north; watch for signs.*

DAY TRIP: Six Flags Great America

Trip time: About 1 hour

Six Flags Great America is one of America's biggest amusement parks, with rides, stage shows, and concessions. The **Eagle** roller coaster is said to be the longest ride in the country. If you like the tipsy-turvy adventure that amusement rides offer, this stop's for you. Many Milwaukeeans find the rides so invigorating that they purchase season passes to Great America.

For more information, call Six Flags at 708/249-1776.

Getting there from Milwaukee: *Take I-94 south to Route 132, in Gurnee, Illinois. Take Route 132 east, and watch for signs.*

DAY TRIP: Wisconsin Dells

Trip time: About 2 hours

The Wisconsin Dells is likely to be one of the state's biggest tourist traps, but kids love it, and many of the historic settlements and Native American exhibits prove educational. The Dells provides such entertainment as Tommy Bartlett's Thrill Show, Noah's Ark water-slide park, Upper and Lower Dells boat tours, hiking and climbing, Wisconsin Ducks tours, and so many more ways to spend your vacation dollars that you'd run out of vacation time just listing them.

One attraction worth viewing is the June **Great Wisconsin Dells Balloon Rally**, when what seems like thousands of hot-air balloons fill the skies and dot the fields. The silk circles of the balloons create a rainbow of shimmering excitement. Hot-air balloon rides are available at this wonderfully colorful event.

Getting there from Milwaukee: *Take I-94 west to Highway 12. Head north on Highway 12 to the Dells exit.*

IMPORTANT PHONE NUMBERS

EMERGENCY
Ambulance, 911
Fire Department, 911
Police, 911
Milwaukee County Sheriff, 278-4700
Coast Guard, 747-7180 or 800/321-4400

MAJOR HOSPITALS
Children's Hospital
9000 W. Wisconsin Ave., 266-2000
Elmbrook Memorial Hospital
19333 W. North Ave., 785-2000
Froedtert Memorial Lutheran Hospital
9200 W. Wisconsin Ave., 259-3000
St. Joseph's Hospital
5000 W. Chambers St., 447-2000
St. Luke's Medical Center
2900 W. Oklahoma Ave., 649-6000
St. Mary's Hospital of Milwaukee
2323 N. Lake Dr., 291-1000
Sinai Samaritan Medical Center
2000 W. Kilbourn Ave., 937-5123
West Allis Memorial Hospital
8901 W. Lincoln Ave., 328-6000

VISITOR INFORMATION

CHAMBERS OF COMMERCE
Cedarburg Chamber and Visitor Center, 377-9620
Door County Chamber of Commerce, 743-4456
Greater Milwaukee Visitors and Convention Bureau, Inc., 273-3950
Metropolitan Milwaukee Association of Commerce, 287-4100

MULTICULTURAL RESOURCES
African American Tourism Coalition, 449-4874 or 483-9800
American Indian Chamber of Commerce, Inc., 383-7531
Hispanic Chamber of Commerce of Wisconsin, 643-6963
Japan-American Society of Wisconsin, 483-9800 or 287-4111
Milwaukee Minority Chamber of Commerce, 226-4105

TOUR PACKAGE COMPANIES
Historic Milwaukee Inc., 277-7795
Milwaukee County Transit, 344-6711
On the Scene with Eleanor Woods & Assoc., 352-2840
Personal Tours-International 258-1066
Quality Tours Inc., 645-1397
Shamrock Coach and Carriage 272-6873

OTHER USEFUL NUMBERS
Disabled Access Information 281-6660
Time, 844-1414
Weather, 936-1212
Weather Service, 848-0077
Ski Hotline—Milwaukee Snow Report, 800/358-7669
Ski Hotline, 789-5000
(The ski hotlines give varying information. Most skiers call both before deciding whether to hit the slopes.)

CAR RENTALS

Avis, 800/831-2847.
Budget, 541-8750 or 800/527-0700
Hertz, 800/654-3131.

National, 483-9800
Thrifty, 483-5870 or 800/367-2277

CITY MEDIA

NEWSPAPERS AND MAGAZINES
Art Muscle, 672-8485
Business Journal, 278-7788
City Edition, 273-8696
Milwaukee Community Journal
   265-5300
Milwaukee Journal Sentinel
   224-2000
Milwaukee Magazine, 273-1101
Shepherd Express, 276-2222
Spanish Journal Newspaper
   271-5683
Wisconsin Jewish Chronicle
   271-2992

TELEVISION STATIONS
ABC	WISN, Channel 12
CBS	WDJT, Channel 58
FOX	WITI, Channel 6
NBC	WTMJ, Channel 4
PBS	WMVS, Channel 10
PBS	WMVT, Channel 36

RADIO STATIONS
90.7 FM	WHAD/Wisconsin public radio
93.3 FM	WQFM/alternative rock
94.5 FM	WKTI/talk and contemporary
95.7 FM	WZTR/oldies
96.5 FM	WKLH/classic rock
97.3 FM	WLTQ/soft rock
98.3 FM	WFMR/classical
99.1 FM	WMYX/'80s and '90s hits
100.6 FM	WYMS/smooth jazz
100.7 FM	WKKV/top 40
102.1 FM	WLUM /alternative rock
103 FM	WLZR/rock
103.7 FM	WEZW/soft favorites
106.1 FM	WMIL/country

620 AM	WTMJ/news and information
920 AM	WOKY/good news and big band
1130 AM	WISN/news and talk
1250 AM	WEMP/oldies
1290 AM	WMCS/community
1340 AM	WLZR/rock

BOOKSTORES

Audobon Court Books Ltd.
383 W. Brown Deer Rd., 351-9140
B. Dalton
Northridge Shopping Center, 7700 W.
   Brown Deer Rd., 354-1240
Southridge Shopping Center, 5300 S.
   76th St., 423-1810
Barnes & Noble
16220 W. Blue Mound Rd., 782-1514
4935 S. 76th St., 281-8222
Bay Shore Mall, 5900 N. Port Washington Rd., 967-0007
Books & Company
1039 Summit Ave., Oconomowoc,
   567-0106
Harry W. Schwartz Bookshops
2551 N. Downer Ave., 332-1181
4093 N. Oakland Ave., 963-3111
Loehmann's Plaza, 17145 W. Blue
   Mound Rd., 797-6140
Pavilions, 10976 N. Port Washington
   Rd., 241-6220
The Little Read Book
7603 W. State St., 774-BOOK
Scribner's
2500 N. Mayfair Rd., 453-3305
Waldenbooks
Northridge Shopping Center, 7700 W.
   Brown Deer Rd., 354-0510
Southridge Shopping Center, 5300 S.
   76th St., 421-4290
Brookfield Square, 95 N. Moorland
   Rd.,921-6298
Grand Avenue Mall, 275 W. Wisconsin Ave., 224-9400

PUBLIC HOLIDAYS

New Year's Day
Martin Luther King Day
Memorial Day
Independence Day
Labor Day
Thanksgiving
Christmas

BANKS

Associated Bank
515 W. Wells St., 271-1786
Bank One
111 E. Wisconsin Ave., 765-3000
Firstar
777 E. Wisconsin Ave., 765-5100
M&I Marshall & Ilsley Bank
770 N. Water St., 765-7700
Mutual Savings Bank
4949 W. Brown Deer Rd., 354-1500
Norwest Banks
100 E. Wisconsin Ave., 224-3775
Tri-City National Banks
10909 W. Greenfield Ave., 476-4500

MAIL

U.S. Postal Service
Main Branch: 345 W. St. Paul Ave.,
    270-2000
City branch office: 606 E. Juneau
    Ave., 289-8336
24-hour service: Airport Post Office,
    5500 S. Howell Ave., 481-4032
United Parcel Service
12400 W. Blue Mound Rd., 785-7232
    or 800/PICK-UPS
Federal Express, 800/463-3339
Dispatch 10 (local delivery)
    800/252-3310

CHILD CARE

Ebenezer Child Care Center, Inc.
1496 S. 29th St., 643-5070
**Wauwatosa Day Care and Learning
Centers, Inc.**
6905 W. Blue Mound Rd., 476-4810
YMCA
5000 W. National Ave., 351-9622